Formations

OF PLEASURE

Formations
OF PLEASURE

'It is not enough to know the ensemble of relations as they exist at any given time as a given system. They must be known genetically, in the movement of their formation.'

Antonio Gramsci

ROUTLEDGE & KEGAN PAUL
London, Boston, Melbourne and Henley

First published in 1983
by Routledge & Kegan Paul plc.
39 Store Street, London WC1E 7DD,
9 Park Street, Boston, Mass. 02108, USA,
296 Beaconsfield Parade, Middle Park,
Melbourne, 3206, Australia, and
Broadway House, Newtown Road,
Henley-on-Thames, Oxon RG9 1EN
Set in 10pt Palatino by
Rowland Phototypesetting Ltd
Bury St Edmunds, Suffolk
and printed in Great Britain by
St Edmundsbury Press
Bury St Edmunds, Suffolk

ISBN 0-7100-9359-4

CONTENTS

ACKNOWLEDGMENTS

Illustrations are reproduced with the permission of Aerofilms Ltd, the
Blackpool Pleasure Beach Co and the BBC. Although every effort has been
made to trace copyright holders, we apologize in advance for any unin-
tentional omission or neglect and will be pleased to insert the appropriate
acknowledgment to companies or individuals in any subsequent edition of
this publication.

NOTES ON CONTRIBUTORS

Fredric Jameson teaches French at Yale University and is the author of *Marxism and Form* (1971), *The Prison House of Language* (1972) and *The Political Unconscious* (1981) . . . **Victor Burgin** teaches photography theory at the Polytechnic of Central London and edited *Thinking Photography* (1982) . . . **Cora Kaplan** teaches English at Sussex University . . . **Frank Mort** is a research assistant in the Arts Faculty at the Open University . . . **Tony Davies** teaches English at Birmingham University . . . **Terry Eagleton** teaches English at Wadham College, Oxford and is author of *Criticism and Ideology* (1976) and *Walter Benjamin, or Towards a Revolutionary Criticism* (1981) . . . **Simon Watney** teaches in the School of Communication at the Polytechnic of Central London . . . **Colin Mercer** is a research assistant at the Open University . . . **Simon Frith** teaches sociology at Warwick University and is rock critic for the *Sunday Times* . . . **Grahame Thompson** lectures in economics at the Open University and is on the editorial board of *Economy and Society* . . . **Tony Bennett** chairs the Open University course on Popular Culture and is author of *Formalism and Marxism* (1979) . . . **Laura Mulvey** teaches film at Bulmershe College and, with Peter Wollen, has directed *Penthesilea, Riddles of the Sphinx, AMY!* and *Crystal Gazing* . . . **Judith Williamson** writes for *City Limits* . . . **Dee Dee Glass** is a television producer-director . . . **Griselda Pollock** is a lecturer in the History of Art and Film at the University of Leeds and is the author, with Roszika Parker, of *Old Mistresses* (1981) . . . **Marie Yates** is an artist and teacher . . . **Fanny Tribble** is a cartoonist.

Fredric Jameson

PLEASURE: A Political Issue

Something on the order of a subject can be discerned on the recording surface: a strange subject, with no fixed identity, wandering about over the body without organs, yet always remaining peripheral to the desiring-machines, being defined by the share of the product it takes for itself, garnering here, there and everywhere a reward, in the form of a becoming or an avatar, being born of the states that it consumes and being reborn with each new state: 'c'est donc moi, c'est donc à moi!' . . . . The subject is produced as a mere residue alongside the desiring machines: a conjunctive synthesis of consumption in the form of a wonderstruck: 'c'était donc ça!' [wow!]

Gilles Deleuze and Felix Guattari *Anti-Oedipus*

At Yekaterina Peshkova's in Moscow one evening, listening to Isaiah Dobrovein playing Beethoven's sonatas, Lenin said:

'I don't know of anything better than the "Appassionata". I can listen to it every day. Amazing, superhuman music! I always think with a pride that may be naive: look what miracles people can perform!'

And screwing up his eyes and chuckling he added without mirth:

'But I can't listen to music often, it affects my nerves, it makes me want to say sweet nothings and pat the heads of people who, living in a filthy hell, can create such beauty. But today we mustn't pat anyone on the head or we'll get our hand bitten off: we've got to hit them on the heads, hit them without mercy, though in the ideal we are against doing any violence to people. Hm-hm – it's a hellishly difficult office!'

Maxim Gorki *Reminiscences of Lenin*

So pleasure, we are told, like happiness or interest, can never be fixed directly by the naked eye – let along pursued as an end, or conceptualized – but only experienced laterally, or after the fact, as something like the by-product of something else. When taken as an end in its own right, pleasure ceases to be that and imperceptibly transforms itself into something quite different, a passion, one of those great inhuman metaphysical 'choices of being', celebrated in his own peculiar way by Sade, and crystallized in great archetypal figures such as those of Don Juan or Herr Jakob Schmidt – no longer hedonists at all, these last, but subjects possessed.

I pause here to register another dimension of our topic – namely history itself, the historicity of our own conjuncture. I am suddenly struck by the fact that no one has mentioned these archetypal (male) quest-figures lately, or any of their accompanying cortège, from the portrait gallery of bourgeois individualism, such as the Adventurer. Is it possible that they have disappeared altogether from consumer society, and that their former passions have been reduced or expanded, either into psychopathology – as in the former 'gluttony' – or into the badge and sign of micro-group behaviour – as in gay promiscuity? At any rate, it becomes clear that the question of the originality of our own situation, consumer capitalism, post-industrial society, or better still, what Ernest Mandel calls 'late capitalism' – will have to be reckoned into any discussion of the relationship between pleasure and politics.

So no pleasure in its own right; pleasurable activities, or something like a 'fading' effect of pleasure after the fact. Yet the word continues to exist, and this suggests yet another qualification or complication in the topic. Will it focus on the experience of the pleasurable, and what that might mean for politics or do to political activity? Or is something else at stake, namely the *idea* of pleasure, the ideologies of pleasure, the political value of slogans which raise the banner of that abstract idea, about which the familiar question might be debated as to its subversive power as a revolutionary 'demand'? New needs, new demands: at once an influential political ideology from our own immediate past takes shape again in the mind's eye – the New Left or Marcusean one. According to this, the cultural contradiction of late capitalism is to be grasped in the way in which the consumption system stimulates new needs and new demands, many of them 'false' or spurious to be sure, yet whose dynamic and pressure can no longer be accommodated within the system, whose very mass therefore threatens to blow it skyhigh. This politico-cultural analysis is part of a larger one, for which, more recently, Rudolf Bahro's conception of 'surplus consciousness' might serve as a motto, signifying the general surplus cultural overproduction of a system that in a new, yet classical, way generates its own 'other' and negation from within itself. We believed this yesterday: do we still do so? If not, why not? What has changed all around us since the 1960s to render this particular political strategy – for it was that too – archaic and outmoded?

Theorising Pleasure

The reminder at least usefully suggests something else at the same time: that there has been a whole series of left political or ideological positions on pleasure and hedonism in our recent past, and that we need to confront a few more of those before 'deciding' what we really think ourselves. (What we 'really' think may simply be a residue of one of those older ideologies, in fact). Oddly, the Marcusean position emerges from its own opposite, that other even more influential tradition in Frankfurt School thought which insists on the determinate relationship between commodification and what we may have been tempted to think of as pleasure. How do you distinguish, in other words, between real pleasure and mere diversion – the degradation of free time into that very different commodity called 'leisure', the form of commodity consumption stamped on the most intimate former pleasures from sexuality to reading? This analysis rests on the more general systemic description of a prodigious expansion of late capitalism, which now, in the form of what has variously been called the 'culture industry' or the 'consciousness industry', penetrates one of the two surviving pre-capitalist enclaves of Nature within the system – namely the Unconscious. (The other one is the pre-capitalist agriculture and village cultures of the Third World.)

The commodification approach raises two questions. The first is an immediately practical-political one: if what people today imagine to be pleasure is nothing but a commodity fix, how to deal with that addiction? Who is to break the news to them that their conscious experience of leisure products – their conscious 'pleasure' in consumption – is in reality nothing but false consciousness? Indeed, even further, who has the *authority* – and in the name of what? – to make such an assessment? What was scandalous about Marcuse's solution could already be measured by the volume of liberal outrage that greeted *Repressive Tolerance*. From out of the cultural baggage of their own 'great tradition', liberals were horrified to glimpse the outlines of Plato's Philosopher-King alive and well in consumer society and offering to lay hands on the media and their 'rights' to free speech. For an anti-authoritarian Left, however, which had begun to raise its own questions about the 'place of truth' and the privileges of 'interpretation', the Marcusean version of Frankfurt School analysis could also at best awaken the proverbial 'mixed feelings', since in the traditions of the Left generally the Platonic sage bears the rather different name of the revolutionary Party.

It is at any rate clear that the problematic of new revolutionary needs and demands and that of the commodification of desires and pleasures are dialectically at one with each other. If the former is an ideological mirage, it is a mirage generated by the correspondingly ideological conception of 'degraded' consciousness and of commodified consumption. On a more populist view, indeed, the question might be raised as to whether all that mindless consumption of television images, that self-perpetuating ingestion of the advertising 'images' of things rather than the things themselves, is really all that pleasurable – whether the consumer's consciousness is really so false and so little reflexive as it dutifully treads the rotating mill of its civic responsibility to consume.

The way to tell the difference between a pleasure and a fix, a therapist once said, is that you can do without the former. But this is surely something the subject is somewhere naggingly aware of, in her 'heart of hearts'. Indeed, the pronoun suggests that the conception of the mindless consumer, the ultimate commodified 'false consciousness' of shopping-centre capitalism, is a conception of 'otherness'. That degraded consumption is assigned to women, to what used to be called 'Mrs American Housewife'. The genealogy goes all the way back to the first collective fantasies about suburban life in the 1950s, Philip Wylie's 'Momism', for instance, and the psychoanalytic terror of a consuming Mom, who not only presided possessively over all the new post-war products but also threatened to eat *you* up as well: a consumption fantasy with teeth in it, according to all the archaic textbooks. As for the exhausted male worker or businessman, according to this stereotype, he has presumably always been more lucid about the worthlessness of the evening images that flicker across his face. But in the raw anti-intellectualism of American capitalism from the outset, was not Culture always something worthless and 'feminine' in all its forms, from European 'high' culture all the way to the substitute gratifications of the pulps and comic books?

What the Frankfurt School theorized in revulsion and historical anxiety as the degradation of culture and the fetishization of the mind has more recently been celebrated, in positive forms, on the other side of the Rhine. It is well-known that the theorists of a French post-structuralism simply change the valences on the old descriptions of Adorno, Horkheimer and Marcuse, so that what used to be denounced as 'commodification' is now offered by Deleuze and Guattari as the 'true hero of desire', the consciousness of the ideal schizophrenic. Behind this peculiar shift lies something more than mere national or generational difference. Both accounts share a secret referent, whose identity they rarely blurt out as such, both aim implicitly to come to terms with the same troubling and peremptory reality. This we can now identify as *American* capitalism, whose historical modifications are, one would think, the determinant of those secondary theoretical ones. From the Manhattan or Hollywood of nascent consumerism and modernization, in which the German refugee intellectuals with some bewilderment retained their Central European cultural pride and dialectical self-consciousness, to the 'delirious New York' and countercultural California of the 1960s superstate, with its very different gravitational pull over the intellectuals of a diminished Western Europe, much has changed, including pleasure itself and its images and functions.

The most consequent and influential French counterposition on pleasure is, however associated, with another name, that of the late Roland Barthes, about whom some remarks are unavoidably in order. What Barthes was, and what he became, is a complicated and interesting subject, only a little of which can be developed here. But as the trajectory is inscribed in *Le Plaisir du texte* in surcharged fashion, the symbolic meaning of that pamphlet cannot, I think, really be grasped without saying something about it. The very date of that influential, fragmentary statement – 1973 – is in retrospect charged with significance. Marking a break dramatized by the emergence of the oil weapon and the onset of a global economic crisis which is still with us (and expressed politically in such different events as the Chilean *coup* and the French common programme of the Left), the general moment from 1972 to 1974 can be seen as the definitive end of whatever, worldwide, came to be known as the sixties. In the area of culture and theory this moment was also the occasion for a range of statements and disguised manifestos which all in one way or another repealed that period and its values and urgencies. They 'called a halt', often in the form of a 'return' to the very moral values the '60s had called into question, as in Lionel Trilling's very different, yet equally symptomatic *Sincerity and Authenticity* (1972). Nothing seemingly so distant from the moralizing of this last, with its defence of tradition and the canon, and its obligatory 'great books' format, as Barthesian hedonism and Barthes' own complacent, stubborn commitment to the *instant*, whether of reading or writing, his self-indulgence (here, self-indulgently, transformed into a very *theory* of self-indulgence), his blissful renunciation of the 'high seriousness' of the Anglo-American critic's sense of the moral vocation of criticism itself – 'nothing to *say* about the *texte de jouissance*'; 'you can't talk *about* it, you can only talk "within" it, on its own terms, abandoning yourself to a voluptuous plagiarism, hysterically reaffirming *jouissance* in its essential void'.

Although it is an attractive alternative to the pieties of Anglo Saxon cultural élitism – not least because the latter still forms *our* particular institutional horizon – on rereading today, *Le plaisir du texte* does strike one as oddly defensive. Its polemic targets are no doubt 'textual puritans' rather than the polymorphous and hallucinogenizing partisans of a '60s 'authenticity', against whom Trilling is concerned to draw the line. The more significant feature here is that for both writers, in their very different national situations, these seemingly antithetical adversaries are both fantasized as images and representations of a dominant *Left* – only where for Trilling, that Left is embodied in the rising tide of the barbarism of a student and black radicalism, for Barthes it takes the form of the 'marxist *gendarme*', the more traditional 'puritanism' of the French Communist Party and of some orthodox Leninism. In both discussions, then, the ostensible subjects of individual gratification (aesthetic on the one hand, that of self-expression or 'authenticity' on the other) prove to be vehicles for some deeper political and ideological position, in which the values of 'decorum', on the one hand, and physical pleasure, on the other, are stimulated and appealed to for confirmation of a repudiation of Left politics by two writers whose theoretical methods have had some historical relationship to left philosophical traditions.

The Politics of Pleasure

Whether the Left has historically been 'puritanical' or indeed whether there is something in the very essence of revolutionary mentality which somehow forever 'dooms' it to a puritanical stance, are questions central to the present topic but quite impossible to answer empirically. The Lenin story, for instance, shows *his* puritanism to have been tactical: he obviously *liked* Beethoven (on the other hand, that line of inquiry opens up the troubled matter of the left-orthodox refusal of modernism and *its* peculiar pleasures). Who says pleasure, however, generally means sex, and it is generally around the end of a properly Soviet cultural revolution in the late '20s (dramatized among other things, in the early '30s, by the exclusion of Wilhelm Reich and the halt to his experiments with a properly 'sexual politics') that the discussion of left puritanism turns. Whatever the contributions of a Freudian habit of analysis may be in this area (the deeper unconscious attitudes of bolshevik leaders themselves for example), it may not be inappropriate to recall the strategic and tactical dimensions of such 'turns', which have to do with the very different matter of the key issues and slogans susceptible of mobilizing (or alienating) working class people. Although this line of discussion does not need to take the condescending framework of some 'stages' theory of consciousness, or to be staged around analysis of the relative backwardness of working class consciousness on sexual matters – 'they're not ready for women's or gay liberation or abortion', 'they need further cultural re-education' – note that precisely those analyses, however condescending, are central to any real discussion of cultural revolution itself, of the programmed habits of subalternity, obedience and the like, which cultural revolution seeks to dissolve.

But there is a different way of understanding working-class resistance to slogans of a sexual politics (always assuming that such resistance exists 'empirically' and is a crucial factor in the construction of political and ideological strategies). That is the class symbolism of such questions. The conception of the primacy of class issues and class consciousness suggests that from a working-class perspective, issues of sexual liberation may not be grasped on their own terms, but rather as so many class ideologies and as the collective expression of groups (such as middle class youth) which working-class people identify as the class enemy. This should at least alert us to the possibility that the discussion of pleasure as a phenomenon may not have much to do at all with the rather different discussion of pleasure, sexual liberation, the Utopian or libidinal body, as a political slogan or value.

It is at least certain that one of the historical merits of Barthes' booklet was to have legitimized the overt discussion of 'pleasure' as a theme on the left (along with other somewhat less influential discussions such as Sebastiano Timpanaro's notion of a 'pessimistic hedonism') – projects like this

symposium are unthinkable without this kind of preparation, or modifica-
tion in the traditional Left problematic. Indeed, the interest in such matters
is clearly part of a more general feeling which emerged from the '60s that
traditional Marxism had failed to address itself to a whole range of essentially 'existential' issues – death and the 'meaning of life', for another; the whole
realm of the Unconscious; religion, the Utopian; the whole area of daily life
and its qualities or modes of alienation, and whether a politics of daily life is
conceivable; Nature finally and the ecology.

I have, however, omitted from this list that political 'issue' in which the
most powerful restatement of a left puritanism 'for our time' has been made;
it seems to me frivolous to describe this as an 'existential' issue, although the
temptation to do so tells us something about the limits of the 'existential'
corrections or completions of Marxism, and about the relationship of
'existential' categories to purely individual experience. The result would
seem to be that while feminism may seem an *existential* issue to *men*, it is a
matter of group struggle for women, which is something quite different. At
any event, paradoxically, the reintroduction of the 'problem' of pleasure on
the Left (thematized by Barthes out of a whole French theoretical culture,
most notably marked by Lacanian psychoanalysis) now paves the way for an
interesting reversal, and for the kind of radical political argument *against*
pleasure of which Laura Mulvey's 'Visual Pleasure and Narrative Cinema' is
one of the more influential statements.[1] Her programme – 'the destruction of
pleasure as a radical weapon' – is based on the theoretical identification of
traditional filmic viewing pleasure with the symbolic expression of male
power in the 'right to look', a right whose ultimate object becomes the
woman's body, or rather, the women *as* body. Something of the politics of
the article could still, I think, be argued in the older class terms evoked
above; the right to look, the defence of sexual liberation, including pornography and whole culture of the libidinal image as such – these would be
slogans attractive to males, but symbolically marked (now in gender, rather
than class ways) for women as the practices of the other, of the oppressor, of
a form of domination analogous to that of the class enemy. The more
theoretical basis for the argument – which rests on the Lacanian account of
the constitution of the male subject (in particular the problem of the
'mother's phallus', the fetish and so forth) – is menaced by the ahistorical
framework of most psychoanalytic approaches, insofar as it may project a
perspective in which men's sexuality will somehow always be formed in this
way and always associated with just such scoptocratic, fetishizing impulses:
Amazonianism or lesbian separatism would then be the only consequent
'solution'. For males of good will, meanwhile, the depth-psychological part
of the argument may well serve mainly to reinforce that tendency to
ideological *examen de conscience*, morbid introspection and *autocritique*, and
the guilt trip, which, in an unusual mutation of older religious practices, is so

often an attractive way for the isolated left intellectual to 'work out his personal salvation'. (Paradoxically, this last is also the promise of Barthesian hedonism.)

At any rate, if it begins to turn out that the value of 'pleasure' as a political slogan is not merely unattractive to working-class people but also to women, then its ideological effectivity is evidently a rather diminished one. As for Barthes himself, returning to him one last time, the concept of pleasure – or more properly of *jouissance* – had a more complicated function, which may be made clearer if we grasp *Le plaisir du texte* as a return to the issues that had pre-occupied him years earlier in *Writing Degree Zero* (1953). The earlier book was still situated within an essentially Sartrean problematic, that of *What is Literature?* (1947), a problematic to which Barthes gave a very different solution from that of Sartre himself, but which shares the latter's vision of history as a nightmare of blood guilt. Sartre had shown, in his book, that the necessary restrictions of all literary languages to the 'signals' of local or limited (non-universal) groups or publics made all literary practices, in the world as we know it, the symbolic endorsement of the class violence of this or that group against the others. Sartre's orthodox solution – the endorsement of the proletariat as the last class, as the only possibility for the emergence for the first time in history of a genuinely universal public – is explicitly designated as a Utopian one. Barthes then ingeniously imagined a rather different way of escaping from the 'nightmare of history', namely the projection of a kind of writing from which all group or class signals had been eliminated: white or bleached writing, a kind of practice of a Utopian neutrality, which would enable an escape on this side (*en deçà*) from the collective guilt inherent in the practice of any of the literary signs as such. Ironically, the whitest writing always slowly turned into a literary institution and a practice of literary signs in its own right, over time: Barthes' contemporaneous example, Camus, no longer looks very neutral to us today, nor do the later practitioners of the then *nouveau roman*.

So it is that in *Le Plaisir du texte*, the operation is staged in a rather different way. It is now through reception rather than production that History may be suspended, and the social function of that fragmentary, punctual *jouissance* which can break through any text will then be more effectively to achieve that freedom from all ideologies and all *engagement* (of the Left as much as of the Right), which the zero degree of literary signs had once seemed to promise. *Atopie* rather than *utopie*: such is the non-place of Barthes' *jouissance*, where the dominant ideology of the sentence and of the institution of literature is to be undermined. Unlike the seemingly related *Tel Quel* or Kristevan formulations, however, where such 'undermining' is saluted as a revolutionary act in itself, Barthes is too wisely cynical to wish to describe such moments in more glamorous terms than those of the local resistance of perversion and the perverse (*leitmotifs* of his essay) to the contaminations of power. In any case, even the flight from history and politics is a reaction to those realities and a way of registering their omni-presence, and the immense merit of Barthes' essay is to restore a certain politically symbolic value to the experience of *jouissance*, and to make it impossible to read the latter except as a response to a political and historical dilemma, whatever position one chooses (puritanism/hedonism) to take about that response itself.

But one cannot conclude all this without some final evaluation of Barthes himself, so ambiguous a figure. Is it necessary to recall that the early Barthes *was* political, and that he furnished (and books like *Mythologies* continue to furnish) us with critical instruments and weapons of an overtly political capability? What the later Barthes meant, however, can perhaps be formulated as follows (the lesson was really there all along, but became more univocal in the later texts): he taught us to read with our bodies – and often to write with them as well. Whence, if one likes, the unavoidable sense of self-indulgence and corruption which Barthes' work can project when viewed from certain limited angles. The libidinal body, as a field and instrument of perception all at once, cannot but be self-indulgent in that sense. To discipline it, to give it the proper tasks and ask it to repress its other random impulses, is at once to limit its effectiveness, or, even worse, to damage it irretrievably. Lazy, shot through with fits of boredom or enthusi-asm, reading the world and its texts with nausea or with *jouissance*, listening for the fainter vibrations of a sensorium largely numbed by civilization and rationalization, sensitive to the messages of throbs too immediate, too recognizable as pain or pleasure – maybe all this is not to be described as self-indulgence after all. Maybe it requires a discipline and a responsiveness of a rare yet different sort, something like free association (outsmarting the instant defenses of the ego or the rationalizing intellect) or boating, sensing and riding with a minimal current. Maybe indeed the deeper subject is here: not 'pleasure' (against whose comfort and banalities everyone from Barthes to Edmund Burke is united in warning us), but the libidinal body itself, and *its* peculiar politics, which may well move in a realm largely beyond the 'pleasurable' in that narrow, culinary, bourgeois sense.

Materialism

So gradually the word 'materialism' begins to impose itself. I have my own reasons for objecting to the current fashionable Left use of this term as an omnibus slogan. Facile and dishonest as a kind of popular-front 'solution' to the very real tensions between Marxism and feminism, it also seems to me extraordinarily misleading and inadequate as an ideological synonym for 'historical materialism' itself. 'Materialism' as a term and as a concept is booby-trapped by its functional association with the eighteenth-century

bourgeois Enlightenment and with nineteenth-century positivism. Whatever precautions are taken, it always fatally ends up projecting a determin-
ism by matter (that is to say, the individual body or organism in isolation)
rather than – as in historical materialism – a determination by the mode
of production. It would be better to grasp Marxism and the dialectic as an
attempt to overcome not idealism by itself, but that very ideological opposition which opposes idealism to materialism in the first place. The work of
Sartre and Gramsci both is there to argue for some position 'beyond idealism
and materialism', and if one does not like the projected new solution – called
praxis – then at least it would be desirable to search for something more
adequate.

　　Still, as far as 'pleasure' is concerned, it may readily be admitted that it is
materialist; whether or not 'consciousness' (the psychological subject) is
always and in all moments of history and modes of production constitu-
tionally and irrecuperably idealistic, the generalization is probably safe *for
us*. (At the very least, it renders the ideal of a 'materialist thinking' problem-
atical: professions of 'materialism' being not at all incompatible with idealist
habits of mind – quite the contrary!) So the bourgeois monad ceaselessly
continues to convert things into the ideas of things, into their images, into
their names, until, at a break in the process, suddenly that taboo and
unimaginable 'outside' breaks the thread for an instant: this fresh, wet air of
spring on my face, the sheer metal taste of a musical phrase that is no longer
just its own idea but the material vibration and timbre of a physical
instrument itself, this 'green so delicious it hurts' (Baudelaire), the irreduc-
ible mystery of flavour itself, as of roots in the earth, or the flush and
comfortable fever of what the great Sartrean description of sexuality calls
'in-carnation'. Pleasure is finally the consent of life in the body, the recon-
ciliation – momentary as it may be – with the necessity of physical existence
in a physical world. (And then at that point, the materialization of what had
formerly been 'idealistic' as well – the materiality of words, once again, and
of images; hardest of all, perhaps, of the 'thinking process' itself, of
whatever the 'mind' is as an activity: the *jouissance* of the great scientific
intuitions, perhaps, or of the great 'deductions' of the mystery story. . . .)

　　Still, all this remains comfort, and comfortable, in Barthes' pejorative
sense – 'house, province, the meal, the lamp, the family in its appropriate
place, neither too close nor too far . . . this extraordinary reinforcement of
the ego (by fantasy); a padded unconscious.' For Barthes, this was still a
privatized and Bierdermeier middle-class experience, a guilty evasion. Yet
we have other class images – Bloch's celebration of the peasant household,
Brecht's plebeian materialism of the worker's soup and cigar, and even
Marcuse's 'erotization of the work process', with its reinvention of the old
material pleasure of handicraft in an advanced technological age. What can
be said of *this* vision of bodily pleasure is not that it is not political, not a

Utopian vision of another way of living: but rather that what it solves is my individual relationship with my own body – which is to say with Earth (Heidegger) or with what used to be called Nature – and not that very different relationship between myself or my body and other people – or in other words, with History, with the political in the stricter sense.

Whence the troublesome unruliness of the sexual question. Is it only that comfortable material question or is it more irredeemably scandalous – as in sexual *ecstasy* (the strongest translation of the Barthesian *jouissance*), or in that even more sombre matter of the will to power in sexual domination? These are harder 'pleasures' to domesticate, their political content more easily assimilable to religions, or fascism – yet another 'pleasure', this last! Therapeutic puritanism thus seems to impose itself again; yet before embracing it, it may be desirable to see what happens if we try to historicize these dilemmas, and the experiences that produced them. Is not, for example, the aesthetics of ecstasy, Barthesian *jouissance*, a properly '60s experience? And if so, would it not be desirable for another moment to explore the historical relations between this new experience – what I will call the *pleasure of the simulacrum* – and its aesthetic objects – henceforth called *post-modernism* – as well as its socially and historically original situation – 'consumer society', media society, multinational or 'late' capitalism, the 'society of the spectacle'?

Or is the experience so new, and without any historical antecedents or analogies whatsoever? Personally, I have found a 'defamiliarisation' and enlightenment in the *Plaisir du texte* of an earlier transitional age, and of the work of one of the most creative and permanently fascinating of the great class enemies, Edmund Burke's *Philosophical Inquiry into the Origins of Our Ideas of the Sublime and the Beautiful*. Here already the great Barthesian opposition, where the pleasurable experience of the Beautiful – described as a comfortable and quasi-sexual relaxation of the organism ('that sinking, that melting, that langour, which is the characteristical effect of the beautiful as it regards every sense') is set off starkly against the 'fearful' experience of the Sublime, which, springing according to Burke from the instinct of self-preservation, causes the body tone to draw together in reaction like a fist, in 'exercise or *labour*; and labour is a surmounting of *difficulties*, an exertion of the contracting power of the muscles; and as such resembles pain, which consists in tension or contraction, in everything but degree.' This last, however, with its train of predictable examples (great buildings or monumental colonnades, darkness, Milton, the Godhead, infinity and also 'infinite' ideas including political ones, such as 'honour, justice, liberty' – but not yet, oddly, the inevitable *mountain* of Romantic sensibility) would not at first glance seem terribly compatible with the Barthesian ecstatic – the sudden stab of *jouissance*, the 'schizophrenic' dissolution of the boring old bourgeois ego, *dérive*, the Nietzschean cry, scandal, break, the cleavage of the subject, the swoon, the 'hysterical affirmation of the ecstatic void' – until one begins to note the insistent negativity of these formulations and to recall Barthes' epigraph from Hobbes, in which his own problematic and that of Edmund Burke suddenly and unexpectedly coincide: 'The only true passion in my life has been *fear!*'

Fear – the aesthetic reception of fear, its artistic expression, transformation, the enjoyment of the shock and commotion fear brings to the human organism – is, on the Burkean theory of the sublime, the apprehension through a given aesthetic object of what in its awesome magnitude shrinks, threatens, diminishes, rebukes individual human life. How one could *enjoy* such an experience is suggested well enough by the grudging appearance at the end of Burke's chain of substitutions of the divine itself: 'I purposely avoided, when I first considered this subject, to introduce the idea of that great and tremendous Being, as an example in an argument so light as this'. The machinery of the sacred, indeed, offers one signal method for the transformation of sheer horror (death, anxiety, the meaningless succession of the generations, the fragility and cheapness of life) into libidinal gratification. What if we substituted for this fragile menaced individual human *body* – in Burke's scheme of things – a threatened menace to and dissolution of that other entity (whose construction on the model of the body image is signalled by the so-called 'mirror stage') which is the psychological subject, the *ego*, the personality, individual identity? Is it possible that the interiorization, the Nietzschean choice, the work of enjoyment, of that second type of fear might well approximate what Barthes designates, in terms that deliberately avoid any suggestion of banal pleasurability, as *jouissance*?

Allegory

In that case, the analogy with Burke may have further lessons for us, since Burke's distinction between beauty and the sublime is already by way of being a structural one: immanence versus transcendence this would have been characterized, in an older philosophical language – beauty being the self-sufficient experience of small-scale objects, the small pleasures of the creation (to develop the religious theme), an experience not dialectically related to that of the sublime but rather simply *different*, distinct from it. (For Burke pleasure and pain are not opposites, but unrelated, self-sufficient experiences in something more like a triad: pleasure, pain, indifference). The sublime, on the other hand, the pleasures of fear, the aesthetic appropriation of 'pain', is a rather different matter, a kind of dual or stereoscopic experience, which I would in the present context prefer to call *allegorical*. That is, the sublime takes its object as the pretext and the occasion for the intuition through it and beyond it of sheer unfigurable force itself, sheer power, that which stuns the imagination in the most literal sense. (The imagination finds no *figure* for that awesome power in and of itself: even Burke's 'ideas of God' is a substitution.)

It then becomes a tempting speculation to specify the historical nature of this terrifying force before which the sublime, in a properly Nietzschean affirmation – choose what crushes you! – finds its gratification and its ecstatic surrender. The capital-logicians have recently made the scandalous suggestion that what Hegel called 'Absolute Spirit' was simply to be read as the transpersonal, unifying, impersonal, supreme force of emergent Capital itself; one does not dare, without more wideranging textual evidence, and under pain of the crassest interpretive dogmatism, affirm anything of the sort for the Burkean intuition (1756). That one can do so for the Barthesian sublime, however, seems to me beyond any question. The immense culture of the simulacrum whose experience, whether we like it or not, constitutes a whole series of daily ecstasies and punctual fits of *jouissance* or schizophrenic dissolutions – *'c'était donc ça! c'est donc moi! c'est donc à moi!'* – may appropriately, one would think, be interpreted as so many unconscious points of contact with that equally unfigurable and unimaginable thing, the multinational apparatus, the great suprapersonal *system* of a late capitalist 'technology' – the ecstasy of the machine once again, as in futurism, yet today without any 'ideology' of the machine or any nascent representations of the excitements of its first great still physical and perceptible embodiments in the tank or the machine gun (Marinetti) or the factory itself (Diego Rivera, Léger). The idea of the computer subsumes those earlier excitements, but beyond any tangible figure or representation (the physical computer now being little more than a box with its brain wires hanging out).

That there is thus a politics and a historicity of *jouissance* seems clear, as does its fundamental ambiguity as a socially symbolic experience. The point, however, is not to awaken some scarcely dormant left tendency to moralize such experiences, but rather to draw the lesson of what might be a radically different political use of pleasure as such. I will suggest, then, that the proper political use of pleasure must always be *allegorical* in the sense spelled out above: the thematizing of a particular 'pleasure' as a political issue (to fight for example on the terrain of the aesthetics of the *city*; or for certain forms of sexual liberation; or for access to certain kinds of cultural activities; or for an aesthetic transformation of social relations or a politics of the body) must always involve a dual focus, in which the local issue is meaningful and desirable in and of itself, but is also *at one and the same time* taken as the *figure* for Utopia in general, and for the systemic revolutionary transformation of society as a whole. Without these simultaneous dimensions, the political demand becomes reduced to yet another local 'issue' in the micro-politics of this or that limited group or its particular hobby or specialization, and a slogan which, once satisfied leads no further politically.

This dual or 'allegorical' focus is indeed what makes for both the uniqueness and the difficulties of Marxism in general as a conception of revolutionary transformation. The dialectic is in itself this dual obligation to invent ways of uniting the here-and-now of the immediate situation with the 'totalizing' logic of the global or Utopian one. So a given economic demand must always be in some sense a figure for a more total revolutionary transformation, unless it is to fall back into economism. So also – to take an example a little more familiar to a public of left *intellectuals* – a given piece of textual analysis must make a punctual or occasional statement about its object, but must also, at one and the same time, be graspable as a more general contribution to the Marxian problematic. And it must do so in both instances, without the concrete local occasion turning back into some mere 'example' of the 'abstract' framework (which it is preferable to call the perspective of totalization). So finally the right to a specific pleasure, to a specific enjoyment of the potentialities of the material body – if it is not to remain only that, if it is to become genuinely political, if it is to evade the complacencies of 'hedonism' – must always in one way or another also be able to stand as a figure for the transformation of social relations as a whole.

Note

1. Laura Mulvey, 'Visual pleasure and narrative cinema' in *Screen*, vol. 16, no. 3, Autumn 1976. I don't mean this example to suggest that 'feminism' is massively puritanical. On the contrary, very different positions on pleasure have been taken within the women's movement – as, for example, in the debate on the vaginal orgasm. And in general, whenever one has to do with the social *repression* of a particular 'pleasure', the issue is at once politicized, at least until the repression is lifted!

Victor Burgin

GRADIVA

SHE WAS RAISED
BY HER FATHER,
A DISTANT MAN,
FOREVER LOST
IN HIS WORK.

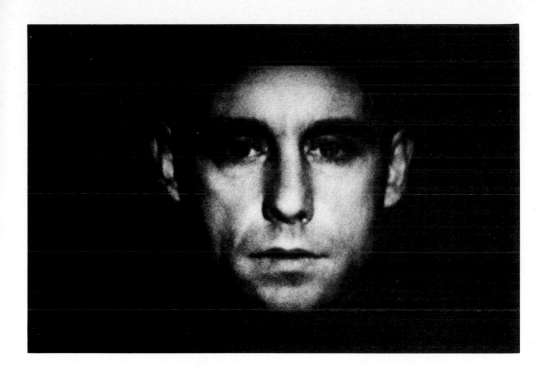

IN CHILDHOOD SHE FOUND COMPANIONSHIP
WITH A NEIGHBOUR'S BOY OF HER OWN AGE.
YEARS LATER, NOW ADULT, SHE ENCOUNTERED HIM AGAIN, BY CHANCE;
HE SHOWED NO SIGN OF HAVING RECOGNISED HER,
WHICH PLUNGED HER INTO DESPAIR.

SHE COULD TAKE NO INTEREST IN ANY SUITOR.
SHE RESIGNED HERSELF
TO THE COMPANIONSHIP OF HER FATHER,
ACCOMPANYING HIM
ON HIS TRIPS ABROAD.

IT WAS WHILE SHE WAS VISITING
THE RUINS OF POMPEII
THAT SHE BECAME AWARE OF
THE FIGURE OF A MAN
WATCHING HER.

ALONE
IN THE RUINED STREETS
HE WAS STARTLED BY THE SUDDEN APPEARANCE OF
THE FIGURE OF A WOMAN
MOVING WITH GRADIVA'S UNMISTAKEABLE GAIT.

IN A DREAM OF THE DESTRUCTION OF POMPEII
HE BELIEVED HE SAW GRADIVA, AS IF TURNING TO MARBLE.
HE RESOLVED TO TRAVEL TO POMPEII
IN THE HOPE OF FINDING SOME TRACE OF
THE LONG-BURIED GIRL.

My gaze slid by chance towards the massive mirror
hanging in front of us and I uttered a cry: in
This golden frame our image appeared like a
painting, and this painting was marvellously
beautiful. It was so strange and so fantastic
that a deep shiver seized me at the thought
that its lines and its colours would soon dissolve
like a cloud.

THE RELIEF REPRESENTED A YOUNG WOMAN, STEPPING FORWARD.
ONE FOOT RESTED SQUARELY ON THE GROUND,
THE OTHER TOUCHED THE GROUND ONLY WITH THE TIPS OF THE TOES.
THIS POSTURE CAME TO HAUNT HIS THOUGHTS;
HE GAVE THE GIRL THE NAME 'GRADIVA' — 'SHE WHO STEPS ALONG'.

Notes

Captions

The text which parallels the images is based on the story *Gradiva*, by Wilhelm Jensen; the story is the subject of a long article by Freud: 'Delusions and Dreams in Jensen's *Gradiva*' (1907), *The Standard Edition of the Complete Psychological Works of Sigmund Freud* (24 Vols), London, Hogarth Press, 1953–74, vol. IX.

Photographs

1 The photograph quoted here is of the frontispiece to vol. IX of the Standard Edition cited above.
2 Image on a cinema screen, New York, 1977. Details of origin forgotten.
3 Roman amphitheatre; Gortys, Crete, 1981.
4 See 2, above.
5 Pl. Defilad, Warsaw, Poland; October, 1981. The building in the background is the Soviet-built *Palace of Culture and Science*.
6 See 2, above.
7 The writing is a quotation from Sacher-Masoch's *Venus in Furs*; the specific source is Gilles Deleuze, *Présentation de Sacher-Masoch avec le texte intégral de La Vénus à la Fourrure*, Les Editions de Minuit, 1967, p. 216.

Cora Kaplan

WILD NIGHTS
Pleasure/Sexuality/Feminism

> . . . till women are led to exercise their understandings, they should not be satirized for their attachment to rakes; or even for being rakes at heart, when it appears to be the inevitable consequence of their education. They who live to please – must find their enjoyments, their happiness in pleasure!
>
> Mary Wollstonecraft, 1792

> Wild Nights – Wild Nights!
> Were I with thee
> Wild Nights should be
> Our luxury!
>
> Emily Dickinson 1861

> I had been a hopeful radical. Now I am not. Pornography has infected me. Once I was a child and I dreamed of freedom. Now I am an adult and I see what my dreams have come to: pornography. So, while I cannot help my sleeping nightmares, I have given up many waking dreams.
>
> Andrea Dworkin, 1981[1]

How difficult it is to uncouple the terms pleasure and sexuality. How much more difficult, once uncoupled, to re-imagine woman as the subject, pleasure as her object, if that object is *not* sexual. Almost two centuries of feminist activity and debate have passed, two hundred years in which women's understandings have been widely exercised, yet most of Mary Wollstonecraft's modest proposals for female emancipation are still demands on a feminist platform. Most distant, most utopian seems her hesitant plea that the social basis for woman's sexual pleasure be 'dignified' after 'some future revolution in time.'[2] Too near, too familiar, is her temporary expedient, the rejection of woman's pleasure as inextricably bound to her dependent and deferential status. Revolutions have come and gone, and sexuality is once more at the head of feminist agendas in the west, the wild card whose suit and value shifts provocatively with history. As dream or nightmare, or both at once, it reigns in our lives as an anarchic force, refusing to be chastened and tamed by sense or conscience to a sentence in a revolutionary manifesto.

In 'the right to choose' the women's movement has reasserted the

the tenets of liberal humanism, laying claim to its promise of individual civil rights for women, and acknowledging the difficulty of prescription in the area of sexual politics. Yet female sexuality remains one of the central contradictions within contemporary politics, causing as much anxiety to feminists and their sympathisers as to their opponents. Within feminist debate, radical and revolutionary feminists argue with their liberal and socialist sisters around definitions of a correct, or politically acceptable sexual practice. The possible positions on this troubling issue which can be identified as feminist range widely from a pro-pleasure polymorphous perverse sexual radicalism, through cautious permissiveness, to anti-porn activism and a political lesbianism which de-emphasises genital sexuality. This muddy conflict on the site of feminism itself, suggests, among other things, how profoundly women's subjectivity is constructed through sexual categories.

The negative meanings which have been historically associated with women's sexuality have been a major impediment in their fight for libera-tion. Historians suggest that the 'ideological division of women into two classes, the virtuous and the fallen, was already well developed' by the mid-eighteenth century. Certainly it received one of its major modern articulations at about this time in Rousseau's *Emile* (1762). In *Emile* the possibility of women's civil, economic and psychological independence is rejected because it would also enable the independent and licentious exercise of her supposedly insatiable sexual appetite. Woman's desire is seen by Rousseau as both regressive and disruptive of the new liberal social order he proposed; women's emancipation would mean a step backward for rational and egalitarian progress. It is important to remember that the notion of women as politically enabled and independent is fatally linked to the un-restrained and vicious exercise of her sexuality, not just in the propaganda of the new right, but in a central and influential work of the very old left.

When feminists sought to appropriate liberal humanism for their own sex they had to contend with the double standard prominently inscribed within radical tradition, as well as with its suffocating and determining presence in dominant ideologies. Female sexuality is still the suppressed text of those liberal and left programmes which are silent on the issues of women's subordination. This silence has had its negative effect upon feminism itself, which must always speak into other political discourses. Where both right and left sexual ideologies converge, associating women's desire with weakness, unreason and materialism, it has been noticeably hard to insist on positive social and political meanings for female sexuality. Only its supposed disruptive force can be harnessed to revolutionary possibility, and then, perhaps, only for the moment of disruption itself. While most feminisms have recognized that the regulation of female sexual-ity and the ideological mobilisation of its threat to order are part of women's subordination, it is not surprising that they have too often accepted the paradigm which insists that desire is a regressive force in women's lives, and have called for a sublimation of women's sexual pleasure to meet a passionless and rational ideal. Rousseau's formulation has cast a long shadow that cannot be dispersed by simple inversions of his argument. As long as the idea survives that a reformed libidinal economy for women is the precondition for a successful feminist politics, women can always be seen as unready for emancipation. This view, explicitly expressed in Mary Wollstonecraft's *A Vindication of the Rights of Woman* emerges in a different form in Adrienne Rich's radical feminist polemic, 'Compulsory Heterosexuality and Lesbian Existence' (1980). This article explores *A Vindication* at some length, and 'Compulsory Heterosexuality' very briefly, as part of a longer project to understand how the sexual politics of feminism has been shaped.

The Rights of Women and Feminine Sexuality: Mary Wollstonecraft

The reputation of Mary Wollstonecraft's *A Vindication of the Rights of Women* (1792), the founding text of Anglo-American feminism, generally precedes and in part constructs our reading of it. We are likely to look for, and privilege, its demands for educational, legal and political equality; these are, after all, the demands that link Wollstonecraft's feminism to our own. If we give ourselves up to *A Vindication*'s eloquent but somewhat rambling prose, we will also discover *passim* an unforgettable early account of the making of a lady, an acute, detailed analysis of the social construction of femininity, which appropriates the developmental psychology of enlightenment and romantic thought. It is certainly possible to engage with *A Vindication* so far and no farther, to let most of its troubling historical meanings and contradictions drop away, so that we may take away from it an unproblematic feminist inheritance. How much use can we make of this legacy without a sense of the history which produced it? Read *A Vindication* for its historical meanings and another text emerges, one which is arguably as interested in developing a class sexuality for a radical, reformed bourgeoisie as in producing an analysis of women's subordination and a manifesto of her rights.

This part of Wollstonecraft's project deserves our attention too, for only by understanding why Wollstonecraft wanted women to become full, independent members of the middle-class, can we make sense of the negative and prescriptive assault on female sexuality which is the *leitmotif* of *A Vindication* where it is not the overt subject of the text.

It is usual to see the French Revolution as the intellectual and political backdrop to *A Vindication*; it would be more useful to see it as the most important condition of its production. As Margaret Walters has pointed out, *A Vindication* sums up and rearticulates a century of feminist ideas,[5] but its immediate stake was in the political advance of a revolutionary vanguard –

the middle-class itself, as Wollstonecraft and others imagined it. Every opinion in the text is written in the glare of this politically charged and convulsive moment, and the area of Wollstonecraft's thought most altered and illuminated by that glare is sexuality. In her two attempts at fiction, *Mary, a Fiction* and *Maria or The Wrongs of Woman*, one produced a few years before *A Vindication* and the other incomplete at her death in 1797, women's feelings and desires, as well as the importance of expressing them, are valorised. But in *A Vindication* Wollstonecraft turned against feeling, which is seen as reactionary and regressive, almost counter-revolutionary. Sexuality and pleasure are narcotic inducements to a life of lubricious slavery. Reason is the only human attribute appropriate to the revolutionary character, and women are impeded from their early and corrupt initiation in the sensual, from using theirs.

Why is *A Vindication* so suffused with the sexual, and so projectively severe about it? This is the question that I will explore at some length below. Wollstonecraft's feminism and her positions on sexuality were, at this point in her life, directly bound up with her radical politics – they can only be understood through each other. In untangling the knotted meanings of the sexual in our own history, our own politics, it is useful to understand the different but recurring anxieties it has stirred for other feminisms, other times.

A Vindication of the Rights of Woman offers the reader a puritan sexual ethic with such passionate conviction that self-denial seems a libidinized activity. And so it was, in the sense that a reform of sexual behaviour was Wollstonecraft's precondition for radical change in the condition of women; permitting the development of their reason and independence. The democratic imperatives – equality and liberty for all classes of persons – have been, for so long now, the well worn staples of liberal and left rhetoric that it is hard to remember that they were being invoked in new ways and with unprecedented exuberance in the 1790s. When we try to puzzle out the meanings of *A Vindication* it is the negative construction of the sexual in the midst of a positive and progressive construction of the social and political which we must question. In that contradiction – if indeed it is a contradiction – our present conflict over sexual politics is still partly embedded.

Written in six weeks at the height of British left optimism about events in France, *A Vindication* came out early in 1792, the same year as the second part of Tom Paine's *Rights of Man*, a year before William Godwin's *Political Justice*. Each was, equally, a response to the political moment. All three were crucial statements about the social and political possibilities of a transformed Britain. An almost millenarial fervour moved British radicals in these years. Their political and philosophical ideas were being put into practice only a few hundred miles away; there were signs of reasoned and purposeful unrest at home among ordinary working people. The end of aristocratic privilege and autocratic rule in France was to be taken as a sign of universal change. The downfall of the Bastille, Thomas Paine exulted, included the idea of the downfall of despotism.

A Vindication engages with radical romantic politics at a moment when the practical realisation of such a politics seemed as near as France itself. Wollstonecraft had already written one short pamphlet, *A Vindication of the Rights of Men* (1790), in support of the revolution, and was still to write a long piece on its behalf.[6] In this, her most important work, she took advantage of an open moment of political debate to intervene on behalf of women from inside the British left intelligentsia. Its message is urgent precisely because social and political reform seemed not just possible, but inevitable. The status of women as moral and political beings had become one fairly muted instance of the unresolved contradictions within the republican and democratic tendencies of the time. The overlapping tendencies of enlightenment and romantic thought emphasized the natural virtue rather than innate depravity of human beings, their equality before God, and the evils brought about by unequal laws and hereditary privilege. Arguments initially directed at a corrupt ruling class on behalf of a virtuous bourgeoisie inevitably opened up questions of intra-class power relations. With *A Vindication* Wollstonecraft challenged her own political camp, insisting that women's rights be put higher up on the radical agenda. Addressed to Talleyrand, taking issue with Rousseau, speaking the political jargon of her English contemporaries, *A Vindication* invited the enlightenment heritage, the dead and the living, to extend the new humanism to the other half of the race. With a thriving revolution under way, the political and intellectual credit of republican sympathisers was as high as their morale. It seemed like the right moment to ask them to pay their debt to women.

The opening pages of *A Vindication* share the aggressive, confident mood and tone that had developed under the threat and promise of the revolutionary moment. Ridiculing the 'turgid bombast' and 'flowery diction' of aristocratic discourse, Wollstonecraft offers the reader instead, 'sincerity' and 'unaffected' prose, the style and standards of the class of men and women to whom she was speaking – 'I pay particular attention to those in the middle class, because they appear to be in the most natural [i.e. least corrupted] state.' Her unapologetic class bias was shared with her radical contemporaries – it is hardly surprising that idealized humanity as it appears in her text is a rational, plain speaking, bourgeois man. Denying any innate inequality between the sexes except physical strength, she promises to 'first consider women in the grand light of human creatures, who, in common with men, are placed on this earth to unfold their faculties', and addresses her sisters boldly as 'rational creatures' whose 'first object of laudable ambition' should be 'to obtain a character as a human being, regardless of the distinctions of sex. . . .'[7]

How to attain this character? In Paine's *Rights of Man* the reader was told that inequality and oppression were the effects of culture rather than nature. The text itself is a politicizing event, first constructing and then working on an uncorrupted rational subject. Paine hoped, and his enemies feared, that some sort of direct political action to unseat despotic power would follow from a sympathetic reading of his pamphlet. The message and intention of *A Vindication* are very different. Nowhere does Wollstonecraft pose women, in their present 'degraded' condition, as either vanguard or revolutionary mass. Like the corrupt aristocracy, to whom they are frequently compared, they are, instead, a *lumpen* group who must undergo strenuous re-education in order that they might renounce the sensual, rid themselves of 'soft phrases, susceptibility of heart, delicacy of sentiment, and refinement of taste' . . . 'libertine notions of beauty' and the single-minded 'desire of establishing themselves – the only way women can rise in the world – by marriage.'[8] Before the middle-class woman can join the middle-class man in advocating and advancing human progress she must be persuaded to become 'more masculine and respectable', by giving up her role both as 'insignificant objects of desire' and as desiring subject.[9]

Even in its own day *A Vindication* must have been a short, sharp shock for women readers. Men might be able to mobilize reason and passion, in them equitably combined, to change the world immediately; women, crippled and stunted by an education for dependence, must liberate themselves from a slavish addiction to the sensual before their 'understandings' could liberate anyone else. At later moments of political crisis feminists could, and would, portray women as vanguard figures, subordinated members of the propertied class who understood more about oppression, as a result, than their bourgeois male comrades. Not here. Read intertextually, heard against the polyphonic lyricism of Paine, Godwin and the dozens of ephemeral pamphleteers who were celebrating the fact and prospect of the revolution, *A Vindication* was a sobering read. Wollstonecraft sets out on a heroic mission to rescue women from a fate worse than death, which was, as she saw it, the malicious and simultaneous inscription of their sexuality and inferiority as innate, natural difference. This was how her political mentor and gender adversary Rousseau had placed them, too weak by nature to reach or be reached by sweet reason. Rousseau's influence was great, not least on Wollstonecraft herself. She accepts Rousseau's ascription of female inferiority and locates it even more firmly than he does in an excess of sensibility. Since lust and narcissism were evil they must belong to social relations rather than human nature; this was Rousseau's own position in relation to men. Accordingly, female sexuality insofar as it is vicious is inscribed in *A Vindication* as the effect of culture on an essentially ungendered nature. By tampering with the site of degrading sexuality without challenging the moralising description of sexuality itself, Wollstonecraft sets up heartbreaking conditions for women's liberation – a little death, the death of desire, the death of female pleasure.

Even if *A Vindication* is preoccupied with the sexual as the site and source of women's oppression, why is woman's love of pleasure so deeply stigmatized as the sign of her degradation? In refusing to interpret women's unbounded desire as a natural mark of sexual difference or the appropriate preoccupation of her mediated place in the social, Wollstonecraft is resisting a whole range of bourgeois positions around gender sexuality, positions which were rapidly hardening into the forms of bourgeois morality which would dominate nineteenth century ruling class gender relations. Her debate with Rousseau is central, because, like her, Rousseau wished to harness his gender ideologies to radical social and political theories. Rousseau's *Emile* is the place where he spells out the theoretical and socially expedient premises which excluded women from equal participation in the enlightenment projects for human liberation and individual transcendence. Arguing for the sexual assymetry of natural endowment, Rousseau insisted that women's 'first propensities' revealed an excess of sensibility, easily 'corrupted or perverted by too much indulgence.' In civil society women's amoral weakness must not be given its natural scope lest it lead, as it inevitably must, to adultery and its criminal consequence, the foisting of illegitimate heirs on bourgeois husbands. The remedy is borrowed back from the techniques of aristocratic despotism, elsewhere in Rousseau so violently condemned: women

> '. . . must be subject all their lives, to the most constant and severe restraint, which is that of decorum; it is therefore, necessary to accustom them early to such confinement that it may not afterwards cost them too dear. . . . we should teach them above all things to lay a due restraint on themselves.'[10]

Acknowledging, with crocodile tears, the artificiality of the social, while insisting on its necessity, Rousseau invokes a traditionally unregenerate Eve partnered to an Adam who has been given back his pre-lapsarian status.

> 'The life of a modest woman is reduced, by our absurd institutions, to a perpetual conflict with herself: but it is just that this sex should partake of the sufferings which arise from those evils it hath caused us.'[11]

Emile lays out, in fascinating detail, the radical project for the education and adult gender relations of an enlightened bourgeoisie, a project which depended for its success on the location of affection and sexuality in the family, as well as the construction of the bourgeois individual as the agent of free will. The struggle between reason and passion has an internal and external expression in Rousseau, and the triumph of reason is ensured by the social nature of passion. Since male desire needs an object, and women are that infinitely provocative object, the social subordination of women to the will of men ensures the containment of passion. In this way Rousseau links the potential and freedom of the new middle class to the simultaneous suppression and exploitation of women's nature.

Rousseau plays on the already constructed sexual categorisation of women into two groups – the virtuous and depraved. By insisting that these divisions are social rather than natural constructs – all women are depraved by nature – Rousseau can argue for social and civil restraints on women. Michel Foucault points out that the process of constructing women first and foremost as a sexual subject was in itself a class bound project:

> '. . . it was in the "bourgeois" or aristocratic family that the sexuality of children and adolescents was first problematized. . . . the first figure to be invested by the deployment of sexuality, one of the first to be "sexualized" was the "idle" woman. She inhabited the outer edge of the "world", in which she always had to appear as value, and of the family, where she was assigned a new identity charged with conjugal and parental obligation.'[12]

Mary Wollstonecraft stood waist-deep in these already established and emergent sexual ideologies. At the time she was writing *A Vindication* she was neither willing nor able to mount a wholesale critique either of bourgeois sexual mores or the wider areas of gender relations. Her life was shortly to go through some very rapid changes, which would, ironically, mark her as one of the 'degraded' women so remorselessly pilloried in her text. A year and a half after her essay was published she was living with a young American, Gilbert Imlay, in France; two years later she was an unmarried mother. *A Vindication* is a watershed in her life and thought, but this crisis is marked in a curiously wilful way. The text expresses a violent antagonism to the sexual; it exaggerates the importance of the sensual in the everyday life of women, and betrays the most profound anxiety about the rupturing force of female sexuality. Both *Emile* and *A Vindication* share a deep ambivalence about sexuality. Images of dirt, disease, decay and anarchic power run as a symbolic undertext in both works, too frequently located in women's sexual being rather than in any heterosexual practice. This distaste is pervasively articulated in *A Vindication*, adumbrated on the first page with an arresting description of French gender relations as 'the very essence of sensuality' dominated by 'a kind of sentimental lust' which is set against the ideal of 'personal reserve, and sacred respect for cleanliness and delicacy in domestic life. . . .'[13] The images of sexuality throughout are so gripping and compulsive that is hard to tear oneself away to the less vivid analysis which insists, with commendable vigour, that these filthy habits are a social construction, foisted on each generation of women by male-dominated and male-orientated society.

The place of female sexuality in *A Vindication* is overdetermined by political as well as social history. Like many of the progressive voices of the late eighteenth century, Wollstonecraft had built her dreams of a new society on the foundation of Rousseau's *Social Contract* and *Essay on Inequality*. Rousseau's writings, insofar as they spoke about human beings rather than men, offered cold reason warmed with feeling in a mixture that was very attractive to the excitable radical temperaments of Wollstonecraft's generation. Rousseau's writing, Paine wrote in 1791, expressed 'a loveliness of sentiment in favor of liberty, that excites respect and elevates the human faculties' – a judgement widely shared. How unlovely then, for Wollstonecraft to consider that in *Emile* Rousseau deliberately witholds from women because of the 'difference of sex' all that is promised to men. Rousseau's general prejudices and recommendations for women – functional, domestic education, nun-like socialisation, restricted activity and virtual incarceration in the home – colluded with the gender bias and advice of more reactionary bourgeois authors, as well as society at large. The sense in which Rousseau's prescriptions were becoming the dominant view can be heard in the different imaginary readers addressed by the texts. In the section on women *Emile* slips in and out of a defensive posture, arguing, if only tactically, with an anonymous feminist opponent for the imposition of a stricter regime for women. Wollstonecraft too is on the defensive but her composite reader-antagonist was a society which believed in and followed Rousseau's novel advice to the letter. *Emile* offered its ideas as a reform of and reaction to liberal ideas on female education and behaviour. Thirty years on, *A Vindication* suggested that female sexual morality had become laxer, operating under just such a regime of restraint and coercion that Rousseau had laid out.

The project of *Emile* was to outline the social and sexual relations of an idealised bourgeois society by giving an account of the education and courtship of its youth. *A Vindication* appropriates part of this project, the elaborate set of distinctions between the manners and morals of the aristocracy and those of the new middle class. The anti-aristocratic critique is foregrounded and set in focus by the French Revolution: its early progress exposed the corruption of the ruling classes to a very wide and receptive audience. When Wollstonecraft suggests that vain, idle and sensuous middle-class women are to be compared with the whole of the hereditary aristocracy who live only for pleasure she strikes at two popular targets. When she identifies the aestheticized and artificial language of the ruling class – 'a deluge of false sentiments and overstretched feelings', 'dropping glibly from the tongue' as the language of novels and letters, she implies that it is also the language of women, or of the society adultress. At one level she is simply producing a gendered and eroticised version of Paine's famous attack on Burke's prose style and sentiments, in *Rights of Man, part I*. At another, the massing of these metaphors of debased and disgusting female sexuality, even when they are ostensibly directed at the behaviour of a discredited class has the effect of doubling the sexual reference. Paine's comment – 'He pities the plumage and forgets the dying bird' – already carries sexual and gendered meanings. Because a naturally whorish and disrupting female sexuality was so profoundly a part of traditional symbol and reference, used to tarnish whatever object it was applied to, it became extremely difficult for Wollstonecraft to keep her use of such images tied to a social and environmental analysis. She herself is affected by the traditional association.

In *A Vindication* women's excessive interest in themselves as objects and subjects of desire is theorized as an effect of the ideological inscription of male desire on female subjects who, as a result, bear a doubled libidinal burden. But the language of that sober analysis is more innovatory, less secure, and less connotative than the metaphorical matrix used to point and illustrate it. As a consequence, there is a constant slippage back into a more naturalised and reactionary view of women, and a collapse of the two parts of the metaphors into each other. Thus, Wollstonecraft tries to argue *against* restraint and dependence by comparing the situation of women to slaves and lap-dogs –

> '. . . for servitude not only debases the individual, but its effects seem to be transmitted to posterity. Considering the length of time that women have been dependent, is it surprising that some of them hug their chains, and fawn like the spaniel.'[14]

But it is the metonymic association of 'slave,' 'women,' 'spaniel' that tends to linger, rather than the intended metaphoric distance, the likeness and unlikeness between them.

The same effect occurs when Wollstonecraft borrows a chunk of contemporary radical analysis of the mob to support her position that women need the same freedom and liberal educations as men. In enlightenment theory a libidinal economy is brought to bear on subordinated groups: mass social violence is seen as the direct result of severe repression which does not allow for the development of self-control or self governance. The mob's motive may be a quasi-rational vengeance against oppressors, but the trigger of that violence is the uncontrolled and irrational effect of sudden de-repression. Sexual symbolism is already prefigured in this analysis, so that when Wollstonecraft draws on it as a metaphor for women's uncontrolled sexual behaviour she reinforces the identification of loose women and mob violence. 'The bent bow recoils with violence, when the hand is suddenly relaxed that forcibly held it' – the sexual metaphor here, as elsewhere, is top-heavy, tumbling, out of control, like the imaginary force of female sexuality itself. Here, and at many other points in the text, *A*

Vindication enhances rather than reduces the power of female sexuality, constructing it, unintentionally, as an intimate and immediate threat to social stability, nearer than the already uncomfortably near Parisian mob. It is no wonder that many nineteenth-century feminists, for whom the mob and the French Revolution were still potent symbols of disorder, found the book, for all its overt sexual puritanism, disturbing and dangerous.

The blurring of sexual and political metaphor so that sexuality is effectively smeared all over the social relations under discussion emphasises Wollstonecraft's deliberate privileging of sensibility and pleasure as the ideological weapons of patriarchy. Picking up on the negative vibes about female sexuality in *Emile*, she beats Rousseau with his own stick (as it seems) by making the sensual both viler and more pervasive in women's lives as a result of his philosophy of education put into practice. Wollstonecraft too wishes bourgeois women to be modest and respectable, honest wives and good mothers, though she wishes them to be other things as well. Yet only by imagining them *all*, or almost all, crippled and twisted into sexual monsters by society as it is can she hope to persuade her readers to abandon a gender specific and deforming education for feminity.

Yet the most incisive and innovative elements of *A Vindication* are deeply bound into its analysis of the construction of gender in childhood. The book gives us a complex and detailed account of the social and psychic processes by which gender ideologies become internalized adult subjectivity. This account is spread across the two-hundred-odd pages of the book and is extraordinary both as observation and as theory. Here is the childhood of little girls brought up, *à la* Rousseau, to be women only:

> 'Every thing they see or hear serves to fix impressions, call forth emotions, and associate ideas, that give a sexual character to the mind. False notions of beauty and delicacy stop the growth of their limbs and produce a sickly soreness, rather than delicacy of organs . . . This cruel association of ideas, which every thing conspires to twist into all their habits of thinking, or, to speak with more precision, of feeling, receives new force when they begin to act a little for themselves; for they then perceive that it is only through their address to excite emotions in men that pleasure and power are to be obtained.'[15]

It is exaggerated; it is even fantasy up to a point. Yet reading this passage, I was both shaken by its eloquence and pricked by its accuracy.

Only an unusual 'native vigour' of mind can overturn such a vicious social construction, for:

> 'So ductile is the understanding, and yet so stubborn, that the association which dend on adventitious circumstances, during the period that the body takes to arrive at maturity, can seldom be disentangled by

reason. One idea calls up another, its old associate, and memory faithful to first impressions. . . retraces them with mechanical exactness.'[16]

Here, in part, is the romantic theory of the unconscious, its operations laid bare to draw a particularly bleak conclusion about the fate of women.

The need to exaggerate the effects of a gender biased rearing and education led Wollstonecraft to overemphasize the importance of sexuality in women's lives. *A Vindication* is hardly a realistic reconstruction of the day to day activities and preoccupations of bourgeois women, the author herself not excepted. Rather it is an abstract formulation of the sort of social and psychic tendencies that a one-sided reactionary socialisation could produce. It is unfortunate that Wollstonecraft chose to fight Rousseau in his own terms, accepting his paradigm of a debased, eroticized femininity as fact rather than ideological fiction. Woman's reason may be the psychic heroine of *A Vindication*, but its gothic villain, a polymorphous perverse sexuality, creeping out of every paragraph and worming its way into every warm corner of the text, seems in the end to win out. It is again too easy to forget that this suffusing desire is a permanent male conspiracy to keep women panting and dependent as well as house-bound and pregnant. What the argument moves towards, but never quite arrives at, is the conclusion that it is male desire which must be controlled and contained if women are to be free and rational. This conclusion cannot be reached because an idealized bourgeois male is the standard towards which women are groping, as well as the reason they are on their knees. Male desire may be destructive to women, but it remains a part of positive male identity. A wider education and eros-blunting forays into the public world of work and politics keeps the rational in control of the sensual in men, and is the recommended remedy for women too. Wollstonecraft thought gender difference socially constructed but she found practically nothing to like in socially constructed femininity. With masculinity it was quite different – 'masculine' women are fine as long as they don't hunt and kill. Yet there could be nothing good about feminised men, since the definitions of the feminine available in *A Vindication* are shot through with dehumanising and immoral sensuality. It's not surprising that women together – girls in boarding schools and women in the home – can only get up to unsavory personal familiarities, 'nasty, or immodest habits.'[19] This description backs up an argument, possibly forceful in its own time, for mixed education and a freer association of adult men and women; it rounds off the denigration of women's world in *A Vindication*.

Ironically, it is the revolutionary moment, with its euphoric faith in total social transformation which permits Wollstonecraft to obliterate women and femininity in their unreformed state. Although *A Vindication* outlines a liberal and unsegregated programme for female education and a wider scope for women's newly developed reason in the public and private world, it has nothing complimentary to say about women as they are. Their overheated sensibility is never seen as potentially creative. One can see how the moral analysis and the social description in *A Vindication* could be appropriated for a more conservative social theory, which might advocate a degree of exercise for women's adolescent bodies and minds, but would confine them to a desexualised domestic sphere as wives and mothers.

The novels of Jane Austen, Wollstonecraft's contemporary, are the most obvious immediate example of a conservative recuperation of Wollstone-craft. *Northanger Abbey* paraphrases Wollstonecraft on the dangers to the young female reader of the gothic and sentimental novel, and *Mansfield Park* reads in many places like a fictional reworking of *A Vindication*. Possibly influence, partly mere convergence, the voices of the two women whose politics were deeply opposed, echo each other. It is Wollstonecraft who writes that 'while women live, as it were by their personal charms, how can we expect them to discharge those ennobling duties which equally require exertion and self-denial', but it might as easily be Austen on Mary Crawford. In the same sentence, and in much the same terms, Wollstonecraft de-nounces hereditary aristocracy. The appropriation of much of Wollstone-craft's writing for conservative social and political ideologies went unac-knowledged because of her outcast social status and her revolutionary sympathies.

Nevertheless, mid-century women writers and feminists, looking for ways to legitimize their feminism and their sexuality, as well as their desire to write them both out together, found small comfort in *A Vindication*, where the creative and the affective self are split up and separated. In fiction and poetry, that discursive space open to women but sheltered from the harshest judgements of Victorian morality, late romantic women writers, as sick of Wollstonecraft's regime, if they knew it, as she had been sick of Rousseau's, tentatively began to construct the idea of a libidinized female imagination and, through it, women's right to reason and desire. Authority for such an unmediated and eroticised relation to art and life had to be sought in and stolen from male romantic manifestos. Nothing suggests more unequi-vocally how deep the effects of separate gender sexualities went, than a quick look at the 1802 introduction to *Lyrical Ballads* after a long look at *A Vindication*. The bourgeois poet was the romantic radical incarnated. Here is Wordsworth, like Mary Wollstonecraft a supporter of the revolution, telling the reader, as she never could, that the poet is a man 'endued with more lively sensibility, more enthusiasm and tenderness' than other men, 'a man pleased with his own passions and volitions, and who rejoices more than other men in the spirit of life that is in him.'[17] The appropriate, democratic subjects for his art were 'moral sentiments and animal sensations' as they existed in everyday life.[18]

We must remember to read *A Vindication* as its author has instructed us, as a discourse addressed mainly to women of the middle class. Most deeply class bound is its emphasis on sexuality in its ideological expression, as a mental formation, as the source of woman's oppression. The enchilding of women – their relegation to the home, to domestic tasks and concerns, while men's productive labour was located elsewhere – was a developing phenomenon of middle-class life in the eighteenth century. The separation of home and work in an industrial culture affected the working class too, but it was not the men only who worked outside the home: nor was the sexual division of labour along these lines a working-class ideal until well on in the nineteenth century. The romantic conception of childhood, already natural-ised in *A Vindication*, had no place in working-class life. Nor did female narcissism and a passion for clothes have the same meanings for, or about, working-class women, who, as Wollstonecraft observes in *Maria*, were worked too hard at 'severe manual labour' to have much time or thought for such things. The ideal of education, opening up wider fields for the exercise of the mind, was part of a bourgeois agenda for social improvement that would 'lift' the poor as well as women. Sequential pregnancies, exhausting child care in the grimmest conditions, the double yoke of waged and unpaid domestic labour, none of these are cited in *A Vindication* as the cause of women's degradation. *Maria* includes an honorable if genteel attempt to describe the realities of life for working class women. *A Vindication* is more class bound and more obsessive; a brief, though not unsympathetic passage on the horrors of prostitution, and a few references to the dirty backstairs habits which female servants pass on to ladies is the selective and sexualized attention that working class women get in *A Vindication*.

Most of Wollstonecraft's difficulties are with the obviously binding power of the binary categories of class sexuality. Rather than challenge them, she shifts her abstract women around inside them or tries to reverse their symbolism. The middle-class married adultress is magically trans-formed by liberty and education into the modest rational wife. If women in public and in promiscuous gatherings, whether schoolroom or workplace, were considered sexually endangered, Wollstonecraft would eroticize the safe home and the all-girls establishment, so that these harems and not the outside world are the places where modesty is at risk. It doesn't work, but it's a good try. It doesn't work because Wollstonecraft herself wishes to construct class differentiation through existing sexual categories. The nega-tive effects of the text fell on the middle-class women which it is so eager to construct and instruct.

In *Sex, Politics and Society, The regulation of sexuality since 1800*, Jeffrey Weeks, summarising and extending Foucault, reminds us that:

> '. . . the sexual apparatus and the nuclear family were produced by the bourgeoisie as an aspect of its own self-affirmation, not as a means of

controlling the working class; that there are class sexualities (and different gender sexualities) not a single uniform sexuality. Sexuality is not a given that has to be controlled. It is an historical construct that has historical conditions of existence.'[19]

If we apply these comments, we can see that the negative gender sexuality which Wollstonecraft constructs was one of several competing gender sexualities of the late eighteenth century. As Margaret Walters indicates, contemporary femininity grips Wollstonecraft even as she argues against it: a sexually purified femininity was equally a precondition for any optimistic, liberal re-ordering of intra-class gender relations, or female aspiration. But Walters is wrong in seeing this struggle as one between feminism and femininity. There is no feminism that can stand wholly outside femininity as it is posed in a given historical moment. All feminisms give some ideological hostage to femininities and are constructed through the gender sexuality of their day as well as standing in opposition to them. Wollstonecraft saw her middle class, for a few years at least, as a potentially revolutionary force. The men and women in it would exercise their understandings on behalf of all mankind. It was important to her that the whole of this class had access to reason, and that women's liberation was posed within a framework that was minimally acceptable to popular prejudices. That is why, perhaps, she finds herself promising the reader that the freedom of women was the key to their chastity. Within the enlightenment and romantic problematics, reason was always the responsible eldest son and sensibility – emotion, imagination, sensuality – the irresponsible rake, catalyst of change. Class differentiation through the redefinition of sexual mores was a process so deeply entrenched, in Wollstonecraft's time that the moral positions around sexual behaviour seemed almost untouchable. Feminists of her generation did not dare to challenge them head on, although Wollstonecraft was beginning to work over this dangerous terrain, in her life and in her fiction at the time of her death. The combination of equal rights and self-abnegating sexuality in A Vindication has had special attractions for feminists who led very public lives, and found it terrifying and tactically difficult to challenge too many prejudices at once. As a liveable formula for independent female subjectivity though, it never had much going for it – not because an immanent and irrepressible sexuality broke through levels of female self-denial, but rather because the anti-erotic ethic itself foregrounded and constructed a sexualized subject.

As long as the double standard survives gender sexualities will be torn by these contradictions. When Wollstonecraft's ideas for mixed education and wider public participation for women began to be put into practice, women started to query and resist the gender ideologies in which they had been raised. With some help from a popularised psychoanalytic theory, pleasure and sexuality were written into a reworked version of female romantic individualism. Both individualism and these new gender sexualities are, quite properly, heavily contested areas within feminism. Wollstonecraft's project, with its contradictory implications, suggests some of the problems involved in the moralisation of sexuality on behalf of any political programme, even a feminist one.

Feminism and Compulsory Heterosexuality: Adrienne Rich

Between the two texts I have chosen to discuss lie nearly two centuries in which successive feminisms have engaged with recalcitrant issues surrounding women's sexuality. Yet while the specific issues have changed, many of the terms in which they are debated would be familiar to Mary Wollstonecraft. In the 1980s the independent sexuality that seems most threatening to the dominant culture as fact and symbol of women's escape from patriarchal control is lesbianism. Lesbian feminists, in the various political tendencies in the women's movement have for many years now been insisting that the cultural constraints on their sexual expression are central to women's subordination as a whole. Sexuality has never been a hidden issue in modern feminism, but its theorisation has produced many painful if necessary disagreements, none more so than the place of lesbianism as a political stance within feminist practice. Adrienne Rich, the American poet and feminist theorist has developed a range of arguments about the meaning of female sexuality in our culture. Her position on the sexual politics of feminism is powerfully stated in an article first published in the feminist journal *Signs* in the summer of 1980, and widely available soon afterwards in pamphlet form. 'Compulsory Heterosexuality and Lesbian Existence' challenges the normative heterosexist values and repressive liberal tolerance of a large section of the women's movement, arguing that an acceptance of the virtue and centrality of historical and contemporary forms of lesbian experience is the base line for a feminist politics. Like Wollstonecraft, if a trifle more tentatively, Rich also poses a reformed libidinal economy for women as the precondition for the successful liberation of women. It is the common element in their thinking about women's sexuality that I wish briefly to examine in this last section.

The foregrounding of sexuality as the source of women's subordination is the element that most obviously links Wollstonecraft's analysis with radical and revolutionary feminism in the distinct but linked tendencies that have developed in Britain, France and the United States over the last fourteen years. These strands in feminism have taken the lead in privileging sexuality as the central fact and universal symbol of women's oppression. Radical feminism has built its theory and rhetoric around the ideological and actual violence done to women's bodies, while liberal and socialist feminism has been rather nervous of the sexual, working instead to define the specific forms which women's subordination takes in different class, cultural and racial groups, at discrete historical moments. These projects and strategies frequently overlap, but it is roughly fair to say that radical feminism emphasises the identity of gender oppression across history and culture. Revolutionary feminism pushes this analysis farther, posing a monolithic patriarchal tyranny, with sexuality as its weapon. Both tendencies have located the universal truth of gender oppression in a sadistic and insatiable male sexuality, which is empowered to humiliate and punish. Any pleasure that accrues to women who take part in heterosexual acts is therefore necessarily tainted; at the extreme end of this position, women who 'go with men' are considered collaborators – every man a fascist at heart. While Wollstonecraft acknowledged that a depraved sexual pleasure for both men and women was the effect of unequal power relations between them, radical feminism underlines the unpleasure of these relations for women. Where women have no choice over the aim and object of their sexuality, hetero-sexuality, in the words of Adrienne Rich, is 'compulsory' – an institution more comprehensive and sinister than the different relations and practices it constructs. Worse, compulsory heterosexuality is part of a chain of gender specific tortures, both medical and conjugal: hysterectomy, cliterodectomy, battering, rape and imprisonment are all elaborations of the sadistic act of penetration itself, penetration the socially valorised symbol of violence against women. Men use these torments to shore up their own subjectivity. Their pleasure in them is a confirmation of male power. Pornography, in this analysis, is emblematic of all male sexuality, the violent fantasy behind the tenderest act of intercourse.

Rich defines heterosexuality as an institution 'forcibly and subliminally imposed on women' who have 'everywhere . . . resisted it.' Although she admits that there are 'qualitative differences of experience' within hetero-sexuality, these differences cannot alter the corrupt nature of the institution, since a good partner is rather like a good master in slavery, a matter of luck not choice. While Wollstonecraft believed, cynically, that all women took pleasure in their slavery, Rich backs off from admitting that coercion, however subliminal, can produce pleasure. Binary categories, historically differentiated, are operating here. Bad women in 1792 experienced bad pleasure; good women in 1980 experience no pleasure. In both cases the effect is punitive.

Rich's abstract women – they are no nearer to real, historical women than the incredibly lascivious ladies of *A Vindication* – are neither masochists or nymphomaniacs, they are simply women whose natural sexuality has been artificially diverted, from their real object, other women. Women's long struggle against heterosexuality took, according to Rich, a wide variety of forms which she calls the 'lesbian continuum', as distinct from 'lesbian existence' – the natural sexuality of women. Rich has shifted the terms in the nature/culture debate without really altering the paradigm around women and sexuality. In her scenario female heterosexuality is socially constructed and female homosexuality is natural. As in Wollstonecraft, what is bad goes on the outside, what inheres is neutral or good. In Rich's formula, women's libidinal drive is made central, transhistorical and immanent where dominant sexual ideology had constructed it as accidental and/or pathological. Political lesbianism becomes more than a strategic position for feminism, it is a return to nature. In this new interpretation of sexuality a fairly crude libidinal economy is asserted:

> 'Woman identification is a source of energy, a potential springhead of female power, violently curtailed and wasted under the institution of heterosexuality. The denial of reality and visibility to women's passion for women, women's choice of women as allies, life companions, and community; the forcing of such relationships into dissimulation, their disintegration under intense pressure, have meant an incalculable loss to the power of all women *to change the social relations of the sexes*, to liberate ourselves and each other. The lie of compulsory female heterosexuality today afflicts not just feminist scholarship, but every profession, every reference work, every curriculum, every organizing attempt, every relationship or conversation over which it hovers. It creates, specifically, a profound falseness, hypocrisy and hysteria in the heterosexual dialogue, for every heterosexual relationship is lived in the queasy strobelight of that lie. However we choose to identify ourselves, however we find ourselves labelled, it flickers across and distorts our lives.'[20]

The saturating power of this socially enforced – as opposed to naturally lived – sexuality represses, in Rich's view, all creative expression and all radical and revolutionary process. It is eerily like Wollstonecraft's totalizing view of sexuality. Both Rich and Wollstonecraft believe that heterosexuality as it is and has been lived by women is an ideological distortion of the possibilities of female sexuality. At one level *A Vindication* is highly prescriptive: it asks women, at the very least, to resist the appeal of a pleasure which will put them at the sexual and emotional mercy of men. Wollstonecraft stopped short of defining an innate form of female sexuality – she understood after her encounter with *Emile* that arguing difference from nature was ultimately reactionary. Rich, on the other hand, has no qualms about constructing female sexuality as naturally different. She uses her analysis, in the passage cited above, to interpret conflicts within feminism today. The result is that these crucial differences, on whose working through the future of feminism depends, are collapsed into the denial of *some* women of the universal sexuality of *all* women. Any failure of energy or strategy can be reduced the frustration and anxiety around a denied or feared sexuality. Difficulties between women are no longer about age, class, race or culture. All the legitimate problems that inhere to an emergent politics are whittled down to a repressed but supracultural sexuality. In *Compulsory Heterosexuality* the solution for a better politics is contained in the appeal from bad culture back to good nature.

The theme of Rich's revision of female sexuality is the possible construction of a specifically *feminist* humanism. Benign nature is female – affectionate and sensual as well as creative, revolutionary and transcendent. In its political inflection it opposes an innately vicious male nature whose ascendency has produced the bad dream of phallocratic culture. According to Rich,

> '. . . heterosexuality as an institution has been organized and maintained through the female wage scale, the enforcement of middle-class women's leisure, the glamorization of so-called sexual liberation, the withholding of education from women, the image of "high art" and popular culture, the mystification of the "personal" sphere and much else.'[21]

These rather heterogeneous, class specific and ethnocentric devices support heterosexuality rather than capitalism or patriarchal relations. Take away these and other cultural supports and heterosexuality would presumably wither away. Destroy heterosexist culture at any historical moment and lesbian/feminism would emerge triumphant from its ashes. Rich's simple belief in the all-embracing political possibilities of lesbian existence, her rejection of the political integrity of heterosexual feminism constitutes a denial both of the specificity and variety of female sexuality and the specificity and variety of feminism.

The identification of the sources of social good or evil in the sexual drive of either sex, or in any socially specific sexual practice is a way of foreclosing our still imperfect understanding of the histories of sexuality. The moralisation of desire that inevitably follows from such an analysis colludes with those dominant practices which construct human sexuality through categories of class, race and gender in order to divide and rule. The sexuality constructed by a feminist revolution will be a new social relation, with new contradictions and constraints. The dream of an autonomous sexuality, not constructed through the desire of the other, male or female, is a transcendental fantasy of bourgeois individualism. It poses a subject who can stand outside the social. Perhaps, considering its political difficulties in the past, feminism should resist appropriating such a subject, or at least refuse to hang our hopes for sexual pleasure round its neck.

The walls and doors of the women's toilets at the University of Sussex library were, and are, covered with women's writing. From this lowest seat of high learning a polylogic testament to women's entry into discourse can be read in the round. There is, inevitably, a euphoric temptation to read too much out of these expressive inscriptions. For if young women can shit *and* write, not for some patriarchal pedant, but for each other's eyes only, what vestiges of Victorian constraints remain? It is true, of course, that the vast majority of contributors to this particular public/private debate are young, white and middle-class, but not all women's loos so decorated are quite so class and race bound. In the smallest rooms of this academy politics and intellectual matters are informally debated, but sex as the preferred topic wins hands down.

'How do I get an orgasm?' prompted a booth-full of replies and commentary in the early mid-seventies, showing off the range and ingenuity of women's sexual practices and theories. Advice included detailed instructions to be relayed to a male partner as well as the succinct, laconic recommendation to 'Try Women.' There was an address for suppliers of vibrators and an illustration, definitely not erotic, to help one find the elusive clitoris. In the wide variety of responses one was noticeably absent – no contributor contested the importance of the question. No one queried the centrality of orgasm for women's sexual practice or the importance of sexual pleasure itself. No anachronistic bluestocking suggested that intellectual and sensual pursuits were incompatible. No devout Christian was moved to tell her sisters to wait until marriage. Only now, from a different time and place in the feminist debate over sexuality does that apparently unanimous agreement among young educated women that sexual pleasure, however achieved, was an unproblematic desire seem curious. About the means of arriving at pleasure there was plenty of disagreement; if anything that cubicle was a telling reminder that there has never been a single femininity, and that within feminism sexuality and the meaning of pleasure have most frequently been the site of anger, contradiction and confusion, too often illuminating class, cultural and racial division between women. Now, when female sexuality is indisputably centre-stage in feminism debates but pleasure is too rarely its subject and eros rampant is more likely to conjure up a snuff movie than multiple orgasm, that loo wall remains with me as an important event in the history of feminism, a moment whose appearance and significance we must work to understand.

Notes

1. Mary Wollstonecraft, *A Vindication of the Rights of Woman*, New York, W. W. Norton & Company, 1975, p. 119. Emily Dickinson, *The Complete Poems of Emily Dickinson*, London, Faber and Faber, 1977, p. 114. Andrea Dworkin, *Pornography: Men Possessing Women*, The Women's Press, 1981, p. 304.
2. Wollstonecraft, *ibid*.
3. Jeffrey Weeks, *Sex, Politics and Society*, London, Longman, 1981, p. 30.

4. Adrienne Rich, 'Compulsory Heterosexuality and Lesbian Existence', in *Signs: Journal of Women in Culture and Society*, vol. 5, no. 4, 1980, pp. 631–660.
5. Margaret Walters, 'The Rights and Wrongs of Women: Mary Wollstonecraft, Harriet Martineau, Simone de Beauvoir', in Juliet Mitchell and Ann Oakley, (eds), *The Rights and Wrongs of Women*, Harmondsworth, Pelican, 1979, pp. 304–378.
6. *Historical and Moral View of the Origin and Progress of the French Revolution*, 1794.
7. Wollstonecraft, op. cit., pp. 9–10.
8. *Ibid.*, p. 10.
9. *Ibid.*, p. 11.
10. Jean-Jacques Rousseau, *Emile*, (tr. Barbara Foxley), London, J. M. Dent & Sons, 1974, p. 332. Passages from *Emile* can all be found in Book V of this edition. However, I have followed the translation used by Wollstonecraft who cites large chunks of Book V in *A Vindication*.
11. *Ibid.*, pp. 332–3.
12. Michel Foucault, *The History of Sexuality: Volume 1: An Introduction*, London, Allen Lane, 1979, p. 121.
13. Wollstonecraft, op. cit., pp. 3–4.
14. *Ibid.*, p. 82.
15. *Ibid.*, p. 117.
16. *Ibid.*, p. 116.
17. Wordsworth & Coleridge, *Lyrical Ballads*, London, Methuen & Co., 1976, pp. 255–56.
18. *Ibid.*, p. 261.
19. Weeks, op. cit., p. 10.
20. Rich, op. cit., p. 657.
21. *Ibid.*, p. 659.

Frank Mort

SEX, SIGNIFICATION AND PLEASURE

Sex, Politics and Society,[1] Jeffrey Weeks's history of 'the regulation of sexuality since 1800', is a significant contribution to current debates in the field of sexuality. It introduces an impressive amount of detailed archival research which will undoubtedly provide a valuable point of reference for future discussions. It also raises some important issues around the questions of history and politics and history and theory. What follows is an attempt to assess the book's general themes and underlying assumptions, and to draw out their implications for a theory of sexuality and, in particular, for discussions about the significance of sexuality in political interventions around pleasure and desire.

As a prelude to his studies of historical formations from nineteenth-century 'moralism' to '60s 'permissiveness', Jeffrey Weeks introduces a number of debates about culture and ideology in order to develop a critique of essentialist approaches to the study of sexuality. Drawing in particular on the current work of Michel Foucault, he insists that analysis should focus on the historically specific practices and discourses through which sexuality is constructed and regulated This, he suggests, requires some clearing of the ground in order to show that it is *definitions* of 'sexuality' and attendant concepts of 'the body', 'pleasure', 'desire' and 'morality' that are at issue. This historical emphasis also implies a critique of those semiotic and psychoanalytic formulations of language, sexuality and desire which are pitched at such a level of abstraction that they produce an absolute split between history and general theory. Weeks, in contrast, looks at the differentiated languages articulated in specific institutions by a network of intellectual and political agents and tries to discover under what determinate set of historical conditions they have had particular political effects. I would fully endorse these opening emphases. What worries me is the sometimes uneasy divergence between them and the historical analysis that actually follows in *Sex, Politics and Society*. Here questions of language and discourse often seem to be accommodated within the terms of reference of a more traditional social history. It is important to examine this theoretical disjunction because it is symptomatic of the broader attempt to think through the challenge which a Foucauldian-informed approach poses to the dominant practices of writing history.

History and Discourse

The crucial question is how we understand the production of cultural meanings and their power relations. Weeks starts from the premise that, yes, sexuality is historically constructed, but he does not in fact go on to explore the precise nature of its signification. In his opening study of nineteenth-century 'official' debates, for example, Weeks follows Foucault in countering the myth of Victorian repression with the point that 'sexuality became a major issue within Victorian social and political practice.' We are then offered a range of representations which have 'sexuality' as their referent – the family, middle-class domestic ideology, birth control, sodomy, syphilis, female prostitution and the construction of childhood. But *how* was it that certain phenomena were sexualised, or ascribed a sexual definition, while others were not? The claim that sexuality is historically and socially constructed needs to be accompanied by an account of the ways that systems of signification and particular power-knowledge relations are organised to produce *sexual meanings*. We should not assume that a set of domains – 'the family', 'domesticity' or whatever – refer to sexuality, but should try to understand how these fields are themselves delimited in such a way that they define 'sexuality' as integral to their functioning.

What is needed, therefore, is a historically sensitive attention to prevailing systems of signification. As Jeffrey Weeks points out, for example, the moral discourses of nineteenth-century environmentalism and philanthropy were organised around a strategy of class disciplining and regulation. But equally significant was the structuring of those official discourses through a series of oppositions – vice/virtue, filth/cleanliness, animality/civilization and so on – around whose polarities the labouring classes and women were differentially constructed. For many middle-class and aristocratic men, sexual desire was structured by these definitions. If we turn to their private letters, diaries and personal confessions, their sexual pleasure often seems to have been organized in terms of private debauchery, lust and licentiousness. It was *experienced* as pleasurable precisely because it stood in opposition to the sanctioned norms of middle-class domesticity and marital relations. In nineteenth-century pornography, male sexual pleasure frequently centred on the depraved and sexualised female prostitute – seen to be both socially inferior and also suffused, shot through, with male sexual desire. Weeks cites the diaries of A. J. Munby and 'Walter's' *My Secret Life* as two instances of complex sexual meanings.[2] In the repeated encounters with working-class women, female coarseness and animality – the antithesis of the characteristics cultivated by the bourgeois wife – became central to the enjoyment of male erotic pleasure. In a related sense, the male homosexual subculture which developed in the metropolitan centres in the later nineteenth century was often characterised by cross-class encounters between upper-class men and working-class youths. Working-class masculinity was seen as the repository of sexual potency and animal passion by and for a middle-class clientele. The diaries of Sir Roger Casement reveal the life of a prominent civil servant organised around a *public* world of colonial government and administration and a succession of *private* sexual encounters with working-class men and African natives. The anonymous physicality of these private transactions was precisely what gave them their sexual meaning.

Clearly, we should be aware of the network of economic, political and cultural relations within which these particular representations of male pleasure and desire were located. As Weeks demonstrates, the attitudes of middle-class men towards extra-marital sexual encounters were determined by the conditions of bourgeois family life: the ambivalent position of the wife, the preference for late marriages to preserve economic and cultural status, the rigid distinctions operating between the world of work and public life and the sphere of domesticity. But we should equally acknowledge the ways in which representations of those very social conditions figured prominently in structuring male sexual desire – in particular in the opposition between, at one pole, the sexual, the pleasurable, the depraved and licentious female and, at the other, the moral , the civilized, the virtuous woman/wife. What was defined as sexual had to stand in opposition to the virtuous, the moral and the marital in order for it to be experienced as sexually *pleasurable*. This discursive construction organised real historical oppositions and contradictions to produce sexual meaning and particular inflection to male desire. This form remains central to male representations of female sexuality. Paul Willis's study of working-class youth has revealed how definitions of women in terms of the 'slag' or 'easy lay', on the one hand, and the girlfriend, wife, mother or sister, on the other, continue to reproduce male definitions of female behaviour and the power relations which are integral to them.[3]

But if representations of sexuality are to be historically located, then how we characterise the relation between these and their specific conditions of existence remains a problem. In this respect, *Sex, Politics and Society* is carefully distanced from either sociological or marxist functionalism, and the integration of forms of cultural and political struggle constitutes a major part of the book's success. But Weeks takes it as axiomatic that the 'rhythm of economic and, consequently, social transformations do provide the basic preconditions and the ultimate limits within which social forms are organised.' It is only when he reaches the permissive reforms of the 1950s and '60s that Weeks offers a sustained discussion of this original assertion. Following Stuart Hall's work,[4] he attempts to connect the transformations in official definitions of sexuality with wider political and economic shifts through an extended Gramscian model of hegemony. The result *is* a complex account of differing histories which are unevenly yoked together – in legislation, for example, or through the moral economy of Labour Party revisionism, with its emphasis on private, civilised sexual pleasure and desire. But this analysis calls into question Weeks's opening comments about determination. His argument seems to be left oscillating between, on the one hand, a necessary stress on the complexity of causation and, on the other, a much tighter insistence that in the '60s there was an overall 'fit' between economic and political changes and changing patterns of moral regulation which specified new sexual subjectivities and new forms of sexual pleasure. Although the Gramscian paradigm does not work with concepts of direct and monocausal determinacy of the functionalist or reductionist varieties, 'the economic' does still occupy a privileged place within its hierarchy of determinations. It retains the notion of a necessary level of economic causation, and still requires the *levels* of determination to be conceptually ranked and hierarchised. Sexuality is proving to be one of the real limit positions for marxist forms of cultural analysis, both intellectually and politically. That is why I would have liked Weeks to discuss some of these problems in greater depth, to elaborate and justify his position more fully.

History and Contemporary Politics

Connected with this is another aspect of Jeffrey Weeks's project which I think could usefully have been developed further. The emphasis on detailed and sustained historical analysis in *Sex, Politics and Society* does raise particularly clearly the question of how 'history' relates to current political and cultural formations. But if the book is a contribution to a 'history of the present' in the sense of trying to understand how our contemporary political dilemmas have arisen and to supplement forms of political calculation with a historical perspective, then its statements concerning forms of intervention into the field of sexual politics today needed to be less muted and more explicit. I am not advocating that historical analysis should provide direct prescriptions for political strategies, but I do think that the current situation should set the broad parameters for selecting areas and modes of historical inquiry. Otherwise we are still so easily caught up in the narrow discourse of purely professional and intellectual radicalism. In short, political questions and criteria should inform historical research. The advantages of this approach are visible in Weeks's incisive account of the various currents within sexual politics in the early twentieth century: he demonstrates the complex ways in which a set of oppositional politics (feminist, radical liberal and libertarian, and moral purist) were themselves deeply implicated in producing official definitions and knowledges of sexuality. He also traces their differing definitions of sexuality and sexual pleasure to their contradictory professional, class and gender positions. In comparison with such studies, the book's analysis of the current situation seems to be posed with less urgency and complexity, yet paradoxically, struggles over representation are at the heart of contemporary sexual politics – struggles for the power to re-define sexual pleasure, desire, identities and needs. I would therefore like to isolate three cases mentioned rather briefly in the book and draw some further implications from them – these are the commercial gay male subculture, the politics of sexuality within the women's movement and the marginalisation of sexuality within dominant political discourses.

The regulation of male homosexual behaviour reveals how, from the later nineteenth century onwards, irregular forms of sexuality have been continually scrutinised through a range of official discourses – the law, medicine, the churches, the 'psy-complex' of practices. This process has involved the definition of *homo*sexuality as distinct from the heterosexual norm and the creation of a homosexual identity based on a deviant and omnipresent sexuality. The male homosexual is thus presented as saturated with a deviant sexual desire which determines his every action. Such official definitions were consolidated in the *Wolfenden Report* (1957) which recommended the decriminalisation of male homosexuality for consenting adults in private.[5] Yet this regulative strategy has also had profound effects on the development of a gay male subculture in the period after the Sexual Offences Act (1967) was passed. It continues to set the conditions for the terms in which sexual practice, sexual pleasure and sexual politics are conceived by many gay men – terms which often sit very uneasily with forms of feminist politics. In the '70s the male gay scene produced its own leisure industries and services – pubs, clubs, travel, sex and porno shops aimed specifically at gay men and highly effective in interpellating them through this sexualised identity. Frank Ripploh's recent film *Taxi Zum Klo* is a vivid testament to the central features of this subculture: sexual pleasure and sexual contact localised in casual sex and 'cruising'. Heterosexual leisure and consumption undoubtedly contain a sexual component – the body is accentuated by dress and fashion codes and set in motion by rock music or disco dancing. But these sexual emphases are highlighted and foregrounded in the gay subculture. At the same time, sexual practices and sexual identities have proliferated around a variety of macho male images (leather, denim, uniforms and so forth). In short, the development of a gay lifestyle has been centrally organised around sex.

This formation does not merely reproduce official definitions of homosexuality. It mobilizes a distinct repertoire of cultural resistances which, though often only localized and defensive, have pushed and tested the limit positions of the post-Wolfenden strategy. Cruising for sex outside pubs and clubs has involved some gays in protracted struggles and negotiations with local police forces over the policing of public places. The provision of leisure services for economically independent gay men does not merely represent commercial exploitation, but provides alternative sites and facilities where gays can temporarily escape from the pressures of the heterosexual norm. The increasing organization of gay sexuality around male images does not simply mirror the codes of heterosexual masculinity – where promiscuous sex is frequently defined as a natural and unstoppable urge – but reveals an awareness of the highly constructed nature of sexual identities and pleasures. Nevertheless, the central concerns for many gay men are defined through a libertarian or liberationist politics. Sexual freedom and the endless quest for localized sexual pleasure are seen to be the most significant aims. As Jack Babuscio put it recently in *Gay News* in response to feminist critiques: 'I don't really give a shit why I dress the way I do. It's not hurting anyone. It seems the god of some people to make us totally . . . non-sexual in appearance. I don't want that, I'm gay and I'm a man.'[6]

The development of a feminist sexual politics has involved the most thoroughgoing interrogation of those liberationist notions of sexual pleasure and desire. Feminist politics has been initially concerned not with promoting hetero-sexual pleasure but with exposing the intimate relation between the dominant definitions of such pleasure and forms of male power. As Weeks's book illustrates, much post-war writing on sexuality has been centred on a concern with pleasurable sex, (in the '50s within marriage and latterly in pre-marital relations) but in ways which have worked to inscribe women more firmly within a discourse of heterosexuality. Feminism has insisted that progressive heterosexual sex – structured around a hierarchy of techniques leading to penetration – is not necessarily pleasurable *for women*. Moreover, for feminists male defined pleasure is itself part of deeper inscriptions of power and sexuality within social relations. The recent campaigns launched by the Women's Movement against violence against women have forcefully drawn attention to the fact that it is male sexuality which is the problem to be addressed, rather than the norm against which female behaviour should be defined. Responses have been posed through a variety of strategies pitched at different levels: public campaigns against pornography and rape, the construction of a positive lesbian culture, the efforts of women to struggle against dominant definitions within heterosexual relationships. The attempt by women to construct new forms of sexual identity and sexual pleasure is an important component of all these strategies. The debate over heterosexuality and lesbianism (both as a form of political practice and as a structure of sexual desire) has been particularly contentious, but as Beatrix Campbell points out, lesbianism within the Women's Movement has been as much about female sexual autonomy as about homosexuality. As such, it has offered a profound challenge to forms of homosexuality and heterosexuality alike.[7]

It is crucial that these issues are prioritised in feminist and gay politics, and that they are raised at the level of a public debate over sexuality. The effects of the Women's Movement, for example, are beginning to be registered by a range of institutions which hitherto wholly excluded feminist positions – the Labour Party, the trade union movement, the media – but the development of a politics of sexuality poses specific problems. One of the difficulties is that the dominant political traditions of parliamentarianism and labourism have consistently sought to define the political terrain in a particular way that excludes sexuality from their political debates. That narrow definition of politics is currently being challenged by a whole range of new political movements, as is clear from the struggle over 'democracy' within the Labour Party. But dominant representations continue to exercise their hold: constructing sexuality as a subject of voyeuristic interest or as a neutral field, to be administered by experts and unconnected to forms of power and domination. In the 'Yorkshire Ripper' trial and the ensuing controversy about the handling of rape by the courts and the police, public debate was orchestrated in a way that ruled out any broad-based discussion of male sexuality. It was definitions of madness and psychological abnormality that functioned to delimit the nature of the problem.

A significant site of struggle here involves the continuing challenge to dominant definitions of sexual practice and sexual pleasure as private and individual concerns. Within the legal-political sphere, the Williams Report on Obscenity and Film Censorship (1979) and the Working Papers on Sexual Offences (1979 and 1980) have consolidated definitions of privatised consenting sexuality.[8] Although these proposals do contain some liberalising provisions for male homosexuality – such as the lowering of the age of consent from twenty-one to eighteen – they also tend to forestall public debate about the wider issues of sexuality and power. We need to develop this debate as a matter of some urgency, for attempts to construct alliances between different political constituencies would have to be based on the demands it could elicit. Recent statements on women and gays by Tony Benn and Ken Livingstone have tried to introduce such issues into mainstream politics through a discourse on 'rights'. How to develop a popular politics around sexual pleasure remains a much more problematic question, for we need to challenge liberal conceptions of pleasure without being cast into the role of unpleasurable moralists. It is political issues like these that we need to foreground when reading *Sex, Politics and Society*. Although Jeffrey Weeks does not address them as directly as I would wish, this book will initiate a debate around those central questions.

Notes

1. Jeffrey Weeks, *Sex, Politics and Society*, London, Longman, 1981.
2. See Steven Marcus, *The Other Victorians*, London, Weidenfeld and Nicolson, 1967.
3. Paul Willis, *Learning to Labour*, Farnborough, Saxon House, 1977.
4. See Stuart Hall, 'Reformism and the Legislation of Consent', in National Deviancy Conference (eds) *Permissiveness and Control*, London, Hutchinson, 1979.
5. *Report of the Committee on Homosexual Offences and Prostitution*, Cmnd. 247, HMSO, 1957.
6. In 'Supplement', pp. 2–3, in *Gay News*, no. 197.
7. In Anna Coote and Beatrix Campbell, *Sweet Freedom*, London, Picador, 1982.
8. See Policy Advisory Committee on Sexual Offences, *Working Papers on the Age of Consent in relation to Sexual Offences*, 1979, and Criminal Law Revision Committee, *Working Paper on Sexual Offences*, 1980.

Fanny Tribble

FOUR CARTOONS

Tony Davies

TRANSPORTS OF PLEASURE:
Fiction and its Audiences
in the Later Nineteenth Century

*Information or critical perception cannot be acquired by running through 'amusing'
books, or inflated, exciting, flashy novels, at a speed almost as rapid as the railway
carriage in which the reader sits.*

The Spectator, 1854

*It is because I passionately wish to improve the minds of the populace . . . that I
don't want to let them see Helvellyn while they are drunk.*

John Ruskin, 'Railways in the Lake District', 1876.

All Who Ride May Read.   W. H. Smith, 1849

Like many basic words, pleasure derives its meanings from implied oppositions: with pain, profit, duty, melancholy, work. It would be useful to have a
history of these shifting and definitive oppositions, a social etymology of
pleasure. For pleasure is an important and neglected locus of struggle,
marked with the historical accents of resistance and control, evasion and
submission: Blake's Lamb and Tiger. Capitalist societies market pleasure, as
solace, instruction or reward. But it remains unstable, suspect. Pleasure
needs to be censored, regulated, supervised. Coupling it to a necessary,
symbiotic antithesis may be one of the ways of doing this.

There is an ancient association between pleasure and reading, around
just such a regulatory opposition: *Omne tulit punctum qui miscuit utile dulci*
(Horace) – 'the best writing is that which combines pleasure and utility.' But
these antitheses, in societies based on wage-labour as on slave-labour,
encode and conceal real contradictions. And one of the places that bind
potentially destructive oppositions in a neutralising mutuality is texts –
occasions of reading. The articulations of textual pleasure, the ways in which
texts are offered to our consumption and use, may point in their historically
different ways to representations and discursive antagonisms which the
alternation or identity of pleasure-and-its-opposite seek to stabilise. One of
the legitimate 'pleasures of the text' may lie in its capacity to offer its readers,
within, beneath or behind its seemingly immutable notations, a secret
promise: an enchanted garden in which, for a while, the intransigent

polarities of the social and symbolic economy can be held in a poignant imaginary resolution, an aching pleasure of possession and loss.

I'm thinking of a particular text here: Wells's story 'The Door in the Wall'. The story tells of a man, a successful politician, who is haunted throughout his life by the memory of an occasion when, in early childhood, he strayed from home and, wandering through the streets of a north London suburb, came upon a low door in a wall, opened it and found himself in a garden.

> 'You know, in the very moment the door swung to behind me, I forgot the road with its fallen chestnut leaves, its cabs and tradesmen's carts, I forgot the sort of gravitational pull back to the discipline and obedience of home, I forgot all hesitations and fear, forgot discretion, forgot all the intimate realities of this life. I became in a moment a very glad and wonder-happy little boy – in another world.'

On several occasions in later life he catches a glimpse of the door in the wall, always unexpectedly, in different parts of London. But each time, duty or ambition or 'a thousand inconceivably petty worldlinesses' prevent him from opening it again, until one night, walking home from a late session in the House through the deserted streets, he sees the door, opens it, steps through, and falls to his death –

> '. . . in a deep excavation near East Kensington station. It is one of two shafts that have been made in connection with an extension of the railway southward. . . . Did the pale electric lights near the station cheat the rough planking into a semblance of white? Did that fatal unfastened door awaken some memory?'

The story ends equivocally, hesitating as it must between pleasure and duty, reality and desire. In the garden the child is shown a book, 'a story about myself', whose compelling realism returns him at last, heartbroken, to 'a long grey street in West Kensington, in that chill hour of afternoon before the lamps are lit.' So the text must always leave the reader, at last, back in the 'long grey street', on the wrong side of the door. But there remains too an equivocal residue of pleasure, a poignancy of loss, a glimpsed utopia whose memory hangs hauntingly in the chill autumnal hour before the lighting of the lamps. 'You may', muses the narrator,

> '. . . think me superstitious, if you will, and foolish; but indeed I am more than half convinced that he had, in truth, an abnormal gift, and a sense, something – I know not what   that in the guise of wall and door offered him an outlet, a secret and peculiar passage of escape into another and altogether more beautiful world. . . . We see our world fair and common, the hoarding and the pit. By our daylight standard

he walked out of security into darkness, danger and death. But did he
see like that?'

This story can be read in a number of ways. It could be taken, for example, as
another expression, with Stevenson's *Dr Jekyll* and Wilde's *Dorian Gray*, of
the divided psyche of the Victorian bourgeois, torn between duty and
desire, wife and mistress, responsibility and romance, requiring each as a
condition of the other in that 'legitimate antithesis' that Marx identified as
the relation between Carlylean romanticism and political economy:

'It is as ridiculous to yearn for a return to that original fulness as it is to
believe that with this complete emptiness history has come to a
standstill. The bourgeois viewpoint has never advanced beyond this
antithesis between itself and the romantic viewpoint, and therefore the
latter will accompany it as legitimate antithesis up to its blessed end.[1]

But it can also be read as a story about the pleasures and the dangers of
reading, as a mode of fantasy – 'an outlet', a 'passage of escape' into a 'more
beautiful world'. For Wells's son Frank, at any rate, the story was unmistak-
ably a metaphor, in its teasing oppositions of reality and desire, utility and
fantasy, for the act of reading and for his father's work as a whole. As he
wrote in the Introduction to *Tales of the Unexpected* in 1936:

'I do not think you can be interested, after reading the stories, in them
only. They are a door leading to a great mass of good reading and good
thinking that will come out of it. The Door is a real door, leading
through a real wall to immortal realities.'

'Good reading and good thinking', though too briskly utilitarian to do justice
to the tale's uneasy sense that the seductive pleasures of popular reading
may represent in reality a fall into 'darkness, danger and death', is a nicely
unpretentious phrase, wholly without the portentousness of, say, Henry
James's claims for the reading of fiction. Literary criticism has on the whole
thought little of Wells, whom F. R. Leavis declared definitively 'incapable of
the education that can be got through "humane letters"',[2] and who has been
generally deprecated as a self-important busybody, a draper's apprentice
with intellectual pretensions comically above his station. Certainly he
remained, by determination as well as in fact, unabashedly a popular
author. Fiction may be a doorway to 'immortal realities' (a sentimentally
vacuous phrase that Wells *père* would have relished), but access to them lies
not through Jamesian complexities of suggestive figuration or the arcane
adumbrations of literary symbol, but through good stories in traditional
modes, briskly and interestingly told. The setting of 'The Door in the Wall' is
suburban, familiar. The fatal scene is enacted under 'pale electric lights near
the station'. The door itself is glimpsed 'among some rather low-class streets

on the other side of Camden Hill', in 'an unfrequented road near Earl's Court', through the window of a cab to Paddington station, 'on my way to Oxford' on the LNER.

Railway Fiction

This recurrence of stations and railways, like the fatal fall into a railway cutting, is suggestive. James was disturbed, at the turn of the century, by the evidence of degenerate popular reading-habits revealed in 'the flare of railway bookstalls'.[3] Already, twenty years earlier, John Ruskin had deplored the productions of 'the common railroad-station novelist' and compared the characters in a popular novel to 'the sweepings out of a Pentonville omnibus'. And still thirty years after James the very best that Queenie Leavis could find to say of a popular novel of the least distasteful kind was that it was the sort of book 'that in Heaven the lowbrow buys at the railway bookstall to read while travelling and leaves behind him in the train.'[4] The pleasures of Victorian and Edwardian popular reading are associated less with the privacy of the study and the armchair than with the agitated excitements of public transport: the brittle, vivid sociability of the illuminated street, the bustle and adventure of the station platform, the transient romance of travel by bus, train or tram.

To be more precise, the production of cheap fiction from the 1840s onwards has two social destinations: the family home and the railway, corresponding perhaps to 'respectable' and 'disreputable' conceptions of the popular classes. To the former belong the decorous and moral fictions of Simms and McIntyre's 'Parlour Novelist' (1847) and 'Parlour Library' (1849), along with magazines like *The Home Circle* (1849), *Household Words* (1850) and *The Family Paper* (1856). But this field is dominated by Mudie's Select (i.e. carefully censored) Circulating Library, only begetter of the mighty 'three-decker' novel, for family reading. The latter, with the exception of a handful of ephemeral interlopers like Routledge's 'Railway Library', belonged to W. H. Smith and Son. Margaret Dalziel has noted the remarkable speed with which the phrase 'railway literature' registered the impact of Smith's first railway bookstall, established in 1848. In 1845 the phrase still referred to Bradshaws, daily newspapers and the like. By 1851 it had become an established catchphrase for cheap popular fiction.

Though less sanctimonious than Mudie, whose shortlived attempt to compete in the railway market, the 'Run and Read Library', consisted of 'Tales uniting Taste, Humour and Sound Principles, written by competent Christian writers with a view to elevating the character of our popular fiction', Smith made some early gestures towards the moral improvement of his readers. But the railway novel quickly became a metonym for the unregenerate tastes of the 'unknown public'. In 'The Literature of the Rail'

(1851), the *Times* grumbled that 'every addition to the stock was positively made on the assumption that persons of the better class who constitute the larger portion of railway readers lose their accustomed taste the moment they enter the station and present themselves to the railway librarian.' And as the last phrase suggests, Smith soon exploited his dominance of the railway market to supplement the bookstalls with libraries: to use the train not only as a place for reading but as a means of access to reading of a more refined variety, so challenging Mudie on his own ground:

> 'Messrs W. H. Smith and Son, taking advantage of the convenience afforded by their railway bookstalls, are about to open a Subscription Library on a large scale, something like that of Mr Mudie. The book-stalls will, in fact, become local libraries, small but select, with the immense advantage of hourly communication by train.'[5]

Railways profoundly transformed the metropolis, literally undermin-ing it, exposing and liberating its 'mysteries', subverting its social topogra-phy of work and leisure. In *Outcast London*,[6] Gareth Stedman Jones has recorded the dehousing and overcrowding of the traditional 'residuum' of central London in the period of the 'railway crazes' (the 1840s and '50s), as well as the role of the railways in the regulation of labour mobility and the relations between the centre and the new suburbs. And a historian of Chartism has noted the active collaboration of the railway companies with the Home Office and the military authorities in the policing of popular insurrections:

> '. . . the technical changes which accompanied the Industrial Revolu-tion rendered easier the task of those responsible for maintaining public order. . . . The development in the sphere of transport and communication had a contribution to make to the pacification of English social life. . . . The key to the repression of disorder lay in an efficient system of troop movements, and it was here that the railways rendered the greatest assistance.'[7]

For Dickens, too, the railway in *Dombey and Son* symbolised a 'great change', a new era of prosperity, efficiency and order.

> 'Crowds of people and mountains of goods, departing and arriving scores upon scores of times in every four-and-twenty hours, produced a fermentation in the place that was always in action. . . . Night and day the conquering engines rumbled at their distant work, or, advanc-ing smoothly to their journey's end, and gliding like tame dragons into the allotted corners grooved out to the inch for their reception, stood bubbling and trembling there, making the walls quake, as if they were dilating with the secret knowledge of great powers yet unsuspected in them, and strong purposes not yet achieved.'[8]

Yet the railway remains a deeply ambiguous symbol, incarnating the modernising optimism of bourgeois order, profit and legality, but ruthlessly destructive too of older pieties. Dickens' celebration of the 'ringing grooves of change' modulates abruptly, in a dramatic demonstration of Marx's 'legitimate antithesis', to romantic premonitions of disaster.

> 'But Staggs's Gardens had been cut up root and branch. Oh, woe the day when "not a rood of English ground" – laid out in Staggs's Gardens – is secure!'

The (mis)quotation here is from Wordsworth's sonnet 'On the Projected Kendal and Windermere Railway' ('Is then no nook of English ground secure From rash assault?'), published four years before *Dombey*. Writing thirty years later in an attempt to prevent a similar venture, Ruskin was convinced of 'the certainty of the deterioration of moral character in the inhabitants of every district penetrated by a railway', and speculated gloomily about the 'effect on the character of such a population' (the rural labourers depicted 'with absolute fidelity' by Scott and Wordsworth) likely to be produced 'by the influx of that of the suburbs of our manufacturing towns'. These were the same popular classes whom, 'worked on' by 'the ordinary popular literature', Arnold in *Culture and Anarchy* saw breaking loose into rowdy assertions of proletarian pleasure and rage:

> 'that vast portion . . . of the working class which, raw and half-developed, has long lain half-hidden amidst its poverty and squalor, and is now issuing from its hiding-place to assert an Englishman's heaven-born privilege of doing as he likes, and is beginning to perplex us by marching where it likes, meeting where it likes, bawling what it likes, breaking what it likes.'

And, of course, reading what it likes – O'Connor and the Chartist *Morning Star*, no less than the romances of Reynolds and Rhoda Broughton: hence the 'Function of Criticism in the Present Time'.

Ruskin, himself a keen traveller and an avid reader of romances of both the edifying and the lurid kind, was one of the first literary intellectuals to analyse these fictions of the burgeoning metropolis. With the improving works of Maria M. Corant, Mrs Leith Adams and the redoubtably Honourable Mrs Henry Chetwynd he contrasted that 'essentially cockney literature, – developed only in the London suburbs, and feeding the demands of the rows of similar brick houses, which branch in devouring cancer round every manufacturing town'. The social sneer at 'cockney literature' recalls the sarcasms, half a century earlier, of the quarterly reviewers at the expense of the 'cockney poet' Keats – by 1880, of course, a classic, though still an uncertain one. But a newer set of sentiments has clustered around the defensive class-feeling: the 'devouring cancer' of the suburbs, the menace of the urban crowd, the imminent insurrections, fed by the literature of fantasy, of the twin forms of proletarian desire – crime and sexuality. All these elements of the bourgeois nightmare are, for Ruskin, reflected in and directly engendered by the popular literature of the 'confused metropolis'.

> 'In the lower middle orders, an entirely new kingdom of discomfort and disgrace has been preached to them in the doctrines of unbridled pleasure which are merely an apology for their peculiar forms of ill-breeding. It is quite curious how often the catastrophe, or the leading interest, of a modern novel, turns upon the want, both in maid and bachelor, of the common self-command which was taught to their grandmothers and grandfathers as the first element of enduring decent behaviour. . . . The automatic amours and involuntary proposals of recent romance acknowledge little further law of morality than the instinct of an insect, or the effervescence of a chemical mixture.'[10]

Here the object of anxiety is the petty-bourgeois reader, suburban, not unredeemable perhaps, but 'wallowing', in Tennyson's elegant phrase, 'in troughs of Zolaism'. There is worse, of course, much worse. But though angry, repelled, often confused, Ruskin has too some notion not only of the different genres and markets, but of their quite complex relations of representation and exploitation, popular consciousness and capitalist marketing.

> 'Fictitious! I use the ambiguous word deliberately, for it is impossible to distinguish in these tales of the prison-house how far their vice and gloom are thrown into their manufacture only to meet a vile demand, and how far they are an integral condition of thought in the minds of men trained from their youth up in the knowledge of Londinian and Parisian misery.'

The allusion is to G. M. W. Reynolds's immensely popular *Mysteries of London*, and to the famous prototype whose formula it shrewdly exploits, Sue's *Mystères de Paris*. The 'mysterious' metropolis, medieval, labyrinthine and inscrutable, predates the railway in topography and mood, presenting an irresistible incentive to the reforming zeal of engineer and policeman alike:

> 'For Parisians in general and even for the Paris police the hide-outs of criminals are such a "mystery" that at this very moment broad light streets are being laid out in the *Cité* to give the police access to them.'[11]

Reynolds, leading Chartist, writer of the weekly *Political Instructor* (1849–50) and founder of the venerable radical paper *Reynolds' News*, was also the doyen of 'railway novelists', whose name served as a catchphrase and a bogey – one of Mudie's 'selectors' regularly rejected manuscripts she thought morally unsuitable with the comment 'leave it to Mr Reynolds'. His sensational tales of love, crime, poverty and riches – fifty-five novels, four volumes of *Mysteries of London*, eight volumes of *Mysteries of the Court of London* with their scandalous exposés of the private life of George IV, and god knows how much else – outsold Dickens in his heyday. But it may be that Ruskin's fear and contempt were prompted less by the technical virtuosity, brilliant vulgarity and sheer energy of Reynolds's novels and serials than by their republicanism, their persistently enunciated solidarity with popular emancipation and democratic causes, and by the deplorable fact, noted by Margaret Dalziel, that 'his lovers, the women as well as the men, *enjoy* themselves'.[12] Reynolds may indeed be the nearest we have in that (perhaps any) period to a radically-motivated popular fiction, of 'a purely ideological-political character', as Gramsci said of Sue, 'democratic in tendency and associated with the ideology of 1848'.[13] It is probably not surprising, therefore, that the most widely-read novelist of the nineteenth century was feared and despised by his high-minded contemporaries, ignored by their academic successors, and appears in nobody's Great Tradition. At a time when the considerably more temperate and equivocal indignations of his rival and contemporary Dickens have acquired – at a safe distance – a classic status, Reynolds appears to be virtually unknown.

Raymond Williams has remarked that while 'the detail of much of Ruskin's criticism of a *laissez-faire* society was in fact perfectly acceptable to socialists . . . the ideas of *design* and *function*, as he expressed them, supported not a socialist idea of society but rather an authoritarian idea, which included a very emphatic hierarchy of classes.'[14] His politics, though anti-capitalist and leaning to a kind of feudal-syndicalism, were reactionary and patriarchal, drawing their energy and symbolism, in Brecht's words for Lukacs, from the 'good old things' rather than the 'bad new ones'. The 'peculiar forms of ill-breeding' of the 'lower middle orders', the 'vice and gloom' of the urban working class, stand in strong contrast in his discourse both to 'peasants', who 'know each other as children – meet, as they grow up, in testing labour' and, revealingly, to those 'patrician families of the field', whose offspring 'know what they are doing, and marry a neighbouring estate, or a covetable title, with some conception of the responsibilities they undertake'. These ennobling sentiments, with which the Honourable Mrs Henry Chetwynd would undoubtedly have concurred, and from whom they may well be derived, recall another of Gramsci's categories of popular fiction: the 'conservative-reactionary', characterised by an 'admiration for the aristocracy and its devoted flunkeys'.

Reactionary, certainly; but decisively patriarchal too. Here, in a letter to a Swiss friend and protected only by the fig-leaf of a foreign language, is the ideology more ornately on display in Ruskin's tract *Of Queens' Gardens*:

'Le devoir d'un homme est d'entretenir sa femme et ses enfants, celui d'une femme est de le rendre heureux chez lui, et d'elever ses enfants sagement. Aucune femme n'est capable de faire plus que cela. Aucune femme ne doit faire moins.'[15]

('A man's duty is to support his wife and children, a woman's to make him happy at home and to raise his children wisely. No woman can do more than that. No woman ought to do less.')

The doctrine of the absolute, naturally- and morally-sanctioned sexual division of labour and function, as a fundamental precondition of civilised society – a doctrine which Ruskin did much to articulate clearly for the mid-Victorian bourgeoisie – is deep, pervasive and, needless to say, hardly a solitary eccentricity. But if there is one novel that perfectly condensed everything that the author of *Queens' Gardens* found pathologically degenerate in popular romance, it was George Eliot's *The Mill on the Floss*. It was that book, already twenty years in print, whose characters he dismissed as 'simply the sweepings out of a Pentonville omnibus', and whose narrative, he reported, 'hinged mainly on the young people's "forgetting themselves in a boat"'. Bizarre as that description is, it does indicate the extent to which worries about popular reading express not only social misgivings about the effects of popular literacy but also, perhaps pre-eminently, very deep anxieties about the threat to patriarchal authority of women's *pleasure* – of representations of the sexuality and sociality of women. And those anxieties point to the central activity in articulating, shaping, perhaps ultimately immobilising women's pleasures, of the genre and the ideology of *romance*.

Romance

Patricia Stubbs has argued for a close relationship between ideologies of domesticity and the genre of the novel, which

> '. . . grew up as a literary form at a time when industrialisation was beginning both to exclude women from production and to create an artificial split between public and private life. These two developments are closely related, and the connection between them lies in the changing role of women. Increasingly confined to the home, it was they who became the focus of the new value which was placed on private experience.'[16]

However true for the form as a whole – and all such statements about the 'rise of the novel' tend to flatten out the uneven trajectories of social and cultural process – that relationship can be very clearly seen in the remarkable contraction and redefinition, between 1850 and the end of the century, of the meanings and connotations, the literary contents, of romance. Ruskin's use of the word ('the automatic amours and involuntary proposals of recent romance') already suggests an incipient specification: novels of love, marriage, domestic sentiment – 'women's fiction'. But even in the 1880s an older, less clearly gendered usage persists. Indeed, as late as the turn of the century Rider Haggard could reassure his schoolboy readers that *King Solomon's Mines* was a 'romance': that is, that 'there is not a petticoat in the entire history'.

Renaissance romance is didactic, aristocratic and while perhaps predominantly 'masculine', not sharply gendered in either narrative or implied readership. All these features are present in the avowed aim of Spenser's *Faerie Queene*: 'to fashion a gentleman or noble person in virtuous and gentle discipline' (i.e. teaching). That discipline will lead the hero through those trials of manhood and virtue that constitute the greater part of the narrative to the reward of marriage to a virtuous and beautiful woman. The elements of later romance are of course clearly present, but the genre offers little evidence of a formal separation between public and private life, the active and the domestic sphere.

That separation, and the increasingly persistent restriction of 'romance' to what George Eliot in an unsisterly phrase called 'silly novels by lady novelists', occurs in the latter half of the nineteenth century alongside two other, clearly related, developments: the institution of a strong ideological offensive to enforce the separation of spheres, and the (re)emergence of an active, politically adventurous feminism. In that struggle romance is captured, domesticated, circumscribed. But though the genre can from then on seem to inscribe its heroines quite inexorably in their domestic and reproductive function, it is worth remembering that the prototypes of a good deal of later romance – *Persuasion*, *Jane Eyre*, *Wuthering Heights* – are also, however ambiguously, products and affirmations of women's need and right to speak, feel and choose: texts in which the smooth discourse of legitimated pleasure, of the feminine subject 'finding herself' in willing subordination to the patriarchal order, is all the time counterpointed and destabilised by other discourses – the 'unbridled pleasures' of anger, disobedience and desire. Indeed, it may matter less, for its women readers, than it seems that the genre typically subordinates these unlawful pleasures to the concluding imperatives of wifely modesty. Criticism emphasises closure, conformity, the power of endings. But readers need not necessarily do so, and their complicities with texts, like the very act of reading them, may be secretly and enjoyably subversive. Certainly some middle-class readers found, and feared, in *Jane Eyre* not a sentimental education in the necessity of matrimonial duty and the redemptive power of a good woman's devotion, but rather a kind of domestic Chartism. The fall of a stress determines whether the famous declaration 'Reader, I married him' sounds like an admission of self-imposed defeat or the promise of an unspoken and deferred rebellion.

Of course, *Persuasion*, *Jane Eyre*, *Wuthering Heights* are 'classics'. So, for all Ruskin's efforts, is *The Mill on the Floss*. Their textual equivocations, like

their angry, uncertain feminism, have been anaesthetised by many generations of 'readerly' criticism and straightforward misrepresentation. The
gendering of fictional genres and their target readerships can be seen more
clearly in the titles and marketing histories of popular magazines, *feuilletons*
and novelettes. By the end of the century the 'woman's magazine', though
not in itself a new conception (*The Mother's Friend*, 1848; *Englishwoman's
Domestic Magazine*, 1852), stands sharply distinct from the older, all-purpose
family paper like *The Family Treasury* or Dickens's *Household Words*; a
separated discourse of domestic femininity, an institutional consecration of
'woman's place' and 'women's interests' – cookery, childcare and romance.

There is, in fact, an odd, momentary tussle over the word. Haggard's
contentious usage has been noted, and one adventure magazine of the
nineties, clearly marketed for a male readership, is called *Romance – illus-
trated* (with a 'romantic' stablemate, *My Queen*). But within a decade,
Romance is advertised as 'everywoman's story magazine'; and although a
more generalised sense is marginally retained in ideologically neutral uses
(the 'romance of travel' and such like), and a specialised sense in literary
history ('alliterative romances'), the gendered attribution, soon to be signified in popular usage by the phonological shift to *Ro*-mance, becomes
rapidly dominant. By the twenties the titles proliferate: *True Romances*, *Love:
Romantic Magazine*, *Romances Album*, *Love and Romance*, with the separation of
spheres thrown sharply into relief by their masculine counterparts, often
from the same publishers: *Detective*, *Empire Frontier*, *Action Stories*.

While the gendering of romance is an effect of sexual ideologies
energetically mobilised by the marketing policies of popular publishing, its
social and cultural status was being simultaneously mapped into place by
the ethical-aesthetic preoccupations of literary criticism. Ruskin had been
taught in Camberwell by Thomas Dale, and later attended some of his
lectures as the inaugural Professor of English Language and Literature at
Kings College London. Dale, whose course included a lecture on 'The
history of romantic fiction', was a clergyman, and more concerned with
moral improvement than with literary criticism.

> 'Never, in tracking the course of those brilliant luminaries that sparkle
> in the firmament of our literature – never will I suffer the eye of
> inexperienced youth to be dazzled by the brilliancy of genius, when its
> broad lustre obscures the deformity of vice; never will I affect to stifle
> the expression of a just indignation, when wit, taste and talent have
> been designedly prostituted by their unworthy possessors to the
> excitement of unholy passions, the palliation of guilty indulgencies,
> the ridicule of virtue, or the disparagement of religion.'[17]

Dale's curriculum, it can be imagined, tended to be small and decidedly
selective – a kind of Mudie's Library of the intelligentsia. But although

judgments of essentially the same kind continued in the following century to animate the discriminations and exclusions of literary ideology, they took increasingly the form of *aesthetic* judgments and categories: realism, formal unity, intensity of 'felt life'. Hence Ruskin's ostensibly disinterested discriminations of 'fiction fair and foul', Richards's seemingly scientific preoccupation with the 'quality of our reading' and the teaching of poetry 'as a means of ordering our minds', and Q. D. Leavis's curt dismissal of a novel of Dorothy Sayers as 'a vicious presentation because it is popular and romantic while pretending to realism'.[12]

That last phrase says, with characteristic pungency and succinctness, much of what I have been trying to argue in this essay. Romance is the object of a double marginalisation, a conjuncture of bourgeois and patriarchal attitudes. It would be easy to leave it there, to shrug it off as an unredeemably reactionary and incorporated form. But the history of popular reading suggests that its pleasures, the uses to which it puts its texts and genres, the modes of sensation, excitement and escape, as well as knowledge, that it stimulates, may not be as securely locked into the 'legitimate antitheses' of the ideological economy as most socialists, and some feminists, have supposed. Reading, like riding on trains, has its unruly as well as its legitimated pleasures, to which the ticketed destination, the timetable of secure significations, sets only a provisional terminus. In 1931 one of Margaret Llewelyn Davies's co-operative working women looked back sixty years to her time 'in service' as a seventeen-year-old.

> 'I had very little time to myself. If by chance I was seen reading, I was told that I ought to be able to find something better to do . . . The result of this treatment caused me to read when I ought to have been doing my work. I managed to do so when I went upstairs to make the beds, etc. The servant next door lent me some trashy books that came out weekly. These books had tales that were continued week by week, and the tales were so arranged that they left off "to be continued in our next" at a very exciting part of the story. . . . After a while I became so fascinated with the tales that when the day came for the book to come out I had no peace of mind until I had been to the shop to get it and had found the means to read it.'[13]

She was soon taught to despise such 'trashy' stuff; but the passion for reading, for the secret pleasures of escape and self-instruction, remained, in a form that Reynolds, if not Ruskin, might have approved:

> 'A railway time-table with a map in it was quite an education to me. I used to trace the distance of different towns through which trains would have to go, and I learnt the names of all the most important villages and the counties they were in. In fact, I became quite a traveller in my mind.'[14]

Notes

1. Karl Marx, *Grundrisse* (trans M. Nicolaus), Harmondsworth, Penguin, 1973, p. 162.
2. F. R. Leavis, 'The Literary Mind', *Scrutiny*, vol. 1, no. 1, May 1932, p. 30.
3. Henry James, 'The Future of the Novel' (1899), in Morris Shapira (ed.) *Selected Literary Criticism*, Harmondsworth, Penguin, 1968, p. 219.
4. *Scrutiny*, vol. 5, no. 3, December 1936, p. 300.
5. Quoted in Guinevere L. Griest, *Mudie's Circulating Library*, Indiana University Press, 1970, p. 32.
6. Gareth Stedman Jones, *Outcast London*, Harmondsworth, Penguin, 1976.
7. F. C. Mather, 'The Railways, the Electric Telegraph and Public Order during the Chartist Period', *History* (new series), vol. XXXVIII, 1953, p. 41.
8. Charles Dickens, *Dombey and Son*, 1848, chapter 15.
9. John Ruskin, 'Railways in the Lake District', in Cook and Wedderburn (eds.), *Complete Works*, George Allen, 1903–1912, vol. XXXIV, pp. 137–43.
10. Ruskin, 'Fiction Fair and Foul', *Complete Works*, vol. XXXIV, pp. 265ff.
11. K. Marx and F. Engels, 'The Holy Family', in *Marx and Engels Collected Works*, vol. 4, Moscow, 1975, p. 57.
12. Margaret Dalziel, *Popular Fiction 100 Years Ago*, Cohen and West, 1957, p. 38.
13. Antonio Gramsci, *Quaderni del Carcere*, ed V. Gerratana, Turin, Einaudi, 1975, vol. 3, p. 2120.
14. Raymond Williams, *Culture and Society*, Harmondsworth, Penguin, 1961, p. 145.
15. Ruskin, *Complete Works*, vol. 18, pp. 109ff.
16. Patricia Stubbs, *Women and Fiction*, Hassocks, Harvester, 1979, p.x.
17. T. Dale, 'An Introductory Lecture delivered in the University of London', quoted in D.J. Palmer, *The Rise of English Studies*, OUP, 1965, p. 20.
18. I. A. Richards, *Practical Criticism*, Routledge and Kegan Paul, 1964 edn, p. 349.
19. Q. D. Leavis, review of Dorothy L. Sayers' *Gaudy Night*, in *Scrutiny*, vol. 6, no. 3, December 1937, p. 337.
20. Margaret Llewelyn Davies (ed.), *Life As We Have Known It*, Virago, 1977, pp. 27–9.

Terry Eagleton

POETRY, PLEASURE AND POLITICS

A terrible beauty is born.   *W. B. Yeats* Easter 1916

Most people seem to feel that this last line of Yeats's poem is a 'good' one: a
little shopsoiled and cliched by now, perhaps, but still enjoyable. I want to
ask why it is that people like this line, as a modest contribution to a theory of
pleasure. To answer this question will involve taking the line and blowing it
up on some screen of the unconscious – or, to change the metaphor, slowing
down the frames of its reading almost to a standstill so as to catch the
complex effects it has on us as they happen. This in turn will involve a kind
of crazed microscopic pedantry, which has not even the saving virtue of
originality, and which I am not recommending as a paradigm of cultural
analysis, partly because life is too short. All I am claiming is that we shall not
understand the mechanisms of pleasure in art until we have been through
this form of enquiry, if only to leave it behind; and that, though I have taken
this line deliberately at random, simply as one that most people seem to like,
what I do with it could in principle be done with any discourse whatsoever.
To abstract a single line from a poem is in any case to beg all sorts of questions
relevant to pleasure; it is just that the complexity of analysis involved forbids
the inspection of a larger discursive unit here and now.

The first reason why the line is pleasurable is because it is the last one.
After this we can relax, happily freed from further investments of energy.
But this of course also has its ungratifying aspect, presuming that we liked
reading the poem, because it is now about to be removed from us. We
approach the line ambivalently, then, relief mingled with regret, as a
presence already hollowed by an impending absence. Like all human beings
we enjoy certain kinds of work, delight in our psychical investments, yet of
course we don't, and would rather be deliciously inert. Our anxiety at the
impending loss of the object, however, is mitigated by the fact that the line is
so nice and short. We can master those five words almost at a glance, and
none of them is worryingly obscure. The eye incorporates the line at a
stroke, delighting in its own dominance.

As the eye starts to crawl through the line, this pleasure is certainly not
qualified, even if it isn't signally intensified, by the first word *A*. No problem

there: an empty signifier taken easily in our stride, offering a bare minimum of frustrating resistance to our possession. Yet a flicker of anxiety instantly unfurls. A – *what? A*s have whats and this one doesn't, yet. The pleasure of mastery is accordingly modulated by a mild panic, which will not be put to rest even when we have laboured our way over *terrible*, for that is not a noun, and we must still wait, deferred over the work of three whole terrible syllables, to uncover the temporarily lost object. No need to give up, however, for there is an immediate pleasure in store for us to offset this unsettling suspense: the gratifying dental activity of *t*, an aggressively stressed phoneme. Gratifying and unpleasurable, of course, for who enjoys being roused from the happy untongued inertia of *A* to the difficult expenditure of that sound? Who, moreover, would not feel a mild mounting of anxiety at the very typographical sight of that *terrible*, bristling as it is with as yet unresolved problems, a cluster of curls and strokes, a positive mountain range of phonemes to be negotiated?

Yet all is temporarily well. The stressed consonant *t* carries us over to the unstressed vowels and soft consonants which follow, until the plosive of *ble* holds aggression and relaxation in balance, stabbing yet unstressed as it is, the downbeat of the small graph of desire inscribed in the whole word. *Terrible* binds together three different syllables, and we momentarily enjoy the paradox of that, to be immediately offered a new kind of pleasurable binding or repetition in the alliterative *b* of *beauty* – a pleasure which, in its smooth equivalencing, modulates the otherwise stressed, aggressive movement of the syllable. *Ty*, which is unstressed, then permits us to relax a little, as well as narcissistically binding us back to the alliterating and assonantal *ter* and *i*; in fact *ty* incorporates two phomemes from *terrible*, thus granting us the momentary delights of equivalence and identity within a stimulating play of difference. Having finished with *ty*, we now know what *A* belongs to, which yields some epistemophilic pleasure. (Epistemophilia in Freudian thought refers to the pleasure taken in knowledge and the desire to know, considered by Freud to relate to the small child's desire to uncover the parents' genitals.) Yet we don't quite know, for what we have is an oxymoron (*terrible beauty*) which gratifies us with its bold equivalence as it disturbs us with its dissonance. The oxymoron generates a pleasurable but anxiety-laden ambivalence, the sense of a knowledge at once in and out of place; it offers a resistance to our incorporation at once frustrating and – since it sets us thinking – enjoyable. It isn't a difficult oxymoron to grasp in the context of the poem, however, so the excitation of ambivalence is fairly quickly released into the pleasurable security of cognition: we 'get' it and like the fact that we do, enjoy surmounting the frustrating object and subduing it to our desire. *Is* binds assonantally with *ty*, its soft consonant and unstressedness providing an indolent moment before the gratifying lip-working labour of *born*. This pleasurably repeats and binds the previous *b*s, an easy-to-master word which signals the end of labour. Yet it is puzzling too, for how exactly can *beauty* be born? And since birth is a prelude, what is coming next? The pleasure of closure is overshadowed, then, by a mild excitation of deferral, since birth at once ends and opens. Anyway, we have closed our teeth around that final *n*, and that is surely satisfying.

As this excessively crude and fanciful analysis ought to have shown, psychoanalysis always has it both ways and is thus apparently unbeatable. We derive pleasure from both binding[1] and releasing, dominating and being dominated, expending and economising, knowing and not knowing, equivalencing and differencing, articulating and identifying. What matters, of course, is that these various activities are rhythmically modulated or orchestrated in an acceptable way, as the rhythm of the line itself, with its distribution of symmetrical unstressed within stressed syllables, manages a certain economy. What I have tried to show here, perhaps arbitrarily, is a certain way of extracting the graph of desire from the little drama or narrative of a line, tracking the play of unconscious drives in language. This, so far, has largely involved bracketing off the semantic level of the line, attending mainly to what Kristeva would call the 'semiotic',[2] but not entirely so: you can't feel ambivalent about an oxymoron unless you can identify it. Meaning, in other words, is already caught up in the play of pleasure/displeasure from the outset, the semiotic and semantic already mutually imbricated. But what I have aimed for so far is a chiefly 'economic' rather than 'representational' account of pleasure, which is in itself primitive and insufficient; and I want now to develop a little the semantic field of pleasure which the line marks out. To do this will entail that we stop pretending that we haven't read the rest of the poem, or anything else by Yeats.

The Semantic Field

We might begin by looking back at that *terrible beauty*. This refers of course to the Easter rebellion itself, but I think that it also means Maud Gonne. Rose of Ireland and rancorous demagogue, Maud Gonne is the terrible beauty with whom the poem must come to terms; the question posed by that oxymoron is, among other things, the question: What is woman? Two conflicting drives – the drive to idealise and the sadistic impulse to destroy or deface – are condensed in that single *Darstellung* or representation, a condensation which, like punning or metaphor, affords its own economic yield of pleasure; but that economic pleasure is itself overdetermined by the triply condensed gratifications of sadism, idealisation and defence. The entire trope operates as a defence against the threatening phallic woman, whose beauty it must at once tear at, deform, make terrible and yet, in a guilty reparative gesture, reinstate in that very act. (It is beauty, after all, however terrible it is.) The trope is a mechanism by which the line may ward off, disarm, the phallic woman, at once destroy and restore her, dismember the object yet leave it miraculously untouched. The woman still *is* whole, beautiful, somehow, even though she has been unmasked, sadistically, as a whore. If there is Kleinian ambivalence in this,[3] so too is there in the line's response to the political uprising: the oxymoron's function, there again, is to idealise, deface, defend and restore at a stroke. The trope, as it were, is a compromise formation: it releases its aggressivity on the uprising but in the same gesture seals the event in the inviolable realm of myth. Or, to express the ambivalence another way, it lets the pleasure principle rip – this bloody event is a beauty to be celebrated – in the very moment that the reality principle prudently covers its losses, with a canny eye on the event's possible future outcome.[4] The trope rationalises guilt, and this is potentially part of its pleasurable effect.

The problem is to articulate the economic and representational levels of pleasure: to interrelate somehow the play of drives in language (binding, deferring, mastering, expending, releasing and so on) with the play of drives in the representations, the complex business of fantasy and defence, covering and unmasking, repression and uplifting. There is, presumably, no invariable set of relations here, no master-code which might translate the one into the other. What is obvious in any case, once we have 'risen' from the semiotic to the semantic without leaving the former behind, is that the concept of pleasure now has to engage the concept of ideology, and indeed, methodological distinctions apart, did so from the outset. It would clearly be disastrously crude to argue that economies of pleasure/displeasure belong to the id, whereas ideological pleasure/displeasure belongs to the ego, or superego. Activities thought proper to the ego such as cognition and perception certainly involve pleasure; the sadism of the superego is equally a libidinal matter; and as Freud's later work makes clear, both ego and superego are themselves deeply rooted in the id. My pleasure or displeasure at the sexism and political vacillation of *terrible beauty* certainly is a matter of ego and superego, but both those formations are of course also a matter of the id. One could imagine the economic gratifications of the line as a kind of 'forepleasure', which tries to seduce me into admiring its fantasies and defences too, preparing the ground for that particular psychodrama, and this indeed may well happen. Presumably something like this is what happens with people who like the line *a lot*. If I am a woman or an Irish nationalist or both, however, the line is going to have to work harder, more deviously, to secure my gratification. It is perhaps unlikely to achieve this simply by its pulsional economy; it will have to persuade me to participate in the *general* mechanisms of its defence, fantasy, compromise formation and the rest, in a way which might surmount my resistance to its *particular* figuration. Whether it can cajole me into laying down my ideology, so to speak, is by no means merely a question of the pleasure principle seeking to subvert the reality principle, but a matter of whether it can successfully corner for its own ends some of the unconscious energy I invest in my 'beliefs', while reassuring me that I have no need to feel guilty or anxious about this. Or, more exactly, that it is worth trading that quantity of guilt or anxiety for the libidinal gratifications it will afford me. One can imagine my unconscious saying to my superego, in an analogous situation: 'Alright, I know, you really do disapprove of girlie magazines, that's not just hypocrisy. But, come on now, you find them pleasurable too, don't you?' The unconscious will try to placate and accommodate the ego and superego, not just brutally unmask them as hollow.

I know plenty of people, mainly Irish people, who dislike this line intensely, finding in it nothing more than an evasive, posturing rhetoric, a climax of Yeats's shabby political betrayals. This, presumably, doesn't mean that they are immune to its play of drives and masks – simply that, given the unconscious infrastructure of their own ideological formation, such gratifications are in the end not worth the trade-off. Lest this be thought to reduce the 'relative autonomy' of ideology to the immediate traffic of the id, it is worth reminding ourselves that one reason we sometimes dislike lines of poetry, or artefacts in general, is because they are *not true*. Knowing the truth, understanding, is certainly a major source of pleasure, if I may leave aside for a moment the increasingly tedious arguments about whether truth exists. Like any other activity, this doubtless has its roots in the unconscious – Freud relates it to the greed of the eye, the primal scene and the castration anxiety – but it centrally involves the ego. One thing I dislike about the line is that it is extremely vague: it at once rhetorically flourishes and cavalierly withdraws an object of knowledge. (One can show, by a rhetorical and ideological analysis of the whole poem, just how precisely vague it has to be, just how determinate its indeterminacy is.) My dislike may therefore be to do with the demand for an imaginary object, which I fear has not been quite restored to me; but it is equally an 'ideological' demand for political clarity. Enamoured as I no doubt am by compromise formations and defence mechanisms in general, this particular one frustrates me. In this sense, then, my investments in a 'regressive' psychoanalytic structure may be politically 'progressive'; there is certainly no mere homology between the two.

There would seem, then, to be at least three 'levels' of pleasure/displeasure involved in a line of writing, which are only methodologically distinguishable. The first is, roughly speaking, economic, or semiotic in the Kristevan sense. To grasp this is to grasp the play of drives in a mainly somatic way, touched upon but not yet fully stabilised by semantic representation. The second is the level of *general* psychical mechanisms and strategies, always themselves with ideological content, but engaging our investments at this point primarily by their *forms*. The third level is that of concrete ideological meaning, itself of course always deeply cathected or decathected by any specific historical reader. (By these terms Freudianism simply refers to our 'investment' of an object with a certain amount of libido, or alternatively our withdrawal of libido from it.) From the viewpoint of libidinal pleasure, these three 'levels' may be seen as engaged in constant intricate trade-offs. When the loosely articulated drives achieve representation, for example, this will reorganise the pulsional economy itself. For a specific historical reader, these 'levels' may conspire, conflict, or one or two may gang up on the other(s). The mutual articulations of the 'levels', however, depends not only upon the specific historical reader, but upon history itself; it is itself a matter of ideology. For Samuel Johnson, there was absolutely no problem about 'aesthetically' enjoying a work which morally disgusted you. It simply couldn't be done. Johnson would have been incapable of reaping pleasure from a text with the ideology of which he was fundamentally at odds. The very concept would have been ideologically offensive to him, and indeed quite impermissable. If we interpret this merely as 'repression', not to say 'puritanism', we are simply ignoring the power with which certain deeply unconscious ideologies of pleasure help to produce certain historical subjects. In a fine, perhaps hopeless utopian gesture, Herbert Marcuse looks forward to an historical epoch in which we shall produce human subjects biologically incapable of violence. Presumably such people would not need to engage in complex libidinal exchanges in order to enjoy in Yeats's poetry a violence of which they also disapproved, but would just feel sick instead. We, meanwhile, in a certain transitional epoch where, for historical and ideological reasons, an ideology of the 'aesthetic' has been able to flourish, are confronted with a *political* problem about pleasure. I mean by that the problem of knowing how to harness pleasure to political ends, and formulate those ends in terms of pleasure, in a situation where, because of the psychic fragmentation of which the ideology of the 'aesthetic' is a part, the relation between the kind of pleasure people take in art, and the pleasure they derive from striving to realise their political needs, has become extremely obscure. If 'aesthetics' is a symptom of that fragmentation, so is psychoanalysis, one of whose historical conditions of possibility was just such a depoliticisation. The very analytic instruments we deploy are in this sense ideologically guilty.

I have argued, to summarise drastically, that the answer to the question, Why do people like/dislike certain lines of poetry?, lies in an analysis of the mechanisms whereby different 'levels' of potential enjoyment are articulated or disarticulated. To a great extent, this will of course vary from reader to reader, not least when we take into account psychologically random connotations: I derive a certain narcissistic pleasure from the word *terrible* because a fragment of my name inheres in it, although I also feel uneasy at seeing my name incorporated into such a negative term. But some of these mechanisms are general ones, even if there is no reason to believe that they are universal. (The most apparently so – the somatic-semiotic – is surely deeply conditioned by the particular social practices of child-rearing.) One reason why it is worth studying these mechanisms, then, is to be able to produce a more politically effective culture. Another reason is that such study may also tell us something useful about political society itself. We need to know under what circumstances people will exchange the gratifications of relative inertia, imaginary investment, masochistic submission, repetition and the rest for the ambivalent pleasures/displeasures of political excitation. We need to know at what point narcissistic identifications become so paralytic and unpleasurable that they may be traded for the pleasurable anxieties of difference; or what the relations are between the deferments of gratification imposed by capitalism and the deferments involved in political engagement. The compromise formations whose inner instability need more analysis are less those of literary oxymoron than of social ideologies. It would be valuable to know more about how far lack of social mastery can in the end be traded for social fantasy, as well as about the mechanisms of ambivalence which govern collective attitudes of aggressivity/idealisation. And so on. 'Culture', need one say, is not the main or only place of such mechanisms. But finding out what people like, and why, always helps, and art is one good place to do it.

Notes

1. Freud speaks of the need for psychic energy, which he considers as loose or 'unbounded' in its unconscious state, to be controlled and channelled preparatory to its release in gratification. The 'binding' effects of narrative are interesting in this respect.
2. By the 'semiotic' Kristeva means, in a sense special to her own work, the play of bodily drives in such phenomena as rhythm, sound, movement and so on, before the point at which they receive articulation in language.
3. The psychoanalyst Melanie Klein is noted for her work on the ambivalent responses of the pre-oedipal child towards its mother, its tendency to take her as an object of both love and aggression, to destroy the breast in fantasy and then make guilty reparation for this destruction.
4. For a fuller analysis of Yeats's evasions and ambiguities here, see my 'History and myth in Yeats's *Easter 1916*' in *Essays in Criticism*, vol. XXI, no. 3, July 1971.

Simon Watney

THE CONNOISSEUR AS GOURMET: The Aesthetics of Roger Fry and Clive Bell

Recent British developments in the theory of art have occupied a broad territory of ideas, stretching between the extremes of those who read all art in terms of its immediate political 'effectiveness', and those who insist equally fervently on the complete autonomy of art from all other areas of social practice. Yet this distinction between political realism and art-for-art's-sake Aestheticism is itself the product of early twentieth-century aesthetics. It would certainly not have made any sense to those nineteenth-century artists and critics whose names are almost invariably invoked in the cause of one side or the other. At the same time, the discussion of such important European Marxist aestheticians as Lukács, Benjamin, Raphael or Adorno has not been aided by the general neglect of the local context within which their work has been latterly received – namely the values and beliefs instituted within the British art historical and art educational establishments. In this article, I examine that 'cultural unconscious',[1] and in particular the work of two early twentieth-century British aestheticians, Roger Fry and Clive Bell, whose work continues to determine and coordinate the structure of the questions, felt problems, the seemingly 'natural' curriculum around which such establishments are constituted. I also want to consider the cultural significance of the Bloomsbury Group in which both men were central figures. Since much of my analysis will be concerned with the continuities of Romantic thought and ideology in relation to received theories of modern art – itself a profoundly problematic term – it will be necessary to make a few introductory observations about Romanticism itself. The persistence of a wide range of ideas connecting and organizing the quotidian to the institutions of cultural knowledge, 'truth', and power, ideas formulated two centuries ago, remains in need of explanation.

Since the late eighteenth century Romantic aesthetics have emphasised the figure of the visual artist out of all proportion to the size of his or her actual audiences. From this fact alone we may deduce the historical signi-ficance of the visual arts as agencies of social and political legitimation. The artist emerges as a special type of person, someone who gives us, the 'public', access to some allegedly 'higher' and superior level of experience or reality than our own. The complex historical transformations of the social functions of artists in earlier periods were explained away in terms of individual genius, battling against unspecified adversaries to establish their names and supposedly independent of the changing social and economic circumstances of their day-to-day activities and labour. Indeed, the very difficulty presented by considering painting as 'labour' or as a branch of production indicates the continued force of Romanticism as an ideology, mobilizing popular attitudes concerning the relation of the individual to the social, and their representations. But Romanticism has not simply been 'recuperated'. Rather, it has been sustained and transformed within a series of debates about art over the past two hundred years which have purported to question every aspect of artistic production. In fact, their interminable concern with the minutiae of style and technique has enabled the central issue of the category of art itself to remain intact and largely unchallenged.

The Romantic Movement offered its adherents two deeply opposed directions. In one version of Romanticism the rejection of the theory of genres in art – based upon a belief in the intrinsic superiority of some areas of subject matter over and against others in a fixed hierarchy ranging from political allegory down to landscape painting – led to a new attention to the material world. Here lay the grounds for nineteenth-century Naturalism, with all its aspirations to scientificity, and the supposedly 'neutral' observation of the 'natural' world, as well as for Realism, with its pictorial object more firmly planted in the world of social relations, and its profound doubt about the adequacy of Naturalism as a means to historical understanding or analysis. At the same time, both Naturalism and Realism were susceptible to the pull of a marked subjectivism, a tendency towards the 'personal' or 'spiritual', in opposition to the public or scientific. Hence we may detect an overall emphasis on technique as an end in itself through the various manifestations of Romanticism, a shared hostility to what were widely understood as the out-dated academic techniques of traditional art. The tendency towards abstraction which informed so much nineteenth century avant-garde painting cannot simply be contrasted as Art-for-Art's-Sake to Naturalism or Realism, without doing grievous damage to the ways in which the relation of subject matter to technique was adjudicated throughout nineteenth century avant-garde art, in such a way that neither subsumed the other. This Romantic scepticism about the closed or concealed nature of 'Official' painting might profitably be compared to Rousseau's scepticism about language, and his equal desire to reach an audience which he understood as universal.

In all these areas we may detect the same general tendency to assume a *categorical* distinction between the verbal and the visual, which is one of the hallmarks of Romantic thought, and a vital pre-condition for both Realist and Modernist aesthetics. It should also be noticed that Romantic social analysis invariably proceeded from an initially *aesthetic* revulsion at the effects of the new capitalist division of labour. This revulsion underpinned the self-image of the Romantic artist as an isolated individual outside society, doomed to be forever at odds with the times, thus ensuring that the Romantics could never get beyond a sociology in which genius is forever locked in mortal combat with mass mediocrity. Hence the emergence of the necessary illusion of the 'general' public, which in this formulation was held to be in some essential sense 'non-artistic' if not actually 'anti-artistic'. It was this notion of the 'genuine' artist as an actual *type* of person which largely explains the powerful concept of the avant-garde, those artists whose work was felt to be somehow in advance of the period in which it was actually produced. For the Romantics could never explain their exclusion from the official markets and sites of display in bourgeois society as the result of conflicting systems of representation, and therefore invented a sociology which was as consoling as it obscured the fact that many of them enjoyed considerable commercial success and critical acclaim – for example Courbet, Delacroix, Manet and later Picasso or Matisse.

Romantic art theory then attempted to speak across a gulf between the person of the 'authentic' artist, and the anonymous non-artistic general public. It also took for granted the most fundamental distinction in Romantic aesthetics, namely the cognitive distinction between word and image, language and sight, as resolutely as pre-Romantic aesthetics had assumed their inter-dependence and inseparability. In this sense Modernism, with its endless versions of the claim that art is totally autonomous – from politics, from its audiences (still in their terrifying *grand guignol* disguise as the Public), from history itself – was the logical outcome of the original Romantic denial of the most precious tenet of Renaissance aesthetics, summed up in the command *'Ut Pictura Poesis'*[2] the fundamental formal and cognitive relation between the verbal and visual arts.

This brief excursion into the nature of Romantic aesthetics is necessary if we are to appreciate how the ideology of Romanticism was re-organized, re-codified and preserved in mainstream twentieth-century British aesthetics. Conventional wisdom invariably reminds us how Roger Fry and Clive Bell stage-managed the introduction of early European Modernist art in England through a series of highly influential exhibitions and publications[3]. This wisdom does not, however, consider whom this art was envisaged as addressing, or how that introduction was intended to be experienced and, perhaps, enjoyed. My argument is that, for all their polemic against 'Victorianism', Fry and Bell succeeded principally in carrying over an entire inventory of conflicting values from Romanticism into twentieth-century British culture, even and especially when they were attacking a particular local tradition of Victorian anecdotal painting which they read as evidence of some congenital national-aesthetic deficiency. The tradition of Anglo-American formalist criticism which they instituted was fundamentally incompatible with an energetic historical semiology or sociology or art – in fact, both British and American formalism have presented their most influential versions of the relations between painting and the wider social world at precisely the point when the entire significance of any such relation was denied. Nonetheless, for all its talk of 'pictorial purity' and 'significant form', British formalism did produce a relatively coherent theory concerning the relations between the artist and his or her viewers, and I hope to demonstrate that this theory may be recovered from the interstices of its version of aesthetic pleasure and the potential audiences for 'modern art' which it advanced.

It is also salutary here to consider the implications of the steady contemporary recuperation of 'Bloomsbury' as a cultural idyll for a middle-class which can no longer admit more frankly aristocratic social fantasies. At this level the writings of Fry and Bell continue to inform post-war British society, sustaining a thoroughly Victorian and paternalistic notion of 'culture', which distinguishes rigidly between cultural production and consumption, even though they themselves mocked and belittled the actual cultural products and audiences of Victorianism. In this sense I want to open up the question recently posed by Raymond Williams: what actually was the Bloomsbury Group 'culturally and socially, as a question distinct from (though still related to) the achievements of individuals and their immediately perceived relationships'?[4] How, for example, are we to relate such grand institutional projects as Keynes's original plan for the Arts Council of Great Britain, as an eye of power surveying and supervising the totality of British cultural production, to the aesthetic prescriptions of such immediate friends and colleagues as Roger Fry or Virginia Woolf? The influence of 'Bloomsbury' upon the institutions of the British art establishment requires an assessment which is attentive to the conflicts within the group itself across a wide range of cultural theory and practice.

Audience Aesthetics and Bloomsbury Art Criticism

In an article published in 1930, Clive Bell asked himself why so many people were going to 'the pictures'.[5] By 'the pictures' he did not mean the cinema, but rather the extensive exhibition of Italian Renaissance painting which was then on display at the Royal Academy, for which his colleague Roger Fry had been a member of the Selecting Committee. Contrasting the deserted rooms of the nearby National Gallery with the throng at Burlington House, Bell concluded that people were not visiting the exhibition in order to gain aesthetic pleasure, but for other motives. The visiting public is caricatured by Bell as the Jones family – 'Mr Jones, Mrs Jones, and all the little Joneses' who flock along 'as one speaks of a flock of sheep', just as they might 'to the Derby'. Mr Jones is understood to be 'performing an act of culture' but since we learn that only those 'who have cultivated a rare native sensibility can understand so much as what is meant by good drawing' we are led to conclude that the unfortunate Mr Jones, 'a linoleum manufacturer', is wasting both his money and his time. The only pleasure Bell allows him is the delayed relief of a cigarette outside in Piccadilly, after leaving 'with an ill-feigned air of tearing himself away'.

Bell is leaning very heavily indeed here upon the published work of his friend Roger Fry, and in particular an essay of 1925 entitled 'Culture and Snobbism'.[6] Here the real villains of Bloomsbury art criticism emerge: the snobs or Philistines, who sham an aesthetic response to works of art and 'acquire more merit by what they know about the history of a work of art than by what they feel in front of it'.[7] The philistine is the exact antithesis of the contemplative artist, confusing social with aesthetic pleasure, which was for both Fry and Bell regarded as the most spiritual and elevating of human emotions and an indispensible sign of 'cultivation'. In their work, the notion of culture is synonymous with 'the aesthetic emotion', just as the slippage from the Philistine to the Popular is almost automatic. Romantic criticism had at least acknowledged the existence of a divided 'general public', one section of which might be susceptible to artistic, moral and even political persuasion. For Fry and Bell, however, there is only a Manichean divide between those who do and those who do not possess the aesthetic emotion, understood as an innate capacity to appreciate 'good' art. In his insistence that aesthetics should be considered in total isolation from all other areas of social practice, Fry was only revealing his own formative origins within the cultural values of the British aesthetic movement of the 1880s and 1890s. As a good aesthete he deplored anecdotal painting, with which he contrasted an art of pictorial 'purity', a term which is central to his theories. It is most clearly summarised in his introductory essay for the catalogue of the Second Post-Impressionist Exhibition, written in 1912, and in a lecture in 1917 entitled 'Art and Life'.

> 'In proportion as art becomes purer the number of people to whom it appeals gets less. It cuts out all the romantic overtones of life which are the usual bait by which men are induced to accept works of art. It appeals only to the disinterested sensibility, and that in most men is comparatively weak.'[8]

For Fry this two-tier theory of aesthetic capacity is matched by a two-tier theory of society itself, the full implication of which was only systematically followed through by Clive Bell. It was also paralleled by a two-tier theory of art. On the one hand lay the wastes of anecdotalism, illustrative painting, 'non-art', which could only interrupt the goal of pictorial purity to which, on the other, all 'true' art supposedly aspires. The notion of social *orders* was always closer to Fry's mind than the concept of class, with its necessary

Roger Fry lecturing. A sketch by Sickert.

implications of conflict. Fry sought a universal art of absolute aesthetic values. Again, this reveals his debts to Aestheticism, the most extreme version of Romantic solipsism. To the dustbin of non-art was consigned all extra-formal meaning, social, sexual or whatever. Issues of form and technique were defined in stark contrast to those of subject matter. In this respect Fry could scarcely have been further from the epistemological confusions of mid-nineteenth century aesthetics which, even for the most outspoken advocates of Realism, had never contrasted form and content in this manner. Closely following the French critic Maurice Denis, Fry uses such painters as Cézanne, Matisse and Picasso with a general disregard for the specific social contexts within which they worked, seeing them rather as modern examples of a timeless artistic concern with certain unchanging and unchangeable painterly values. At the same time it should be clear that the more ruthlessly Fry fetishizes formal aspects of design and technique, the more densely coded is the implicit sense of social superiority which is derived from their 'correct' recognition, acknowledgement and appreciation.

If the ability to distinguish between art and non-art is the result of some innate aesthetic faculty of discerning sensibility, and if that art is defined in sharp contra-distinction to the rest of social and personal experience, then it is clear that there is not much room left for any kind of sociological enquiry. Indeed, the very idea of such an inquiry would only reveal the sordid presence of the Philistine. Historical enquiry is equally reduced to a kind of aesthete's treasure hunt amongst the non-artistic garbage of world civilization. As Fry explained in 1919, it 'is irrelevant to us to know whether . . . a . . . bowl was made seven hundred years ago in China, or in New York yesterday'.[9] Fry's response to overly biographical or socially reductive and deterministic criticism is a total rejection of history itself. A parallel with other contemporary formalisms is apparent too in Fry's appeals to, and development of, a theory of visual cognition. But unlike the socially motivated theories of, for example, Viktor Shklovsky in contemporary Russia, Fry's concern was not to analyze seeing in relation to larger social evaluations, with the goal of revealing unconscious attitudes at the level of sight itself, but rather to validate a hierarchical sequence of 'ways of seeing'. According to this formulation human vision is organised into four modes of perception, which are held to be universal, thereby displacing critical attention once more from any consideration of the relation of viewers to images in any but a physiological sense. First there is 'Practical Vision' or everyday seeing. Secondly, 'Curiosity Vision' is the substance of the 'socio-historical imagination' and, presumably, non-art. Thirdly, 'Aesthetic' or 'Disinterested' vision corresponds to some domain of pure denotation, drained of any of the meanings of the first two categories. And lastly, at the apex of visual experience, teetering on the very edge of a full transcendental mysticism, is 'Creative Vision' – the sole prerogative of the artist, generalising, undifferentiated, perceiving only a world of 'pure' functionless formal relationships. This is the vision to which Lily Briscoe aspires, and which she finally achieves, in Virginia Woolf's *To The Lighthouse*, a novel profoundly informed in its conception of the artistic personality by Fry's contemporary monograph on Cézanne.

It should be clear that these four modes of seeing correspond, in Fry's mind, to four distinct types of people. As such, they embody a kind of aesthetic eugenics, against which any appeals to education would have seemed pointless. In this sense Fry evacuated the Romantic tradition of its last notional traces of the idea of 'improvement' through art. Modernism is set free from all social obligations whatsoever. However much he detested the effects of industrialism, no connection could henceforth be made between 'art' and 'society' without calling forth accusations of Philistinism. The soul was only to find release and relief through the disinterested contemplation of pure form. The belief that the artist is above politics was axiomatic for many of Fry's circle. But even before his death in 1934, a younger generation had begun to question the validity of a theory of aesthetic response in which the public is portrayed not simply as a tasteless and biologically inferior mass, but as *irredeemably* so. This picture was most eloquently drawn by Clive Bell.

As early as 1914 he could confidently describe most people faced with works of art as 'deaf men at a concert',[10] lamenting the absence of a leisured class in England. In the cultural theory I have outlined, such a class has little option but to defend the signs of its own beleaguered privilege against the threatening masses, the 'gross herd'.[11] This lament took its most elegaic and politically reactionary form in his book *Civilization* (1927).

> 'To be civilized society must be permeated and, what is more, continually nourished by the unconscious influence of this civilising élite . . . a leisured class is indispensable. The majority must be told that the world of thought and feeling exists. . . . To point the road is the task of the few.'

Such writing helps to explain why the generic and highly misleading notion of 'Bloomsbury' continues to arouse both opprobrium and respect in different audiences. It is also, I fear, one reason why at least one version of Bloomsbury will retain its élitist appeal. For what could have been more flattering to a middle class clinging tenaciously to its social and political privileges than to be told not only that its taste in curtains was evidence of biological superiority, but that in its taste in curtains lay the prospects for all that was best in the species? Bell concluded his personal manifesto with an unambiguous call for a ruling symposium of like-minded aesthete-intellectuals, imposing its own 'thought and feeling' on a populace so sunk

in the dim consciousness of merely practical vision that they could supposedly neither think nor feel for themselves. Less extreme, but equally
emotive, was Fry's application of Baudelaire's celebrated metaphor for the
greatest figures in western art as lighthouses or beacons shining out across
the landscape of history. But, Fry regrets, 'the lighthouses of art do not
burn with so fixed and unvarying a lustre' as actual lighthouses. On the
contrary:

> 'The light they give is always changing insensibly with each genera-
> tion, now brighter, now dimmer. . . . But we sometimes forget that the
> lights have to be tended or they grow faint and may expire altogether.
> For them to burn brightly they must be fed by the devotion of some few
> spirits in each generation:[12]

There is little separating these 'few spirits' from Bell's 'civilizing élite'. The
social exclusions which had given rise to the explanatory theory of the
avant-garde in Romantic culture were now admitted to be insurmountable
in biological terms – thereby establishing the contradictory picture of a
supposedly universal culture speaking to and for no more than a handful of
individuals in any given society. The political implications of such a frankly
mandarin teleology of culture are not obscure. Hence the pre-emptive
fatalism of much Bloomsbury cultural theory as, in the guttering light of Mr
Jones's cigarette, we detect the anxious figures of Bell and Fry cupping their
hands protectively around the lamp of beauty, confident at least in their
contempt for the 'general' public (now also seen as 'the people'), over whose
inanely chattering heads they carefully pass on the priceless, timeless flame
of art to the next generation of initiates and acolytes.

The Role of Pleasure in Bloomsbury Aesthetics

In the art theories of Roger Fry and Clive Bell there was little space for any
discussion of subject-matter, social usage, or the conditions of cultural
production and distribution. Art was regarded as a trans-historical essence,
constantly restoring itself to a condition of pristine Edenic purity, against the
power and will of the hopelessly Philistine masses. A uniform audience for
art is thus envisaged, an audience which is not divided by class or sex or race
or age, but by immanent degrees of sensibility. In this context the actual
direct experience of looking at pictures assumed an enormous significance,
since it was this intimate moment of aesthetic revelation which displaced all
other potential questions concerning the relation of the viewer to the
pictorial commodity. Hence the immense convenience of Fry's concept of
the aesthetic emotion, which ensured that both the creation and viewing of
works of art would continue to be seen as fundamentally private, states of
blessed communion between self and canvas. Cézanne was for Fry the

embodiment of the artist in this scheme of things, a figure as completely outside society as the ideal ascetic art critic.

> 'Cézanne realized the type of artist in its purest most unmitigated form . . . a character in which everything is due to the compulsion of inner forces . . . the most purely disinterested and the most frankly egoistic of men . . . where others are shaped he grows.'[13]

It is in the cult of Cézanne that Fry's art criticism remains most widely influential, standing for an art which regards only relations of forms, colours, and materials with 'no reference to actual life . . . unconditioned by considerations of space or time'.[14] The contemplation of such art leads to a pleasure which is incompatible with that derived from the recognition or exchange or contestation of motivated signs or symbols. The pleasure of true art, for Fry, is temporary transcendence, a loss of consciousness, the perception of a higher and more stable order of reality; this can only be effected by the suppression of pictorial reference to the material world as anything more than a pretext for formal pictorial analysis.

The rôle that Fry does allow subject matter in art is in fact extremely close to the theoretical level of denotation in classical Saussurean semiotics. Both are equally idealist insofar as they ascribe a theoretical ascendancy or priority to the supposedly non-social. Aesthetic pleasure is thus understood as the highest faculty of consciousness and partakes of a hypothetically universal set of values. Characteristically, it was Clive Bell who described this state of aesthetic Nirvana most frequently and most dramatically. 'The critic's business,' he explained, 'is to help the public . . . to put the public in the way of aesthetic pleasure.'[15] We are also informed that: 'Connoisseurs of pleasure – of whom I count myself one – know that nothing is more intensely delightful than the aesthetic thrill.'[16] And since the essence of art is the same in all times and all places, it follows that pleasure is similarly universal. All art has but one intention, to interpellate us, the audience, into a recognition of its absolute and sovereign metaphysic. It is only *criticism* which changes, he argues, in its more historically specific attempts to express this universal pleasure, at least for those 'born with a peculiar sensibility, who enjoy art naturally, simply, and at first hand as most of us enjoy eating, drinking and kissing.' Such attempts to convince us of the ecstasy of his raptures are not immediately persuasive. We learn again of the 'bald miracle' by which 'we are transported into a world washed clean of all past experience aesthetic or sentimental': we are promised that 'we can be thrown into . . . extraordinarily lucid and unself-conscious transport wherein we are aware only of a work of art and our reaction to it by aesthetic response alone.' Here is the old Romantic dream of an art which requires no conventions, which speaks directly to the viewer regardless of his or her circumstances or the context in which it is viewed. But is a Romanticism ruthlessly stripped of any relevance to the rest of our lives.

Bell was fond of the analogy between eating and the aesthetic emotion. The identification he makes with his readers is that of the connoisseur as gourmet. He connects the names of Picasso and Matisse, for example, comparing them to 'Shelley and Keats or Fortnum and Mason', an alignment more revealing about Bell and his assumed audience than about the painters. The double meaning at work within his use of the word 'taste' is equally telling. 'In the fine arts,' he argues, 'taste is bound to be very much directed by people blest with peculiar gifts and armed with special equipment'[17] – whilst explaining at the same time that 'you may dine at any one of the half-dozen "smartest" restaurants in London, pay a couple of pounds for your meal, and be sure that a French commercial traveller, bred to the old standards of the provincial ordinary, would have sent for the cook and given him a scolding.' There is a deep anxiety here. Would Clive Bell have given the cook a scolding? Are 'standards' or 'taste' national characteristics and, if so, are there nations more intrinsically artistic or tasteful than others? Is taste itself not a threat to the theoretically innocent and conceptually empty moment of pure aesthetic pleasure? And lastly, is the humble French commercial traveller somehow in closer touch with 'good taste', by reason of his very Frenchness, than the self-styled (*soi-disant*) English country gentleman? Questions such as these will always gather around any unitary theory of culture in a class- and gender-divided society. Fry too exhibited in much of his writing a stolid Anglophobia, which was no more than the other side of his Francophilia. Such beliefs could only force their holders into ever more preposterous attitudes – the better to demonstrate their own superior tastefulness, their culturally assumed French identities, which equated the existence of a more powerful avant-garde in France with innate national differences. Ultimately, however, the gastronomic analogy is always self-defeating. It attempts to combine two distinct types of satisfaction, one of them simultaneously proclaimed to be independent and distinct from *all* other varieties of pleasure. Food may vary, but it does not throw one into extraordinarily lucid and unself-conscious transports, even if it should come from Fortnum and Mason's. Nor can pictures be regarded as objects for consumption without doing grave damage to the internal consistency of the overall formalist position, conceding as it does the existence of appetites other than those of the aesthetic emotion, and a process of production which problematizes the fetishized moment of artistic perception. Eating satisfies grossly practical needs and has equally practical consequences. As a metaphor it necessarily implies a social relation to the object of consumption which is bound to interrupt the ideal frame of 'disinterestedness'.

This is the central conflict within Bell's picture of aesthetic pleasure. Form 'transports us from the world of man's activity to a world of aesthetic exaltation',[18] which at the same time is restricted 'to those who have and hold a sense of the significance of form.'[19] It is thus in the very nature of civilization to be continually threatened and abused, since 'few are born with the ability to discover for themselves that world of thought and feeling whence come our choicest pleasure.'[20] But at no point can they begin to explain why any one object rather than others should be able to stimulate our aesthetic sense. No matter how society might be transformed, the world would still apparently consist of intrinsically retarded individuals. The capacity to appreciate the 'right' pictures stands in Bloomsbury art theory as the supreme and decisive social arbiter. It is championed in opposition to the familiar middle-class vices of greed, hypocrisy, superstition and snobbery. It was in effect the ultimate sign of the free individual, placing the ideally equipped viewer in the very boots of the painter, re-enacting his or her specific aesthetic responses and perceptions, which are invariably those of the socially transcendent hero of Romantic art theory. Hence the appeal to Fry, as to many of his contemporaries, of the Romantic analogy between art and music, both of which are distinguished from language as domains of pure formal relations.

For all Fry's strictures against Victorian culture for its 'impure' social symbolism, it is apparent that his own work was equally steeped in social evaluations and moral assessments. It was the codes of response which had changed. The lofty moralism of Ruskinian aesthetics was effectively intro-jected into a new concern with brush-strokes and paint density, and away from the narrative conventions of much Victorian painting. The Romantic balance between issues of form, or art-for-art's sake, and subject matter was abandoned as the values which the latter had supported were collapsed into the intricate new codifications of Modernist art and criticism.

Fry's and Bell's art theories may therefore be seen to move from the exposure of what they understood, in Victorian cultural terms, as snobbery, to the development of a complicated body of beliefs concerning the primacy of the aesthetic over all aspects of the social, and from there to the tacit assumption of the primacy of the aesthete over the rest of humanity, especially English humanity. It is worth noting that Fry himself explained the rise of what he described as 'popular or commercial' art in the seventeenth century 'in open rivalry to the old tradition of the profession, a tradition which appealed to other sanctions than those granted by the gross public in recognition for the gratification of its untrained instincts.'[20] There is no room here for the recognition of any transformations in the social conditions of artistic employment. Hence the idiosyncratic nature of Bloomsbury avant-gardism. Fry and Bell never claimed to be ahead of their times, or vanguardists opening up areas into which others might follow. Rather, they sought to distinguish the true from the false artist, the 'genuine' tradition of European art history as opposed to the general. Cézanne emerges, for example, as above all a *traditional* artist, but one working in a tradition recognizable only by the few – and actually constructed retrospectively from their own readings of contemporary art. Hence their hostility to such tendencies as Futurism or Cubism, which articulated an idea of innovation fundamentally at odds with their own notion of the 'revolutionary' artist as one who, against all the odds, perceives the central – if hidden – tradition of Art. In their versions, art history and art criticism are involved in a perpetual rearguard action, identifying the lighthouses of Art behind the blocks of flats and factories set up all around them. Pleasure identifies the dissident modernist aesthete in the wastelands of the modern world, a world doomed to remain incomprehensible since any attempt to understand it is regarded as incompatible with the status of the 'true' artist, a world therefore theorized exclusively in terms of aesthetic absolutes and universals. By placing a total interpretational embargo on works of art, Fry and Bell condemned artist and viewer alike to an aesthetic solipsism which was unrelieved even by a Leavisite sense of an organic social order which had been lost but which might, with effort, be recovered. There may be a great tradition of painting, but it leads only to the recognition of itself. This is the deeply pessimistic conclusion of the Anglo-Saxon formalist tradition, from Fry to Clement Greenburg, from art to non-art, from culture to kitsch. It marks a terminal separation of artist from public, without ever being able to question the profoundly ideological nature of these two concepts which it finds indispensable, since it takes them for granted as immutable and, in the final analysis, biologically given categories.

In this context, it is worth considering the one major institutional formation with which Fry in particular was involved in the early days of his association with the Bloomsbury Group. In 1913 he financed the establishment of the Omega Workshops in Fitzroy Square, London. The innovative significance of the Omega Workshops lay in their approach to the relation of production and distribution. They did not consist of a shop-front, in the Morris tradition, but were modelled on the *haute couture* fashion market in France. There were no contracts to artists, whose work was thus tacitly acknowledged to be intrinsically privileged and distinct from other forms of labour. This was partly a response to the contemporary trend to turn painters into gallery employees, but also an intervention into the whole problem of artists' employment and support. However, its collectivist approach to matters of design was undercut by the class market in which it attempted to operate. The anonymity in which products were designed and sold marks Fry's significant concern with the idea of Design, but frequently came into conflict with the individualistic approach of particular artists, like Wyndham Lewis. Anonymity also served to disguise the division of labour between out-workers, such as carpenters and weavers, and the artist-designers employed at the workshops on a fixed daily wage with parity for all. The range of products was radical, rather than their mode of distribution – the merging of 'Art' with 'utility' production in relation to a theory about the socially regulative effects of 'good' design, whose values were understood to be fundamentally the same as those of painting. After the economic collapse of the workshops in 1919, the Bloomsbury artists tended to work in areas of interior design over which they had more control, such as pottery, embroidery, and wall decorations. But the importance of the initial challenge to the Victorian distinction between high and low art, or between art and craft, has been insufficiently noticed. The Omega has generally been judged against the inappropriate model of late nineteenth-century craft organisations, rather than as a precursor of later twentieth-century attempts to question the actual occupation of artists in modern society. Cézanne might remain the dominant model of the artist as an isolated producer, outside society, his work 'recognized' by gifted 'artistic' individuals. But Cézanne, like Fry, had a private income.

Conclusions

Much has been written about the concept of pleasure developed by the Cambridge philosopher G. E. Moore and supposedly handed down to 'Bloomsbury' like the tablets of stone. Basically, Moore had denied that goodness can be defined. Certain things are simply good in themselves, things equated with 'certain states of consciousness, which may be roughly described as the pleasures of human intercourse, and the enjoyment of beautiful objects.'[21] Such a transparently anti-utilitarian philosophy elevates consciousness above material life, which it sees as the direct product of mental activities. It also begs the entire question of usage, elevating the aesthetic above all other possible responses to works of art. Whilst it would be wrong to ascribe a single, consistent criterion of pleasure to the diverse group of people that constituted 'Bloomsbury', one can nonetheless detect a general tendency to elevate states of mind above the idea of moral action in the social world. And it was certainly in relation to Moore's example that Fry and Bell developed their picture of art as the means to our 'highest' pleasures, even if that involved a sense of inhabiting a vulnerable escarpment, perched just above the swirling flood-level of popular taste or 'pseudo-art'. The relation of culture to society was not so clear-cut for other members of the group.

Virginia Woolf was deeply torn between two rival theories of artistic practice, as Michèle Barrett has demonstrated.[22] On the one hand, she regarded writing in relation to the social position of the writer in the prevailing economic conditions of literary production. But this materialist analysis was constantly operated in tandem with a conflicting picture of art as transcendent individual 'creativity' – a conflict represented in the person of Lily Briscoe in *To The Lighthouse* where, as I have suggested, Fry's direct influence may be detected. For Lily the artistic problem is how to transform the temporal actuality of life into the supposedly timeless domain of art. She attends to the physical world in order to lose her ordinary 'practical' awareness of it. Yet, 'as she dipped into the blue paint, she dipped too into the past.'[23] Lily's conflict lies between her belief in the timelessness of art, and her immediate understanding of the world as a woman. The final achievement of the novel, Lily's completed picture, is in fact an extremely unstable moment in which the 'aesthetic emotion' and her intense personal relations with her subject matter are simply collapsed into the 'vision' of art, as understood by Roger Fry. The importance of the notion of pleasure, in the discourse of Bloomsbury criticism bears witness to the influence of the idea that in one's aesthetic pleasures lies an impacted simulacrum of one's total individual identity, prior to the operations of class or gender.

It is clear to any reader that Virginia Woolf's importance does not consist simply in her ability to structure abstract relations between forms. Yet her own theory of art, which deserves more serious attention than it has so far received, depended upon an absolutely categorical distinction between word and image, sound and silence, which is a central tenet of Romantic art theory. She felt that, 'like most English people', she had been trained 'not to see but to talk'.[24] Thus, by definition, painters cannot write, just as writers are not supposed to be able to paint. This distinction was fundamental to Bloomsbury's view of itself; it was axiomatic throughout the group. It also guaranteed a certain jealous rivalry between writers and painters which surfaced frequently. They were united in their hostility to high bourgeois society and its cultural symbols – Virginia Woolf rejected the award of Companion of Honour in 1935, for example, and Duncan Grant refused a CBE in 1950. But in the absence of any general group theory of culture or of politics, the art criticism of Roger Fry and Clive Bell was able to inflect the received image of 'Bloomsbury' with their theory of civilization and all its implications of minority privilege, social exclusivity and, occasionally, *individual* change in a manner which would have shocked even Matthew Arnold. At the same time, as Raymond Williams has recently pointed out, there remains a danger of simply reading off a verdict of élitism against the totality of the group's cultural production. This is nowhere more obvious than in relation to the work of the group's two principal artists, Vanessa Bell and Duncan Grant, whose reputations have been ludicrously vulnerable to the buffetings of the prevailing winds of Bloomsbury-phobia and Bloomsbury-mania over the past forty years, to the virtual neglect of their actual work in all its unusual diversity.

An art criticism structured around the figure of the individual artist finds it difficult, if not impossible, to accommodate the position of two or more artists working in close alliance. This same problem has afflicted the historical understanding and visibility of much women's art. It is also ironic that the general disregard for twentieth-century English art on the part of English critics and art historians should reveal so clearly the continued influence of the cultural priorities of Roger Fry and Clive Bell. For the specific achievements of Bloomsbury painting and design run counter to Fry's and Bell's entire aesthetic position, reaching out as they did into a wide range of decorative projects in commerce, education and industry, with their striking and emphatic iconographic concerns with sexuality, domesticity and a wide variety of complex social significations. But it is through the institutional legacy of John Maynard Keynes that a particular monolithic picture of Bloomsbury culture and cultural values has been most broadly disseminated, preserving intact the divisive concept of high art at the very point at which the objects of Victorian culture which had originally legitimated such a notion, were being openly derided. Fry and Bell enthusiastically toppled the icons of Arnoldian and Ruskinian culture, whilst energetically dismantling any consideration whatsoever of the social relations in the work of art. Indeed, the very manner in which both Fry and Bell approached Victorian culture as an affront to 'good taste' is the clearest sign of their own residual Victorianism, obscuring its plenitude of cultural forms, audiences and pleasures with a rhetoric of 'autonomy' which remains as prevalent as it is conveniently mystifying.

Bloomsbury art criticism thus presented a hierachy of pleasures responsive to painting. However, since painting itself was divided onto logically between Art and Pseudo-art, it follows that there is also pleasure and pseudo-pleasure, the latter being understood as the 'popular' taste of the 'average man'. Such slides and elisions of meaning were part and parcel of the way in which the powerful Romantic notion of universal cultural values and aesthetic criteria was detached from one set of signifiers, namely Victorian anecdotal painting and High Art, and transferred to early French Modernist painting and art theory. The degree of hostility aroused by this new art is seen as index-linked to the degree of the artist's or critic's aesthetic superiority, which is also the measure of his or her humanity. In this context one can scarcely place sufficient weight on the political significance of Romantic art theory, and its place in contemporary cultural practice, both as a conscious and as an ideological force. And it is this version of Bloomsbury which has been the subject of a spectacular recuperation in recent years, with the characters of the group being endlessly paraded in biographical, dramatic, theoretical and fictional forms. Hence, for example, Edna O'Brien's recent play *Virginia*, which lifts Virginia Woolf and her immediate circle of friends out from all the unacceptably complex realities of their everyday working lives, and effortlessly transports them onto the misty stage of 'genius'.[25] We might also consider the current campaign to preserve Charleston, the Sussex farm-house which was for half a century the home-cum-workplace of Vanessa Bell and Duncan Grant. Now I have no doubt that the house should be preserved; it contains the finest extant Bloomsbury wall-paintings and is the only complete surviving example of their influential work as interior designers and decorators. At the same time, the house is clearly being afforded the status of a new kind of stately home, enshrining the view of Bloomsbury as a picturesque idyll for exotic Edwardian aesthetes. This is a convenient pastoral fiction whereby all the important concrete issues of Bloomsbury's political and artistic conflicts, both among themselves and with the dominant culture of Edwardian England, are displaced and deflected. If we are to learn anything from the ways in which Bloomsbury art criticism produced and regulated a specific economy of aesthetic desires and pleasures, it must stem from an understanding of the ways in which the nineteenth-century sense of a *necessary* conflict of interest between culture and popular taste was re-positioned in relation to early twentieth-century French art, and the subsequent ways in which that sense of conflict has been sustained.

I would like to thank Michèle Barrett for her advice on an earlier draft of this paper.

Notes

1. Pierre Bourdieu, 'Intellectual Field and Creative Project', in M. F. D. Young (ed.), *Knowledge and Control*, Collier Macmillan, 1971.
2. See Rensselaer W. Lee, *Ut Pictura Poesis: The Humanist Theory of Painting*, W. W. Norton, 1967.
3. See Francis Spalding, *Roger Fry: Life and Art*, Granada, 1980.
4. Raymond Williams, 'The Bloomsbury Fraction', in *Problems in Materialism and Culture*, Verso 1980.
5. Clive Bell, 'Why do they go to the pictures?', in *Les Arts à Paris*, no. 17, mai 1930.
6. Roger Fry, 'Culture and Snobbism', in *Transformations*, Chatto and Windus, 1927.
7. *ibid.*
8. Fry, 'Art and Life', in *Vision and Design*, Chatto and Windus, 1920.
9. Fry, 'The Artist's Vision', in *Vision and Design*, op. cit.
10. Bell, *Art*, Chatto and Windus, 1914.
11. See the footnote by Anne Olivier Bell to Virginia Woolf's diary entry for 22 November 1917.
12. Fry, 'Fra Bartolommeo', in *Transformations*, op. cit.
13. Fry, '"Paul Cézanne" by Ambrose Vollard' in *The Burlington Magazine*, August 1917.
14. Fry, 'The Artist's Vision', op. cit.
15. Bell, 'Criticism', in *Since Cézanne*, Chatto and Windus, 1922.
16. *ibid.*
17. Bell, 'Standards', in *Since Cézanne*, op. cit.
18. Bell, *Art*, op. cit.
19. *ibid.*
20. Fry, 'The *Seicento*', in *Transformations*, op. cit.
21. G. E. Moore, *Principia Ethica*, Cambridge, 1903.
22. Michèle Barrett, 'Introduction' to *Virginia Woolf: Women and Writing*, The Women's Press, 1979.

23. Virginia Woolf, *To the Lighthouse*, The Hogarth Press 1927.
24. Virginia Woolf, *Walter Sickert: A Conversation*, The Hogarth Press, 1933.
25. Edna O'Brien, *Virginia*, The Hogarth Press, 1981. See also my review 'Versions of Virginia' in *Gay News*, no. 208, 5–18 February 1981.

Colin Mercer

A POVERTY OF DESIRE:
Pleasure and Popular Politics

It was Ernest Bevin, of all people, who observed in the 1930s that the British suffer from a 'poverty of desire.'[1] It's an intriguing comment, not least because in this context it seems to echo Brecht's contemporary project of constructing new forms of popular enjoyment and pleasure. But it is important to hold onto the difference between the *mobilization* and the *reconstruction* of popular pleasures as strategies within a cultural politics. The former has recently given rise to new political styles in this country – 'alternative' festivals like the People's Jubilee, the carnival elements in Rock Against Racism or the Anti-Nazi League rallies, the theatrical impact of Reclaiming the Night or the People's March for Jobs, the new directions and emphases of CND. These are not simply knee-jerk reactions to a new political scenario: they represent a new articulation of politics and popular culture. But do they call into question the pleasures they invoke? Some do more than others, obviously, but the reconstruction of existing forms of pleasure can perhaps be seen more clearly in the theoretical traditions which in the past decade or so have drawn not only on a Brechtian cultural politics but also on semiotics and psychoanalysis. No longer dismissing ideology as 'false consciousness', these approaches have attempted to understand ideology as a 'lived relationship' and hegemony as the process whereby we not only consent to forms of domination which we know, rationally and politically, are 'wrong', but even *enjoy* them. The question here is not whether we ought to enjoy, say, Hollywood or pornography, but *why* we do. Or, to come clean myself, what is the pleasure I derive from Frankie Howerd's humour, the *Carry On* films or even the prose of Enoch Powell? The point of the question is not to wallow in individual guilt, but to trace the history of such pleasures and their formation within popular memory. For they do have a real cultural hold, one that resists political opportunism as well as simple interpretation.

A political strategy which would both mobilize *and* reconstruct popular pleasures would clearly have to overcome a basic contradiction. Popular pleasures, as Pierre Bourdieu and before him Mikhail Bakhtin have insisted, require a wholehearted and unselfconscious involvement in a cultural event, form or text.

'The desire to enter into the game, identifying with the characters' joys and sufferings, worrying about their fate, espousing their hopes and ideals, living their life, is based on a form of *investment*, a sort of deliberate "naivety", ingenuousness, good-natured credulity ("we're here to enjoy ourselves") which tends to accept formal experiments and specifically artistic effects only to the extent that they can be forgotten and do not get in the way of the substance of the work.'[2]

Popular enjoyment, in other words, is inhospitable to the sort of distanciating analysis implicit in the strategy of deconstruction – hence Bourdieu's antagonism towards Brechtian deconstructors, whom he sees as asserting the old authority of the traditional intellectual within the very heart of popular culture. Certainly he has identified a real political danger, but it would equally be a mistake to place too much faith in the spontaneous eruption of the contradictory or oppositional elements in popular negotiations of provided forms. Laura Mulvey was right to place the destruction of pleasure on the political agenda[3] – not the puritan suppression of displeasing or offensive forms, but the radical rewriting of the codes and grammar of pleasure, within our culture.

The engagement of politics and cultural analysis with pleasure does not only challenge the complicity of popular forms. It also dissolves the certainties and authority of the theorist. No longer can the contradictory *play* of ideology be reduced to questions of meaning and truth. You can ask whether people 'believe' what they hear on the News or on *Nationwide*, but it's by no means clear what people would 'believe' in light entertainment or comedy. Once enjoyment and pleasure are reintroduced – those jokers in the game – we have to change the rules and go beyond the 'message'. Barthes saw this:

'Simply, a day comes when we feel a certain need to loosen the theory a bit, to shift the discourse, the ideolect which repeats itself, becomes consistent, and to give it the shock of a question. Pleasure is this question . . . it is an oblique, a drag anchor, so to speak, without which the theory of the text would revert to a centred system, a philosophy of meaning.'[4]

It may be that in this loosening of cultural theory we could find, if not answers, then at least some terms and ideas that could be incorporated into a new politics of pleasure.

From Text to Politics

Some of Barthes's ideas seem *enabling* in just this way. In *The Pleasure of the Text*, he attempted to get beyond not only the idea of the text as reducible to a message, but also beyond those socio-ideological analyses of literature which, from Aristotle to the early Barthes himself, had agreed on the *deceptive* nature of literature. In their obsession with finding out what a text really signified, Barthes now argued, they had forgotten the formidable underside of writing:

> 'bliss: bliss which can erupt, across the centuries, out of certain texts that were nonetheless written to the glory of the dreariest, of the most sinister philosophy.'[5]

Bliss there is a poor stand-in for the French *jouissance,* which signals at once orgasm, possession, enjoyment and, in a strand of French literature very familiar to Barthes and at the head of which stands Baudelaire, *death.* But let's be British about it and say that it stands for something like loss of stasis, loss of the fixity of relationship between the key terms of 'signifier' and 'signified' and the consequent absence of a fixity of meaning (for the text, the ideology, the commodity) and in favour of a sense of movement, of play.

This stress on ideological play opens up several paths, and we don't necessarily want to follow Barthes's own drift into theoretical *hubris* or his almost falstaffian expeditions in search of the 'profound hedonism of every culture'. Nor, like some of the psychoanalytical approaches which have inserted themselves into the gap between signifier and signified and whose curriculum is dominated by Freud's *Interpretation of Dreams*, need we make 'the text' the unique and privileged scenario for the construction of human subjectivity. Politically, Barthes's break-out from the prison of message and meaning is most helpful insofar as it shifts our attention away from the fact of language, style and so forth towards their productivity, their active articulation, their utterance, their *economy*. This emphasis enables us to stop and scrutinise the conflict of forces (say) within a text:

> 'In the text of pleasure, the opposing forces are no longer repressed but in a state of becoming: nothing is really antagonistic, everything is plural. I pass lightly through the reactionary darkness.'

This nimble footwork is more than just a way of reading. For Barthes it is a mode of existence within a language which 'fights for hegemony':

> 'If power is on its side, [language] spreads everywhere in the general and daily occurrences of social life, it becomes *doxa*, nature . . . A ruthless *topic* rules the life of language: language always comes from someplace, it is a warrior topos.'

The cardinal point for the analysis of pleasure, though, is to find out what sort of *reading* will make it possible to survive in this hegemonic language, this reactionary darkness.

> 'We read a text (of pleasure) the way a fly buzzes around a room: with sudden, deceptively decisive turns, fervent and futile . . .'

Barthes's own reading in *The Pleasure of the Text* attempts to match this movement without stopping it dead in its moment of 'meaning'. He will not say what a text means, he will gesture at what it does. Stephen Heath suggests what is involved: 'an abrupt and unexpected loss, outside of the cultural field, bliss (*jouissance*) cannot be explained in the language of criticism (one comes up against the impossibility of accounting for individual *jouissance*.)'[6]

In Heath's gloss we can see some dangers for the analysis of pleasure: of reducing the problem to non-theorisable dimensions of personal experience (there are a few), or of making it synonymous with the 'other side' of culture, order, the social. Barthes was no doubt aware of these dangers, and a book like *The Pleasure of the Text* may have been intended as a perverse 'bending of the stick' too far in one direction in order to focus our attention on the problem of pleasure. But leaving aside his possibly polemical hedonism, how can we move from a text-bound conception of pleasure towards a political deployment of the term? To be sure, we would have to be careful in transferring textual hedonism *à la francaise* to the more sober climate of political analysis and action. Barthes himself was never less than a political writer in the sense of the slogans 'everything is political' or 'the personal is political', but that does not mean that terms for analysing texts can be instantly translated into political terms. Beyond those slogans lies an even more pressing demand for a differentiation in the space they have opened up. This takes us back to where I started: the transfer of 'enabling' formulations on the question of pleasure in the realm of textual analysis (deconstruction) to the area of political analysis (mobilization) has to be transacted through that other problem area, the *popular*.

Does the theoretical guilt associated with ideology-analysis have a counterpart in the contemporary political inflexions of the terrain of popular culture and the emerging desire for a popular politics that I identified in aspects of the Women's Movement, in the ANL and so forth? There is something about the repertoire, the 'particular language' of these social and political movements which signals a break from the duffle-coated days of existential affirmation. They represent the emergence onto the political and cultural stage of a *collage*, perhaps better seen as a *bricolage*, not just of different social forces but of different styles. These terms are taken from Dick Hebdige's analysis of contemporary spectacular subcultures, in which the combination of disparate stylistic elements constitutes a 'semiotic guerilla warfare'.[7] It is here that we can establish some common ground for the transfer of the terms of a cultural enquiry into pleasure into the realm of its actual political deployment. Both areas indicate a common theoretical absence: a means of grasping not the singular meaning (a revolt against capitalism!) but the pluralism of the play of styles, codes and languages which can now be seen to constitute the realm of the popular – the popular, that is, properly understood not as something pejorative, not as 'mass culture' nor as some collusive 'folk culture', but in terms of a critical repertoire which could assess the significance of 'pleasure' and 'the popular' as at once democratic and socially managed, as contested and controlled, as a structured balance of forces rather than a con-trick. To formulate a cultural politics on this basis, a politics which could both mobilize and reconstruct popular pleasures, would require a differentiated reading in the realm of culture as well as in the realm of politics. Before arriving at that point, though, there are a few other connections of pleasure and the popular with which we have to settle accounts.

The Social Management of Pleasure

Unlike leisure, pleasure has attracted no sociology. This makes things at once easier and more difficult. Easier in the sense that pleasure did not – like leisure – become, at some stage in the nineteenth century, the necessary and legislatable counterpart to *work*. More difficult in the sense that because of this it is not an easily definable 'area'. When the late eighteenth and early nineteenth century magistrates and social reformers pressed for legislation against blood sports, football and fairs, were they arguing against pleasure or leisure? The moral tone of their condemnations suggests that they were inveighing against the former with the result of producing a controlled and privatised version of the latter. A profound ambiguity around the question of pleasure began to emerge, which focussed on popular recreations. A petition got up in 1875 against annual fairs in Sawbridge, Hertfordshire, deplored the diminution of the original function of the fairs – the sale of stock:

> 'Whilst these fairs are of the smallest possible conceivable worth in a commercial point of view, indefensibly and indisputably they are the prolific seed plots and occasions of the most hideous forms of moral and social evil – drunkenness – whoredom – robbery – idleness and neglect of work . . .'[8]

The documentation of such responses is considerable. The response was, of course, not just a moral one. Economic considerations had a major part to play in the increasing legislation against recreations and their associated pleasures in the transition to a fully industrialised economy. A hierarchy of work and leisure had to be established and maintained and 'pleasure', however ambiguously conceived would have to fall in behind the latter, preferably out of the sight of the legislators.

But even so, pleasure could still create problems and it would be mistaken to assume that pleasure simply became the underside, or the 'other', of political, moral, economic and legislative order. This abiding conception surfaces in the twentieth century in the work of Herbert Marcuse and other writers more immediately associated with the ''60s Generation'. Michel Foucault has argued that the familiar 'repressive hypothesis' with regard to the nineteenth-century treatment of sexuality is fundamentally misplaced: the Victorians did not suppress or repress it, but made it a major issue in producing definitions of it, regulating it, disciplining it, *producing* it as an object of discourse. It is possible to argue the same for pleasure. The plethora of moral, religious and political tracts concerned with the nexus of recreations and pleasure which emerged in the latter half of the eighteenth century and throughout the nineteenth were not concerned with any simple repression of recognised pleasures, but with defining, regulating and locating them in their appropriate sites. Above all, perhaps, they were concerned to shift pleasures from the site of mass activity (fairs, football matches with unlimited players, carnivals verging on riot) to the site of private and individualised activity. As Robert Malcolmson points out, 'the degree of a diversion's publicness significantly conditioned the extent to which there might be a concern for its regulation.'[9] He cites one writer who, in relation to blood sports, argued that: 'The Legislature ought to interfere for the protection of animals, wherever public control can be extended, although it may be deemed impossible to regulate the conduct of individuals in regard to their own property.' That significant separation between public and private is beginning here to exert its influence on the realm of pleasure – both defining, locating and justifying pleasure in the prescribed new site called the domestic. There was still, of course, the problem of the pub and the music hall later in the century but these were to negotiate their own position within the general economy of pleasure.

Concern about the management of pleasure and/or its attainment (concern, therefore, over the very ambiguity of pleasure) was not restricted to local reformers and legislators. Pleasure came to function as the centre of an *episteme* – a sort of social 'grammar' – which would set the terms for many subsequent and contemporary debates over the issue. It was not a new problem – Plato had had problems in attempting to balance out the dialectic of pleasure and pain for the good of the *communitas* – but now it was to assume a new form: how to deal with pleasure in the face of the exigencies of an organised labour force and how to regulate pleasure in relation to the sovereign category of the *individual*. The focus on the domestic as a primary site of pleasures was one way in which both of these demands could be held together but it was by no means sufficient or monolithic or even fully effective in this function: there were points of resistance which announced their own particular pleasures. The two bodies of thought which constitute the binary poles of this episteme of pleasure are Utilitarianism and Romanticism.

The Catalogue of Pleasures: Jeremy Bentham

In *An Introduction to the Principles of Morals and Legislation*, the Utilitarian philosopher Jeremy Bentham wrote:

> 'Nature has placed mankind under the governance of two sovereign masters, *pain* and *pleasure*. It is for them alone to point out what we ought to do, as well as to determine what we shall do. On the one hand the standard of right and wrong, on the other the chain of causes and effects, are fastened to their throne.'

The recognition of this governance, of this subjection is the basis of Bentham's *principle of utility* which, he adds in a footnote, has more recently been termed 'the *greatest happiness* or *greatest felicity* principle'. Bentham confesses that he had problems in establishing a sufficiently strong lexical and connotative connection between the words 'pleasure', 'happiness' and 'utility'. Nonetheless the words would have to do for his attempt to found a scientific jurisprudence and a moral legislation initiated by a phrase he found in Joseph Priestley's pamphlet *Essay on Government* in 1768, 'The greatest happiness of the greatest number'. What is emerging here is a philosophy of *consent* and of *sanction* to be measured through the principle of utility. All previous forms of legislation would have to be measured against this principle and judged as good or bad accordingly. Against 'Natural Law' and the notion of an 'Original Contract' binding State and subjects, Bentham posed a specific form of calculation and intervention to be assessed through the precise measurement of quantities of pain and pleasure:

> 'Pleasures then, and the avoidance of pains, are the *ends* which the legislator has in view: it behoves him, therefore to understand their *value*. Pleasures and pains are the *instruments* he has to work with: it behoves him therefore to understand their force, which is again, in other words, their value.'

What follows is a detailed catalogue of criteria for the calculation of pain and pleasure 'To a person considered *by himself*'. There are seven circumstances by which the value of pleasure or pain is to be assessed; there are fourteen types of 'simple pleasures of which human nature is susceptible' and twelve simple pains. These are further subdivided into more or less complex types. The process is then straightforward:

'Take an account of the *number* of persons whose interests appear to be concerned; and repeat the process with respect to each. *Sum up* the numbers expressive of the degrees of *good* tendency, which the act has, with respect to each individual, in regard to whom the tendency of it is *good* upon the whole . . . [do this again with respect to the bad tendency] . . . Take the *balance*; which, if on the side of pleasure, will give the general *good tendency* of the act, with respect to the total number or community of individuals concerned. . . . [etc].'

What is extraordinary about this catalogue is not so much the extent of what is considered to be an object for calculation or legislation, nor what appears, in historical hindsight to be an 'eccentric' and over-rational set of demands, but the actual *confidence* through which an infinitely transparent web is constructed which would link individual, pleasure, community, calculation and legislation together in an untroubled network of regulation. Above all perhaps it is the *individualisation* of pleasures which reminds us of another of Bentham's projects   the Panopticon. This was a plan for an 'inspection house' which would comprise a central tower with windows giving out to segmentary cells comprising a circular outer building. From the vantage point of the central tower, the 'inspector' would be able to look into each of the outer cells without great disturbance and, because of the distribution of light, without being seen. Each cell would contain one person (a prisoner, a patient, a schoolboy, a worker) whose every action, posture or complaint would be visible to the controlling central presence. Michel Foucault, who has made of the Panopticon a metaphor for the creation of 'disciplinary mechanisms' comments that this building reverses the principle of the dungeon: 'The seeing machine was once a sort of dark room into which individuals spied; it has become a transparent building in which the exercise of power may be supervised by society as a whole'.[10]

There are other articles in this issue which deal with the more precise ways in which the individual body became the site of a controlling and regulating set of disciplines and which mark out the ways in which the nexus pleasure-sexuality came to assume distinctively new forms and these are not my immediate concern here. In Bentham's project, though, and in that of subsequent Utilitarian philosophy, we can begin to detect the theoretical accompaniment of that political and ideological practice which was to constantly strive towards the privatisation and individualisation of pleasure and the attempt to construct a jurisprudence for that transparent network of individual subjects. Paraphrasing Foucault, we could say that Bentham's project represents the first stage in the introduction of individual pleasures into the field of documentation and social regulation.

Naked Dignities

It would be wrong to assume that Utilitarianism represented an 'official ideology' of the emergent bourgeoisie. The distribution of its effects was more complex and negotiated than that. Parts of Bentham and Mill smacked of a rather unsavoury and 'continental' desire for regulation which did not sit well with the decidedly *amateur* status of traditional intellectuals in early nineteenth-century Britain. There were degrees of assimilation and negotiation with another body of thought, the resultant of which is sometimes called the 'Liberal Imagination'. This would have found Bentham's 'catalogue' a totalitarian document and would want to stake its position rather closer to a Wordsworth or a Coleridge. This 'imagination' would abhor the overt images of control in Bentham and Mill and would continue to fear them through fictional reconstructions of its dangers like E. M. Forster's *The Machine Stops* or Constantine Fitzgibbon's *When the Kissing Had to Stop*. Another form in which this opposition occurs is in Margaret Thatcher's populism: on the one side social regulation, totalitarianism, control and 'burgeoning collectivism'; on the other side individual pleasures, initiatives and endeavour and a certain historically formed conception of the 'private' (the family, medicine, education). This binary scheme, the duality of pleasure and the social order is a familiar one, constantly and variously deployed from fiction to political discourse. (One 'libertarian' bookshop near Covent Garden displays in its window books by Ayn Rand, Edward Thompson, A. S. Neill, Milton Friedman and Timothy Leary – Libertarianism is here clearly on the side of pleasure.)

The 'Liberal Imagination' – that set of ideologies from which our dominant conceptions of pleasure take their bearings – is a peculiar historical fusion of political and juridical Liberalism and cultural Romanticism. It would want to take the sovereignty of the individual from Bentham and clothe it (or disrobe it) with a Romantic solipsism. One of the most articulate theorists of the Liberal Imagination, Lionel Trilling, has charted some of the meanings of this ambiguity and this fusion in an article entitled *The Fate of Pleasure*. Wordsworth it was who wrote of 'the grand elementary principle of pleasure' which constitutes the 'naked and native dignity of man', the principle by which he 'knows, feels, lives and moves'. (There's an echo here of Louis Althusser's favourite apostle, St Paul, who, Althusser claims, states that it is in 'the Logos, meaning in ideology, that we live, move, have our being.') Trilling argues that it was Keats who substantively modified this affirmation. It was Keats who '. . . may be thought of as the poet who made the boldest affirmation of the principle of pleasure' but also he who '. . . brought the principle of pleasure into the greatest and sincerest doubt.' Trilling goes on to claim that 'he therefore has for us a peculiar cultural interest, for it would seem that at some point in modern history, the principle of pleasure came to be regarded with . . . ambivalence.'

For Trilling that moment came when commodity and meaning began to converge in a particular way in the early nineteenth century. It is, the claim goes, with the growth of a luxury market and the proliferation of certain commodities as *signs* of pleasure that, for the artist, this profound ambivalence begins to emerge. This ambivalence is produced by a breach between on the one hand, a 'politics directed towards affluence, fulfilment and pleasure' and, on the other hand, the 'stern and even minatory gaze of the artist' at all that is implied by affluence. Now Trilling may be touching on something quite important here, but as the generalisation stands we have little more than the myth of the 'Romantic Artist' embarking on the tradition- al critique of commercialism. Here is the representative figure – the artist. Here is the historical background – the growth of industrialism and of a consumer market. Here are the effects in the work – ambivalence around the question of pleasure. But Trilling goes a little further than this in noting that the effect of this convergence of commodity and meaning on 'social and moral ideas' was '. . . an influence to be observed in the growing tendency of power to express itself mediately, by signs or indices, rather than directly, by the exercise of force.'

This last statement is more germane to the argument. The history of the formation of particular conceptions of pleasure is not to be seen as some history of ideas against a recognisable historical backdrop. What is happen- ing at this 'point in modern history' is rather more substantial than that. It is not just a question of commodities affecting ideas, but a complete trans- formation of the social terrain on which notions of pleasure can actually be thought. Commodities and the growth of a consumer market certainly have a role to play, but we also have to make connections with the ways in which pleasure was conceived juridically, politically and ideologically through a transformed social network. Would Wordsworth and Keats have been able to formulate their works outside the reorganisation of the public and the private, of work and leisure, of the country and the city? Indeed, it may be argued that their work is precisely a *writing* of those transformations and a rescheduling of the possibilities and constraints of pleasure within a trans- formed framework – a response, in particular, to that transformation in which, as Trilling puts it, '. . . what was once a mode of experience for a few has now become an ideal of experience for many.' This moment of the writing, the production, the location of pleasures for what was now a distinctively transformed populace and social network has left us with many legacies, the most pervasive of which, with respect to the question of pleasure, is that particularly potent fusion of 'Liberalism' and 'Imagination' which has marked up the agendas, historically, for almost all discussion of pleasure.

Under the Cobble Stones . . . the Beach!

Many of the roads in the fifth *arrondissement* of Paris – the Latin Quarter – are now covered in uncharacteristic tarmac. The working-class quarters in the north of the city are not so dubiously blessed with this reality principle: they retain their cobbles. The tarring of the roads on the Left Bank was a response to a practice – the use of the cobblestones against the riot police in the 1968 'events' – and to a slogan – *sous les pavés, la plage!* The situationist slogan is further testament to that binary – or perhaps 'ambiguous' – location of pleasure in our common culture. Beneath order (the city, the cobblestones) is pleasure (sand, the beach). It is *on the other side*. It is not a recto-verso but a qualitative opposite: this is the grammar of pleasure and pain. Similar structures are discernible, with a different lexicon and emphasis, in the discourse of a Reagan or a Thatcher – away with overweaning government! The peculiar convergence of 'sixty-eightist' demands and the New Right of the 1980s is something which has been noted, at another level, by Stanley Aronowitz who has pointed out that many of the struggles for local control of the community have now resulted in Reagan's concession of just that in the USA to the extent that they are now told in the language of the New Federalism to balance their own budget.[12] We know what effect that is having on local government in this country as well. What is the point of convergence, of unnoticed complicity here? How were those demands for satisfactions and pleasures assimilated within a neo-authoritarian discourse? These are general political problems which we cannot hope to answer here. Equally, though, we cannot fail to notice a certain complicity in the 'grammar' of these demands which indicates a need for the reformulation of political and cultural objectives which both acknowledges and displaces that complicity.

Part of this complicity lies in the acceptance of the essential dualism of pleasure/order most obviously manifested in, for example, our attitudes to the city or at least to the image of the city. The situationists would dismantle it to establish a new semiotics of pleasures. Others of a less radical inclination would simply move out to a cottage in the country or turn their existing home into a country kitchen. This tactic represents a peculiarly British pleasure and is one reason why the 'inner city' or 'urban deprivation' remains an abiding problem. We have no political language – at least not until recently – which could conceivably hold together images of city and pleasure in a sustained way. The 'pleasures' associated with the city have been historically dubious, to say the least. One response, within this existing grammar of 'country' and 'city' has been, of course, the 'Garden City' – all very well if you have the resources and space to create such entities but no real answer to the problem of inner city areas.

At a more general political level the work of Herbert Marcuse has had a role to play within this dualistic structure of social thought about pleasure. The role of pleasure within bourgeois society, according to Marcuse, is to liberate people yet to keep them in check:

> 'From the beginning the prohibition of pleasure was a condition of freedom . . . The prohibition against marketing the body not merely as an instrument of labour but as an instrument of pleasure as well is one of the chief social and pyschological roots of bourgeois patriarchal ideology.'[13]

Within this particular form of social and economic organisation, Marcuse argues, a general taboo is exercised when the body becomes an explicit bearer or manifestation of the sexual function. This is the case not only with prostitution'. . . but for all production of pleasure which does not occur for reasons of "social hygiene" in the service of reproduction.' This goes part of the way, but the problem is surely not just one of prohibitions, taboos, and the exchange of one substantive quality – pleasure – for another – freedom. The problem is more explicitly posed by Marcuse in the political preface to *Eros and Civilisation* where he argues that the new direction would have to 'activate repressed or arrested *organic* biological needs; to make the human body an instrument of pleasure rather than labour' and this 'old formula' as he puts it, 'seemed to be the prerequisite, the content of liberation.'[14] Among others, Jeffrey Weeks has pointed out that this equation of pleasure with liberation and pleasure with 'non-work' could have strange effects:

> '"Sexual liberation" was confined to the heterosexual libido, and the belief in the release of the "real man" and "real" woman could have its bizarrely oppressive effects.'[15]

Again the problem seems to reside in the language of prohibition and repression through which we are accustomed to dealing with the problem of pleasure. Pleasure is simply there to be liberated, released, redistributed and accordingly the language of pleasure becomes a language of essentialism. Pleasure in itself is not a problem for this particular language; its dubious accomplices are.

Pleasure and Subjectivity

Pleasure and pain; pleasure and order; pleasure and work. Why must definitions of pleasure within what we have called the Liberal Imagination always have their opposites? We don't necessarily think of the opposite term when we think of, for example, culture or ideology or politics, even though their opposites exist within the language. Pleasure, on the other hand, almost always invokes its chosen antonym – this is perhaps the point about its 'profound ambiguity' – and this is probably because it also implies the unspoken figure to which it applies – the individual. Pleasure is about individual tastes and preferences. More than any other notion (except perhaps those of taste or choice) it entails individual sovereignty. This is the 'unsaid' of pleasure, its presupposition when mobilised in any discourse. (Collective pleasures are always a bit tacky!) This is a question of language and of history and of the inevitable association, discussed in Cora Kaplan's article, between pleasure and sexuality. We know now that individualism, sovereignty and the 'subject' have their own paths of formation and that the project 'legislated' by Bentham where pleasure and the individual would co-exist in a relationship of transparent and unbreakable filiation was not only historically specific but historically necessary. This recognition provides one way out of that pervasive grammar of opposites. Once you begin to examine in some detail the precise foundations and mechanisms and disciplines which have constructed and held that sovereign category of the individual, then the whole substratum of that grammar of pleasure begins to crumble as well. The linch-pin which holds together the binary poles of pleasure and pain begins to disintegrate. But easier said, perhaps, than done.

Recent semiotic and psychoanalytic and 'deconstructionist' approaches have made dismantling of the 'subject' their explicit aim. The languages, codes, discourses which actively construct and position the individual subject have come under scrutiny. But although much of this work has been productive, it has not, on the whole, been able to escape another problematic dualism – that of text and subject. Most of it has been developed in the area of film and literary studies and one of the most innovative early contributions to this was Laura Mulvey's 'Visual Pleasure and Narrative Cinema', whose clear statement of its purpose I mentioned earlier:

> 'It is said that analysing pleasure, or beauty, destroys it. That is the intention of this article.'

The mechanisms of pleasure inscribed within the dominant structures of narrative cinema, and particularly the function of the 'look' are analysed in depth with a methodology drawing upon psychoanalysis, semiotics, feminism and Marxism. The pleasure of the look, theorised though concepts of scopophilia, voyeurism and fetishism, has conferred upon the sign 'woman' a certain condition of 'to-be-looked-at-ness'. Woman, 'from pin-ups to striptease, from Ziegfeld to Busby Berkeley . . . holds the look, plays to and signifies male desire.' Within the diegetic process of the narrative film itself, this look is structured in a *textual* way through the co-ordination of camera position and movement to exclude any idea of intrusive camera presence or any obvious sense of an organisation of figures, lighting, position, editing and thereby to create a seamless flow of sexuality in the image of the women. This analysis has been rightly influential in the feminist analysis of film and in the production of feminist film practice. But if Mulvey's article marks out the trajectory in one direction for the analysis of the mechanisms of pleasure in narrative film, in another sense it provides simply a starting point. This is signalled by another proposition, that,

> 'Women, whose image has been continually been stolen and used for this end . . . voyeurism . . . cannot view the decline of the traditional film form with anything much more than sentimental regret.'

This 'sentimental regret' is not to be discounted. Once you have specified the *mechanisms* of pleasure within that privileged relationship to text and subject, or, to use another metaphor, once you have established its currency, you still have a problem on a larger scale – that of the *economy* of pleasure. Sentiment, regret, nostalgia, desire, ambition and identification play a rather more significant role in this economy of pleasure than Mulvey's analysis would allow. They are the problems to be confronted especially if we want to engage with pleasure at the level of the popular. These are the impulses, historically embedded in consciousness, with which we start out when we watch a film, a television programme or whatever. They are the actual, historical and concrete substratum of ideology, common-sense – call it what you will – and they will resist incursions or interruptions no matter how well these are formulated. Sentimental regret will keep returning.

In effect, this is a problem of history, which those modes of analysing pleasure structured around the new dualism of text and subject cannot confront. This is not meant to score a crudely 'materialist' point. History is not something to be added to textual analysis to prove your radical credentials: it is not a 'background', nor is it a guarantor of effectivity. Rather, it is the history of the *formation* of systems of representation or of 'traditions' of entertainment paying heed, for example, to the 'socialisation' of voyeurism. Before saying that Ziegfeld and Busby Berkeley dancers hold the look we would need, for example, to look quite closely at the formation of vaudeville and burlesque both prior to and after its negotiation with the cinematic apparatus. This would give us a conception of the look quite different from that, say, in Hitchcock. We would need to look quite closely at the formation of the particular languages, systems of signification which gave this tradition what Barthes would call its particular texture or 'grain' and we would need to know something about the reasons for the historical acceptability and popularity of these traditions. These are issues which cannot be easily engaged with at the level of representations or theorised at the level of psychoanalysis. There are trajectories, connections, lines of strength and weakness which have their genesis not in the space between text and subject but elsewhere.

These apparently 'textual' problems have a political resonance. At the beginning of her article, Mulvey states her purpose as the analysis of '. . .

the ways the unconscious, (formed by the dominant order) structures ways of seeing and pleasure in looking.' The dominant order is indeed at stake here but the problem – and here we return to the question of the economy of pleasure – is surely that of how the dominant order stays dominant, or perhaps we should say hegemonic, in a *multiplicity* of directions. Interrupting the ways in which structures of voyeurism and scopophilia support this order is certainly one of the ways in which this critique can be sustained, but it is rather like trying to catch Barthes's fly. As soon as you've done it, and especially in a tropical region like pleasure, another appears to torment you from a different direction.

Poverty of theory/poverty of desire

How might these excursions through various conceptions of pleasure help in formulating a cultural politics which would not be disabled by Bevin's 'poverty of desire'? Analysis of régimes of representation and the ideological formation of subjectivity is important because it lays the ground for a critique of the connection between pleasure and subjectivity. To recognise that the subject is not a natural fact but an ideological and juridical construct is only the first stage, though. A political analysis of subjectivity requires other terms. As Gramsci put it:

> 'It is not enough to know the *ensemble* of relations as they exist at any given time as a given system. They must be known genetically, in the movement of their formation. For each individual is the synthesis not only of existing relations, but of the history of these relations. He is the précis of all the past.'[16]

How would such genetic knowledge enable us to read this subjective précis with respect to the histories and trajectories of pleasure? For one thing, we would need to abandon interpretative frameworks which seek out definitive meanings in the mysterious connections between signifier and signified, between film text and the unconscious and so on. This has often been a useful methodology in the analysis of ideology. It leads to a politics of interrupting the normal mechanisms for producing meaning and so may be able to illuminate 'the *ensemble* of relations as they exist at any given time as a given system'. But it says little about the genetics or historicity of pleasure. What is needed at this level of analysis of pleasure is something analogous to the history of 'discursive unities' which Foucault traces in the *History of Sexuality* – of the *hysterisation* of women's bodies, the *pedgogisation* of children's sex, the *socialisation* of procreation and the *psychiatrisation* of perverse pleasure. Is it possible, for example, to speak of the pleasures of pornography from a purely textual point of view, without taking into account some of those developments in the *enunciation* of sexuality? Is it possible to speak of it in isolation from the diverse disciplines associated with the development of photography in its capture of the individual? Foucault's nouns of process – they tend to end with -ation – insist that the mechanisms, strategies, negotiations and formations of pleasure are simply not reducible to sociological exegesis or deciphering in whatever variant. We have first of all to examine not only our contemporary and unavoidable complicity with pleasures, but also to chart the lines of historical materialisation and sedimentation of that pact.

So, for example, I would have to see in the curious sense of humour and the sneaking admiration for Enoch Powell's prose to which I owned up my own complicity with certain pleasures of 'Englishness', a particular national, gender and ethnic formation which I cannot simply stand outside. Nor does all my theorising enable me simply to interrupt it, any more than it could be recuperated by dusting off the anachronistic imagery of the 'free-born Englishman' which gave ideological coherence to a radical cultural politics in the nineteenth century. For not only are such popular forms of subjectivity complicit with particular pleasures; these pleasures are themselves complicit with specific political relationships – the carnival surrounding the Canberra's return from the Falklands was a striking example. It's because of this complicity that these pleasures cannot be wrenched free from their political location and mobilised by different political forces. It is interesting to see how intellectual disdain at the mobilization of popular enjoyment and self-identity among the English around jubilees, royal weddings and even nationalist wars is increasingly giving way to expressions of sentimental regret that the left cannot provide an alternative. One response is to reinvent a suppressed Englishness waiting to be liberated – Tony Benn's litany of 1945, the Chartists, the Diggers and Wat Tyler. Certainly, today's queen-and-country populism presents an impoverished repertoire of desire in comparison with the utopian visions of earlier English radicalism. But that is really to dodge the political issue.

The alternative, at the level of analysis, may lie in the shift of focus towards the ways in which pleasures are not only textualised but are also institutionalised and politicised. This would enable us to break from the coherence of utopian visions of the good life and the liberated person and to engage with the differential and fundamentally incoherent effects of pleasure: not the pleasures of 'mass culture' or 'reification' or 'fetishism', nor the simple pleasures of the 'passive reception' of the codes of a culture. The whole area has been thrown into disarray partly because of the emergence onto the political stage of different languages of pleasure associated most evidently with feminism but also with those divergent styles of which Dick Hebdige has been the most eloquent archivist. It has equally become clear that these languages are not assimilable to a unitary discourse of revolt – in spite of the *Riot for Pleasure* slogans along the Covent Garden/West Hampstead axis. As Hebdige himself puts it, 'the objections are lodged, the contradictions displayed.'[17] It is in these contradictions, in these blunt statements of desire, that the poverty of those pleasures complicit with a pervasive hegemony can be seen most clearly. Their political importance lies in their insistence that it is possible to learn to desire differently.

Notes

1. Quoted in Charles Barr, *Ealing Studios*, London, Cameron & Tayleur, 1977 p. 17.
2. Pierre Bourdieu, 'The aristocracy of culture', in *Media, Culture and Society*, vol. 2, no. 2, 1980, pp. 237/8.
3. Laura Mulvey, 'Visual pleasure and narrative cinema', in *Popular Television and Film*, London, BFI and Open University Press, 1981, p. 206.
4. Roland Barthes, *The Pleasure of the Text*, London, Cape, 1976, pp. 64/5.
5. Roland Barthes, *Image-Music-Text*, London, Fontana, 1977, p. 188.
6. Stephen Heath, *Vertige du deplacement*, Paris, Fayard, 1974, p. 161.
7. Dick Hebdige, *Subculture: The Meaning of Style*, London, Methuen, 1979, p. 105.
8. Robert Malcolmson, 'Popular recreations under attack', in Bernard Waites *et al.* (eds) *Popular Culture: Past and Present*, London, Croom Helm and Open University Press, 1982, pp. 34/5.
9. *ibid* p. 39.
10. Michel Foucault, *Discipline and Punish*, New York, Vintage Books, 1979, p. 207.
11. Lionel Trilling, 'The Fate of Pleasure' in *Beyond Culture*, London, Penguin, 1969, p. 70.
12. Stanley Aronowitz, in *Socialist Register 1981*, London, Merlin Press.
13. Herbert Marcuse, *Negations*, London, Penguin, 1973, pp. 115/6.
14. Herbert Marcuse, *Eros and Civilisation*, London, Sphere Books, 1972, p. 13.
15. Jeffrey Weeks, *Sex, Politics and Society*, London, Longman, p. 283.
16. Antonio Gramsci, *Selections from the Prison Notebooks*, London, Lawrence and Wishart, 1971, p. 353.
17. Hebdige, op. cit. p. 17.

Simon Frith

THE PLEASURES OF
THE HEARTH: The making of
BBC light entertainment

*Broadcasting, in short, is the greatest ally that the divine Muse ever had on earth. It
is the final step in the democratisation of music that had its beginnings in a
community singsong among missing links in a primeval forest – who knows?*
BBC Handbook 1928

1

The cultural prospect in Britain in the 1920s was, in F. R. Leavis's words,
dismal: 'the American stage of our developing industrial civilisation was
upon us.' The spectre of Americanisation has always been an aspect of the
mass culture critique and in the 1920s there were good material reasons for
Leavis's terms: the mass media in Britain were becoming subject to American capital and American ideas. By the end of the decade Hollywood films
organised the cinema experience, American agencies dominated the advertising world, the popular papers were copying US tabloid techniques, and
popular musicians played American or *ersatz* American songs. If mass
communication made possible a new national culture – as everyone in the
country read the same news, walked past the same hoardings, hummed the
same tunes – Britain's traditional cultural intellectuals were detached from
it. The mass media were forms of cultural production in which they had no
obvious place, and their aesthetic response to popular prose and film and
music combined bafflement, hostility and fascination. This was, in Bernard
Bergonzi's words, 'the first literary generation in England to have to face
mass civilisation directly, though with a sensitivity formed by traditional
minority culture.'[1]

The Americanisation of popular culture was, in other words, a threat to
the cultural hegemony of Britain's intellectuals and there were a variety of
reactions to this threat – not only the straight hostility of Leavis and Orwell,
but also attempts at participation. Mass cultural forms could be used in high
cultural production (by Auden and Isherwood, for example), and even the
most Americanised media were still sources of intellectual employment.
Numerous would-be literary and artistic figures came down from Oxbridge
and found jobs in advertising agencies or wrote for the tabloid press or, like

Anthony Powell, became screen-writers – he worked for Warner Brothers. They brought to their work a contempt for their audience which marked (and maintained) their own sense of detachment from the new cultural forces. The serious artist became, by necessity, an observer, a recorder, a camera. The most complex expression of this position was, perhaps, Mass Observation. Its project – to make public behaviour a matter of aesthetic as well as political contemplation – combined the approaches of anthropology, surrealism and market research. Other intellectuals registered, more simply, a sort of cultural resignation. Graham Greene, for example, used popular songs and song titles throughout his work (in *Brighton Rock*, most obviously, as well as in 'entertainments' like *The Confidential Agent*) to encapsulate the irony of mass produced signs of private love and tenderness. Such songs (and Greene often wrote his own, efficient lyrics) *stood* for 'bitter sweetness' but it was clear that Greene himself felt no involvement in mass culture, whether as producer or consumer. Like other writers, he was concerned to use popular forms for serious purposes, but he was not interested in any attempt to take control of the mass media themselves, to use the new *means* of cultural production.

For more explicitly socialist intellectuals the task was to oppose the media, to nurture 'real' working class culture. Communists, for example, committed themselves to the folk song movement, while the British documentary film-makers, whether state-sponsored educators like John Grierson or more explicitly proletarian agitators like Kino, the Progressive Film Institute and the Workers' Film and Photo League, defined their work against Hollywood – realism was to replace escapism. Mass culture was resisted in the name of a working class 'community' that was itself, though, more often than not, the product of a decidedly middle class nostalgia. 'Can these dry bones live?' asked C. Day Lewis in *Letter to a Young Revolutionary*. 'Can they live on the tinned foods, cheap cigarettes, votes, synthetic pearls, jazz records and standardised clothing which the town gives them back, as a "civilised" trader gives savages beads for gold? They damn well can't, and you know it. And it's up to you, if you want to see the country sound again, to put its heart back in the right place, even though it means what the progress-mongers call "putting the clock back".'[2]

2

This is the background against which we have to understand the BBC. BBC culture was, first of all, another response to the fear of Americanisation. Reith himself always related mass culture to America. The development of the popular press, for example, had 'subverted the role of the printed word as an instrument of religious, cultural, social and political enlightenment,' and so left the British vulnerable to the influence of American films ('silly and vulgar and false') and music. In 1929 the BBC's director of Outside Broadcasting was commissioned to prepare a report on the 'ramifications of the Transatlantic octopus.' The company had become concerned about American control of the most popular musicians, composers, writers, performers: 'it is even possible that the national outlook and, with it, character, is gradually becoming Americanised.'[3]

The BBC, similarly, opposed the concept of the mass audience. Its attitude to its listeners was summarised in its statement to the Beveridge Committee in 1949:

> 'Under any system of competitive broadcasting all these things would be at the mercy of Gresham's Law. For, at the present stage of the nation's general educational progress, it operates as remorselessly in broadcasting as ever it did in currency. The good, in the long run, will inescapably be driven out by the bad. It is inevitable that any national educational pyramid shall have a base immeasurably broader than its upper levels. The truth of this can be seen by comparing those national newspapers which have circulations of over four millions with those whose circulations are counted in hundred-thousands. And because competition in broadcasting must in the long run descend to a fight for the greatest possible number of listeners, it would be the lower forms of mass appetite which would be more and more catered for in programmes. Any effort to see whether some of that appetite could appreciate something better would be a hostage to fortune. It would be far too dangerous; the winner in *that* race being the loser in competition. This is not merely a matter of BBC versus commercial broadcasting. Even if there were a number of public service corporations they would all be similarly and involuntarily driven down.'[4]

If the BBC was in general terms anti-mass culture and anti-American, its position was in other respects quite different from that of the other media critics. Most obviously, the BBC was not socialist, had no interest in developing or articulating 'authentic' popular culture in working class terms. As Tom Burns puts it:

> 'BBC culture, like BBC standard English, was not peculiar to itself but to an intellectual ambience composed out of the values, standards and beliefs of the professional middle-class, especially that part educated at Oxford and Cambridge. Sports, popular music and entertainment which appealed to the lower classes were included, in large measure, in the programmes, but the manner in which they were purveyed, the context and presentation, remained indomitably upper middle-class; and there was, too, the point that they were only there on the menu as ground bait.'[5]

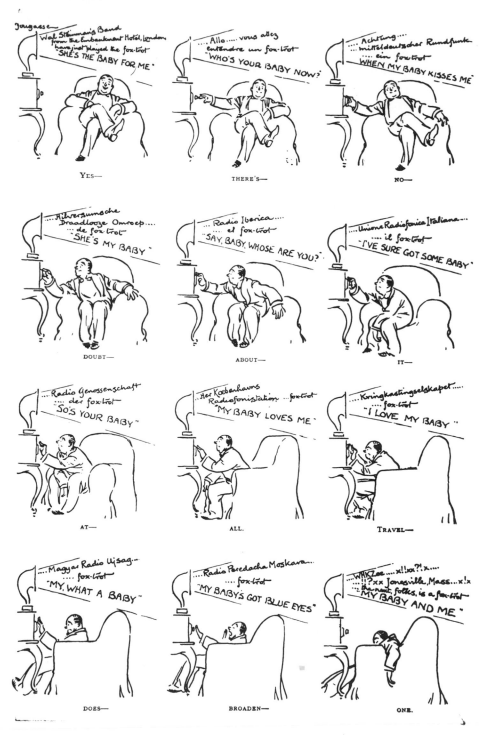

The 'Americanisation' of popular music. Cartoon by Fougasse.

At the same time, though, broadcasting was a mass medium and the BBC's upper middle-class staff couldn't ignore the popular effect of their work. Neither could they get much support in their shaping of British radio from outside the company. 1920s and 1930s intellectuals were remarkably uninterested in the wireless. The literary establishment was, to use Barbara Coulton's term, wary of the BBC, and journals like the *New Statesman* and the *Spectator* rarely acknowledged its existence – though they would occasionally register their disdain for the BBC's reflection of 'popular taste'. It took the post-war development of the Third Programme to make the wireless a medium for high culture.[6]

In terms of the mass culture debate, then, the BBC's production staff found themselves in an odd position. Working in a mass medium with explicitly anti-mass cultural principles, they had daily to answer the questions that other intellectuals avoided. What did it mean to *construct* a national culture? Who were 'the people'? What did it mean to 'please' the public? If market measures (listening figures, advertising revenue, profits) were rejected, how could the 'success' of a programme be defined? The very intensity of Reith's hostility to mass culture armed his staff against the detached cynicism of other media intellectuals. The BBC's programme makers were attempting to use a mass medium for their own, serious, purposes.

Historians of British broadcasting argue that these purposes involved, in practice, tensions and contradictions between two quite different broadcasting principles – 'public service' and 'entertainment'. What made the BBC unique was its commitment to public service; what linked it to the general development of broadcasting was its need to entertain an audience, to offer its listeners some 'ground bait'. Even Paddy Scannell and David Cardiff, by far the most acute radio historians, use this contrast, suggesting that in the late 1930s the emphasis of BBC programming shifted. Scannell and Cardiff point to the BBC's increasing use of audience research, to the growing competition from the commercial stations on the continent, to the departure of Reith in 1938. They describe the routinisation of programme schedules, the changing style of radio talk, the discarding of the pretence that the BBC could unify its audience. A large section of the radio public did use the wireless exclusively for entertainment, as a background sound; the BBC had to distinguish its 'serious' and 'popular' listeners and make programmes to appeal to them accordingly. The rise of 'popular radio' was unstoppable: 'the BBC no longer sought to lead and reform public taste; it now tried to match or anticipate it.'[7]

The argument is that the BBC began by pitting public service against entertainment broadcasting but had, eventually, to come to terms with its popular audience, had to adopt, for such listeners, the programming ideas of the commercial stations (a change of policy that was to be repeated, thirty years later, with the creation of Radio 1). This may be true, but the argument has had an unfortunate consequence for research: much more attention has been paid to the BBC's notion of public service (the Reith problem) than to its equally problematic idea of entertainment. It is the latter idea that I want to examine, and I am concerned to challenge two assumptions in particular: first, that 'light entertainment' (the BBC's own peculiar term) can be defined separately from public service; and, second, that the popular/serious distinction describes a class division, with serious programmes aimed at the bourgeoisie, popular programmes reflecting working class tastes and interests. Rather, BBC light entertainment was a 'middlebrow' form shaped itself by the idea of public service. The paradox is that this new sort of pleasure quickly became a significant strand in British commercial entertainment too.

3

According to John Reith, public service broadcasting had four key components. It was not meant to make money. It involved national coverage – BBC programmes aimed to reach the greatest possible number of homes. These programmes were subject to 'unified control', rather than being made in *ad hoc* response to pressure groups (or target audiences defined by advertisers). And it treated the radio listener as 'capable of growth and development'.[8]

None of these principles excludes entertainment as the proper concern of a broadcaster but they do put constraints on it. The central Reithian principle was that the wireless listener should be treated as active rather than passive, and the recurring BBC distinction between 'serious' and 'tap' listening was applied in particularly pressing terms to entertainment programmes precisely because their staple content, light music, was so obviously liable to 'passive consumption'. The 1928 *BBC Handbook* was positively school-teacherly about this – 'each individual member of an audience . . . must give his or her best receptive faculties if the full entertainment value is to be received and appreciated' – and throughout the 1920s the BBC employed its own radio critic, Filson Young, to spread the message that there was 'a right and a wrong way to use Broadcasting'.

> 'I would urge listeners to cultivate the art of using their wireless receivers intelligently and artistically, so that the immense care and trouble that are taken in compiling and presenting the programmers' skill achieve their true direction and effect.'[9]

'Active' listening meant discriminating listening – what mattered was less what people listened to than that they had chosen to listen to it. This theme was sounded by programme makers of all sorts. Hilda Matheson, who had worked in the Talks Department, made a contrast between listening as a vice ('like gin or opium') and listening as 'a source of pleasure, wonder, excitement and stimulus.' Background sounds were, by definition, meaningless; background music meant 'trifling, tea-time sentimentality'. Turning on the radio should be 'an act of will, like choosing a book, or buying a ticket for a concert.' C. A. Lewis, the BBC's first Programme Organiser, called constantly for 'selective' listening – the point of the *Radio Times* was to make audiences planning possible and, indeed, the BBC deliberately left silence between programmes to discourage casual listeners. Val Gielgud, who took charge of Drama and Variety in 1929, explained that

> '. . . a service which is "on tap" for all the day and much of the night; which encourages every listener to believe that by the payment of his almost insignificant license fee he is entitled as of right to find something which be personally desires to hear at his disposal at any moment, can never hope to establish a genuine artistic or aesthetic prestige.'[10]

The problem was that people could *over*-use radio, 'over-familiarise' themselves with what should be unique experiences. Roger Manvell later commented that 'for the majority of people keeping a radio set which is not giving off its natural sounds is like keeping a parrot without encouraging it to talk,' but it was precisely this analogy, wireless as parrot, that the BBC was determined to avoid, and this meant not only 'balance' (interspersing popular programmes with silence and unpopular programmes) but also 'presence' – entertainment programmes too had to be presented (and heard) as special events.[11]

This approach reflected the BBC's obligation to develop its audience's listening skills. If no-one in Britain really knew how to listen to the radio – there was no experience to draw on – then it was up to Reith and his staff to train them, to give them the means to discriminate. An important aspect of Reithian programming was the education of the listener in the process of radio listening itself. The BBC sought to determine what it meant to be a 'listener', and Reith himself believed that his development of the proper skills and standards among the BBC audience would have a significant cultural ripple effect. The classic statement of his position was his valedictory speech.

> 'That broadcasting should be merely a vehicle of light entertainment was a limitation of its functions which we declined to accept. It has been our endeavour to give a conscious, social purpose to the exploitation of this medium. Not that we underrated the importance of wholesome entertainment or failed to give it due place; but that we realised in the stewardship vested in us the responsibility of contributing consistently and cumulatively to the intellectual and moral happi-

ness of the community. We have broadcast systematically and increasingly good music; we have developed educational courses for school children and for adults; we have broadcast the Christian religion and tried to reflect that spirit of common-sense Christian ethics which we believe to be a necessary component of citizenship and culture. We have endeavoured to exclude anything that might, directly or indirectly, be harmful. We have proved, as expected, that the supply of good things creates the demand for more. We have tried to found a tradition of public service, and to dedicate the service of broadcasting to the service of humanity in its fullest sense. We believe that a new national asset has been created . . . the asset referred to is of the moral and not the material order – that which, down the years, brings the compound interest of happier homes, broader culture and truer citizenship.'[12]

Reith is usually – and rightly – described in terms of moral and cultural arrogance but his position also rested on a number of psychological assumptions about people's 'needs'. At the beginning of his wireless career, in 1924, he wrote that:

'. . . entertainment, pure and simple, quickly grows tame; dissatisfaction and boredom result. If hours are to be occupied agreeably, it would be a sad reflection of human intelligence if it were contended that entertainment, in the accepted sense of the term, was the only means for doing so.'

For Reith 'pure entertainment' meant 'to occupy agreeably' but he rejected the suggestion that 'jazz bands and sketches by humorists' could do this for long. Pop music, as C. A. Lewis put it, had 'nothing really satisfying in it. It is a drug, and when one drug fails to operate a new one must be prescribed.' The BBC's music policy was, therefore, to encourage 'better, healthier music'. To begin with, pop music had to be broadcast but tastes would soon be 'lifted' – listeners' 'present standard of musical appreciation' simply reflected the fact that most of them had never had the chance to go to the Albert or Wigmore Halls. Once they heard classical music, though, they'd realise its superiority to popular tunes:

'*The music doesn't wear*. It cannot be repeated, whereas good music lasts, mellows and gains fresh beauties at every hearing. It stands, like Shakespeare, through the centuries. No passing craze can shake it. It is the product of greatness, and greatness leaves its mark and endures.'

The constant repetition of classical music was Lewis's confident response to the listener complaint that the BBC didn't broadcast enough popular sounds:

'I prophesy that ere many years have passed a Beethoven symphony or a piano concerto will be every bit as popular an item in our programmes as half-an-hour's dance music.'[13]

Tom Burns, like many other commentators, has concluded that with reference to music, at least, Reith's arguments about broadcasting and enlightenment were justified: 'perhaps the greatest single achievement of the BBC has been to transform this country from what was musically the most barbarous nation in Europe into what has some claims to be the musical capital of the world.' This seems to me an unduly complacent reading. The BBC's music policy – its early financial involvement in opera and the proms, for example – was less significant as an exercise in national education than as an expression of support for an existing way of musical social life. Other, non-middle class uses of music were not treated with such 'discrimination'.[14]

The same set of attitudes was obvious in the Drama Department. Val Gielgud later wrote that his producers' task was to introduce drama to people who had never been to a theatre, to educate in them a 'willingness' to listen, to teach them 'that drama can be a satisfying and rewarding entertainment.'

> 'Radio drama never made, by its essence, it never could make what is called "easy listening" . . . its audience had to be "built up" . . . an audience which in the beginning was bound either to be "minority" and in consequence cranky or "majority" and in consequence "moronic". To have chosen the latter target would have been as fatal as it would have been easily popular. And but for the Consistency of Policy at the highest level, and consistency of control at my own, backed by strong personal beliefs and convictions, BBC Drama might have fallen into the transatlantic trap, and gained nothing from its freedom from the quirks, whims and occasional imbecilities of commercial sponsors.'[15]

In practice, though, Gielgud's chief concern was with the norms of the established middle class theatre. His department mostly broadcast West End plays, classics and adaptations of novels. There were 'young experimenters' on Gielgud's staff, but as he wrote, 'much credit is due to the more old-fashioned stalwarts, such as Howard Rose, who got little of the limelight reserved for the more youthful experimentalists, and yet was quietly building, by steady, unostentatious and perhaps prosaic method, the regular audience of the middle class fireside.' For Rose and Gielgud radio drama was most suited to 'the presentation of characters and situations which the audience can easily identify with its own experience', experience symbolised by the BBC's first soap opera (or 'family serial'), *The English Family Robinson*, which began in 1938. If Gielgud's difficulty 'was to hold a reasonable balance between the claims of intelligent, interesting aesthetics and of normal, accepted standards of entertainment,' he had, apparently, no difficulty in deciding what were 'intelligent aesthetics', what were 'normal standards of entertainment.'[16]

4

The BBC's work in putting together a new sort of national audience was not confined to its coverage of politics and public affairs. Its account of 'normal standards of entertainment' was equally important. C. A. Lewis, using typical BBC rhetoric, praised radio for 'bringing all classes of society into closer touch with their neighbours, and so fostering that mutual trust and understanding which is essential for the well-being of a great democracy.' Reith argued that if radio was to become 'valuable as an index to the community's outlook and personality . . . it was of first importance that the service should be trusted; it must not abuse the confidential footing it had obtained on every man's hearthrug.'[17]

Entertainment's contribution to these ideas of democracy, neighbourliness, the community's personality, lay in its organisation of family life: what bound listeners together was *where* they listened. In 1923 the Marconi company claimed that:

> '. . . many of the older people regret the scattering of the young folk to their various occupations and amusements, and think sadly of the old-fashioned "family" evening. But broadcasting has brought this back again.'

And the 'radio hearth' featured heavily in the advertising of all wireless manufacturers. Lewis, from the BBC, argued the point even more aggressively:

> 'Broadcasting means the rediscovery of the home. In these days when house and hearth have been largely given up in favour of a multitude of other interests and activities outside, with the consequent disintegration of family ties and affections, it appears that this new persuasion may to some extent reinstate the parental roof in its old accustomed place, for all will admit that this is, or should be, one of the greatest and best influences on life.'[18]

The BBC celebrated the radio hearth in numerous ways, quickly associating itself with the development of the Royal Family, for instance. The implications of domestic listening were clearly symbolised by the *Children's Hour*, 'the pause in the day's occupations' (the quote was taken from Longfellow) when the company's senior personnel became Aunts and Uncles. The *Children's Hour* was obviously part of middle class family routine and Reith was clear about the significance of this model for working class

TO THE WOMEN OF BRITAIN

The Radio has undoubtedly helped you to keep your husband and boys away from the club and kept them at home where they thus experience the benefits of your gentle charm and influence, but you must now go *one step further* and make your home comfy and cheerful by having Hailglass Shades and Globes on your lights.   Hailglass is made only by Hailwood & Ackroyd, Ltd., Morley, near Leeds.   It is made in beautiful opals and is decorated or tinted with lovely colours and designs.   Each piece is marked "Hailglass."   Don't let your supplier foist upon you foreign glass which is made under sweated conditions.   Your supplier gets a reasonable profit on our glass.   We are putting up a hard fight in the face of unfair foreign competition and against certain atrocious British dealers who want *excessive profits*.   Please help us to keep the Trade and British Money in Britain.   Your menfolk, as they listen to the Radio in a home made bright and comfy by our charmingly coloured glassware, will indeed feel that they are in a real "Heaven on Earth," and **you** women of England will mutually join in this pleasure.   We have an enormous range of sizes, shapes and designs.

Head Office and Works: MORLEY, Near Leeds

Showrooms { 98 Mansell Street, LONDON, B. 1
32 Shaftesbury Avenue, LONDON, W. 1
21 Waterloo Street, GLASGOW

Women and the wireless: from the *BBC Handbook* 1928.

children: it offered them 'a happy alternative to the squalour of the streets and backyards.'[19] This idea of domesticity as warm, glowing, safe and loving became just as important for commercial broadcasters – the Ovaltineys live on in television advertisements.

In terms of light entertainment, the contrast of the home and the street had an even wider class significance. As Michael Chanan has written about the development of nineteenth-century pleasures: 'the family cradled the consciousness of the middle classes while popular working-class consciousness was formed on the streets and on the public stage.' Working class entertainment was collective, disorderly, immediate – 'vulgar' by definition. Middle class entertainment was orderly, regulated and calm, and it was this aesthetic that informed the BBC's understanding of listeners' leisure needs. Reith, for example, acknowledged the BBC's obligation to provide relaxation: 'mitigation of the strain of a high-pressure life, such as the last generation scarcely knew, is a primary social necessity, and that necessity must be satisfied.'[20]

Entertainment-as-relaxation meant that no-one should be *disturbed*. A 'hearty laugh', music hall style, was fine, but as Hilda Matheson observed, 'humour on the microphone has to take into account grand-mothers and schoolboys, navvies and invalid ladies, town and country, north and south, rich and poor, sophisticated and unsophisticated,' and none of these listeners must be laughed *at*. For the BBC Music Department, meanwhile, the problem was to find 'good light songs', 'music with attractive melodies, used and harmonised with distinction of thought and fancy.'

> 'Generally speaking, when a man gets home tired and "fed up" he wants to be cheered by a good, lilting tune and harmony that is distinctive without being so "modernistic" as to disturb the increasing tranquillity of his mental state. Sullivan and Edward German fill this want so adequately that a programme of works by these thoroughly "English" composers is always welcomed.'[21]

Relaxation was earned by hard work and only made sense in reference to it. The spread of suitably entertaining radio programmes would, in C. A. Lewis's words, 'of necessity, promote a healthier and more cheerful mental outlook on work and life, and this in its turn will react on their work itself to the benefit of all concerned.' By the 1930s radio was playing a significant role in the organisation of the rhythms of work and leisure. The BBC Sunday, for example, reflected not only Reith's Protestantism, but also his staff's wider set of assumptions about the place of the weekend in the organisation of family life. As the *Radio Times* music editor put it in 1930, 'the BBC has always tried to frame these Sunday programmes in a way which might blend the maximum of wholesome brightness with the atmosphere of quiet leisure about the hearth.' Quiet leisure was so central a BBC idea that it is a jolt to read that D. G. Bridson (then a producer based in Manchester) wanted to use radio drama to capture something of the *spectacular* appeal of 'film makers like D. W. Griffith and Cecil B. de Mille.' Bridson believed that radio should be a source of emotion – he used verse, for example, to 'charge' his features, not simply as a sign of artistic seriousness, and so in the 1930s he remained an unusual (and unusually high-brow) BBC figure. More typical was Jack Payne, leader of the BBC's first in-house dance band, who described his job as 'to put happiness and sunshine over the air.' His arrangements were made to provide 'moments of relaxation' – not rhythm, but variety: 'plenty of solo work and clever orchestrations are necessary before the microphone, and the melody must be brought out.' A popular song was, he wrote, 'one which everyone can pick up and hum and sing as they feel disposed. After all, no one wants to listen to jazz seriously.'[22]

5

In his history of music and the middle class in the nineteenth century, William Weber shows how 'classical' concerts became important public occasions as the link between the bourgeois family and bourgeois society. Shared tastes became symbolic of shared class interests, and concerts were public displays of a particular sort of exclusive community. (And thus they provided a suitable setting for courtship – all the young people on display could be guaranteed eligible.) Artistic judgements were, in other words, tied up with questions of status. 'The art must not be degraded,' wrote a columnist in the *Music World*. 'To play the finest music to an audience which has been admitted at a shilling apiece is what I can never give my consent to.'[23]

It was this model of how entertainment could work to bind together a community that underlay the BBC's vision of a 'common culture' in the 1920s and 1930s. BBC ideology too implied that membership of (and exclusion from) the listening 'public' was, in fact, a matter of right attitudes, shared interests. In one sense, the BBC, as a mass middle-class medium, faced an obvious problem: how to articulate the *borders* of middle class taste while being accessible to everyone. But in practice radio use was something that spread down the class ladder and in Britain, at least, the wireless was defined initially as an aspect of middle class leisure. Even though half the population had a radio by 1934, for example, ownership remained concentrated in the South East and Midlands and was sparsest in the North East and South Wales. Mark Pegg argues, indeed, that the BBC didn't really have a solid working-class audience until the spread of the 'utility' set of the 1940s. Even such populist pressures on BBC programming as the *Daily Mail* radio ballot of 1927 were, essentially, middle class pressures. When the Radio Manufacturers Association began its campaign for audience research and popular shows in the mid-1930s it was in the face of the exhaustion of the middle-class consumer market. New sales meant attracting *new* radio listeners – it was their tastes that needed investigation. There is little evidence that the demands of the *existing* audience for entertainment (reflected in the rising audience figures of the commercial stations, for example) were working-class demands. What was at issue was not different sorts of popular programme, but more of them.[24]

The Reithian principle of broadcasting as enlightenment meant, in practice, that BBC programmes offered listeners direct access to the middle-class community. The pleasure of a BBC 'talk', for example, rested on the assumption that a BBC talker had a particular kind of class authority. Early in the BBC's life, Reith wrote to his regional directors:

> 'In some stations I see periodically men down to speak whose status, either professionally or socially, and whose qualifications to speak, seem doubtful. It should be an honour in every sense of the word for a man to speak from any broadcasting station, and only those who have a claim to be heard above their fellows on any particular subject in the locality should be put on the programme.'[25]

As D. G. Bridson commented:

> 'That the man in the street should have anything vital to contribute to broadcasting was an idea slow to gain acceptance. That he should actually use broadcasting to express his own opinions in his own unvarnished words was regarded as almost the end of all good order.'[26]

When Bridson did eventually get *Harry Hopeful's Northern Tours* on air (this was an early version of *Down Your Way* – Harry Hopeful, actor Frank Nicholls, travelled to towns and villages in Yorkshire and Lancashire and talked to inhabitants about their lives and work) it was described in the BBC *Yearbook* as a programme of interviews with 'peasants from remote northern districts.' The BBC's usual treatment of 'common' speakers was showcased, rather, by *In Town Tonight*, started by Eric Maschwitz in 1933 on the assumption that his listeners were interested in 'the human verities, the simple fascinating things that humble folk do, and the high points achieved by men and women of distinction.'[27]

The language here – humble folk, men and women of distinction, Reith's sense of honour – reflect the way in which the BBC's 'common culture' was, at the same time, hierarchically ordered. Listeners were equally honoured to have distinguished people in their homes. This was most obvious in the BBC's treatment of public events. The Outside Broadcasting section was soon providing the most 'popular' programmes of all. In these orchestrated dramas of royalty, sport and patriotism, the listener was addressed as a loyal, grateful spectator/citizen/subject. The listener, in other words, was carefully fixed at the bottom of the chain of privilege that ran from the performers through the commentators into the home.

The same principle was apparent in light entertainment. Producers pointed to the difference between the radio listener – domestic, private – and the usual musical or show-biz public, a crowd gathered for a special occasion. The problem was to fit entertainment as occasion into an intimate routine, to take pleasures that were essentially live (with elements of risk and uncertainty) and script them so that nothing untoward happened. The solution lay in the development of a particular sort of *voice* – intimate and authoritative – and a particular sort of *personality* – relaxing and knowable. The radio star was public figure as private friend. As Leonard Henry, one of Britain's first successful wireless comics wrote: 'it is one of the great charms of broadcasting that we manage to get this intimate family kind of atmosphere through the mike and out of your loudspeakers.' The honour for the listener in this case was to be invited to sit at someone else's hearth.[28]

6

The BBC began broadcasting dance music in 1923 – the Savoy Havana Band from the studio, live music from the Carlton. By 1924 the Savoy Orpheans' relay was a weekly routine. By the end of the 1920s the BBC finished each weekday with a band: Lew Stone from 10.30 to 12 on Tuesdays, Harry Roy

The family audience. John Gilroy, *Radio Times*, 15 April 1938.

on Fridays, Ambrose on Saturdays, and so on. There were various attempts to change this pattern. Jack Payne, for example, argued that 'dance music should not just become a habit; there must be something else worthy of concluding each day's task – conversely I never saw any reason for putting the bulk of dance music right at the end of the day.' But Payne, as leader of the BBC's own dance band, broadcast every afternoon, as well as in the evenings, and there continued to be an audience demand for live name bands, outside broadcasts, dance music as late evening listening.[29]

Dance music was American music and the bands were often taken by the BBC's critics (and by subsequent commentators) as symbols of the sort of popular entertainment that Reith had to broadcast, despite himself. But this is misleading. From the beginning this American music signified a British way of life: syncopation in 'a high class setting', entertainment defined in terms of upper class glamour and relaxation. The dance bands came from West End hotels or exclusive clubs like the Embassy. This was not 'popular' music in proletarian terms. Rather, the radio hearth became the setting for vicarious high living. As Albert McCarthy has commented:

> 'The locations of the major dance bands in England were hotels like the Savoy and the Mayfair, bastions of a class society, with a clientele that was conservative in both politics and taste, and unlikely to extend a welcome to an influx of younger people from the lower orders.'[30]

For this audience jazz was an occasionally exhilarating novelty but too complicated for normal dancing needs. When the Fred Elizalde Band tried playing 'real American music' in 1927, 'the paying customer at the Savoy complained that the band was difficult to dance to; radio audiences complained that they couldn't recognise their favourite tunes dressed up as they were in the filigreed finery of a jazz orchestration.' Elizalde was soon off the air, and his experience became that of any band leader who wanted to 'swing' his tunes: 'the BBC and the recording companies would raise their hands and cry "not commercial" anytime the bands tried something more adventurous.' In 1935 the BBC formally banned 'hot music' and scat singing, citing listeners' objections. Jazz remained, in Philip Larkin's words, 'a fugitive minority interest'. As *Melody Maker*, the paper for 'dance band *afficionados*', and Edgar Jackson in the *Gramophone* slowly put together a critical vocabulary to distinguish 'hot dance music' from 'popular rhythmic music' and began to explain the superiority of black musicians in terms of greater art rather than 'less polish', the BBC employed as their resident dance band leaders Jack Payne and Henry Hall, who were inspired by Paul Whiteman and Jack Hylton and the idea of 'symphonic jazz'. Their bands put on a show, featured 'personalities', used crooners who, with the aid of the electric microphone, could blend their voices coolly into the easy-on-the-ear harmonies.[31]

By the end of the 1930s the distinction between commercial and non-commercial 'light' music, between 'real jazz' and pop, between respectable and disreputable entertainers was well established, and the BBC had become central to the organisation of the music as commerce. It took the war and military service to free musicians from 'the commercial duress their civilian counterparts were subject to – the demands of the dancers, the caution of the recording companies and the rapacity of the bandleaders.' Only in military bands (like the RAF's Squadronaires) could would-be jazz players pursue these interests. For these musicians the BBC had never represented a non-commercial, alternative way of making music or entertainment. Rather, it was radio that determined the conservatism of band leaders and record companies. The BBC listener was taken to be 'neither a hopeless low-brow nor a supercilious head-in-the-air highbrow.' The BBC demanded familiar tunes in 'interesting settings' and with familiar rhythms – in other words, waltz or fox-trot. As Terpsichorean, dance music reviewer for the *Gramophone Critic* observed, the average British listener did not understand 'jazz language': to describe something as 'loud and crazy but mean' was to talk nonsense. The British were fans of 'straight' dance music.[32]

The BBC was well aware of its own commercial significance, and there were numerous discussions about how to prevent song or record plugging – in 1929 bands were banned from announcing song titles or singing title choruses, for example. But the BBC's importance for pop was not just as a means of advertisement. The BBC was also instrumental in the spread of dancing and the dance band as a normal part of middle class and respectable working class leisure. Dancing became a regulated, decorous form of fun, an evening out according to the 'strict tempo' of Victor Sylvester and his schools of dance. The upper-class bands the BBC used found themselves with a reputation, a popularity, that spread far beyond their initial exclusive clientele. Band leaders like Jack Payne could sell out provincial theatres and dance halls all over the country; dance bands were added to the attractions of the newly opening holiday camps. And if 'records were important in spreading the popularity of the dance bands,' it was, as McCarthy notes, 'success gained from broadcasts that led to bands being sought after and built up by record companies.'[33]

The relationship between radio and the record companies marked a general shift in cultural power in the 1930s – from Tin Pan Alley to Broadcasting House. The emergence of the BBC as the most significant source of musical entertainment meant a change in the organisation of popular music – from the publisher/showman/song system to the record company based star system. In 1933, for example, the BBC changed its song plugging rules: dance programme producers now dealt directly with the band leaders rather than with the venue managers. Dance programmes were organised less and less as 'transparent' broadcasts of live events, more and more as specially designed radio shows. The judgement (and judges) of what was a good number, a good performance, shifted accordingly. The 'popularity' of pop music became measured by its radio suitability and by record sales – immediate, live, collective audience response mattered less and less.[34]

Christopher Stone, the BBC's first disc jockey, suggested that 'the broadcaster's job is to provide the equivalent of a bath and a change for the tired man's and the tired woman's mind,' and, in general, Stone was the voice and had the tastes of the BBC's middle-brow listeners. Ronald Pearsall has suggested that the BBC's 1920s music policy is best understood as a middlebrow attempt 'to make classical music popular and popular music classical', but this approach was not confined to Reithians or the BBC. The British record industry was, equally, run by men and women with little experience of or interest in popular culture or popular taste. They too began with the assumption that pop music was worthless – it was its worthlessness that made it commercially exploitable.[35]

The BBC's account of popular music reflected, then, more generally changing attitudes of cultural entrepreneurs towards their audiences. These changes were the effect of the mass media themselves on the power structure of entertainment. The BBC and the record companies spoke differently about audience needs – the record companies in terms of market choices, the BBC in terms of 'giving the public something slightly better than it now thinks it wants'. But with regard to popular music, they both treated listeners the same way: as a mass public with a mass taste, rather than as a number of specific publics with specific tastes. The pop audience was seen as a series of individuals, listening and buying privately rather than publicly. And so there were not really many differences between the BBC's use of pop and Radio Luxembourg's – record companies like Decca learnt from the BBC how to use the time they could buy from Luxembourg and Radio Normandy. The real contrast was with pre-BBC, pre-radio, pre-record entertainment. Popular music had been dominated by promoters and music hall owners and publishers; their skill had been to manage an immediate experience, to understand and service *particular* publics. And the rise of the mass musical media meant too a new sort of performing star, with domestic 'charm' rather than larger-than-life appeal.

Not surprisingly, the BBC had an uneasy relationship with British show business. Promoters and managers, and the performers themselves, held aloof from broadcasting. In the 1920s, for example, outside trans-missions from music halls and theatres were not allowed: the Society of West End Theatre Managers did a deal with the BBC for the broadcast of play excerpts in 1925, but the Variety Artists Federation remained hostile. The BBC's variety producers themselves were neither recruited from this world nor knew much about it. In 1934 the head of Variety claimed that the 'war' with music hall was at an end, but it was clear by then that radio variety bore little resemblance to traditional music hall performances.[36]

This partly reflected the long broadcasting boycott itself. George Black, for example, reintroduced the radio ban on his acts in 1931. By 1932, when his agency, management and theatre company, GTC, merged with Moss Empires, he controlled almost half the performers the BBC had been using. But in developing its own comedy and musical acts, the BBC was also developing its own performing conventions, and music hall stars, even when available, were often unsuitable – too visual, too ribald, too spontaneous, too large; the more middle class concert parties and revues were a better recruiting ground. Meanwhile, though, the new radio stars also had to make a living. They couldn't survive on BBC fees alone but had to use their radio name as the draw for a new type of public show – the appearance of the voice, the local display of national attractions, the 'in-person' performance of stars who were much better 'known' in the living room than they ever could be in a theatre. By the end of the decade the BBC was no longer getting its performers from the stage but, rather, the stage was getting its entertainers from the BBC. Even Christopher Stone had appeared at the Palladium and toured the provinces playing records. The BBC's 'non-commercial' principles of entertainment now determined what commercial entertainment itself sounded like.

7

'Whole sections of the working class,' wrote George Orwell influentially in *The Road to Wigan Pier* in 1937, 'who have been plundered of all they really need are being compensated, in part, by cheap luxuries which mitigate the surface of life.' Orwell included radio in his list of working class palliatives, but 'cheap luxury' doesn't really seem to describe British broadcasting, and reading the memoirs and public statements of the BBC's employees themselves I was reminded rather of an Orwell passage that other middle-class socialists didn't much like:

> 'All my notions – notions of good and evil, of pleasant and unpleasant, of funny and serious, of ugly and beautiful – are essentially *middle-class* notions; my taste in books and food and clothes, my sense of honour, my table manners, my turns of speech, my accent, even the characteristic movements of my body, are the products of a special kind of upbringing and a special niche about half-way up the social hierarchy.'[37]

The same is true of all the BBC's tastes and notions – notions of entertainment included. Eric Maschwitz, the head of Variety from 1933, had a taste for Viennese opera and wanted to organise BBC light music round European rather than American standards. Val Gielgud, the head of Drama, had a taste for well made plays and despised the semi-educated 'puppy-like' mass audience. Jack Payne (who in 1926 volunteered to drive a London bus) wanted to make jazz 'tasteful'.

The suggestion has often been made (by Asa Briggs most powerfully) that between the wars the BBC was the site of a cultural struggle – entertainment versus enlightenment – which was not resolved until Reith-ianism was finally routed in the 1940s. Reith's achievement, in other words, was to *prevent* radio being used as mass culture, as a cheap luxury. But this is to accept Reith's own definition of mass culture – as the lowest common denominator of taste, as 'vulgar' by definition. Reith feared an Americanised popular culture that would exclude Britain's educated, 'cultured' élite from the processes of both production and consumption, and the BBC repre-sented his counter-stroke. By keeping broadcasting in cultured hands, he would halt the emergence of the mass audience. In practice, though, Reith faced the same problems as any other broadcaster: how to build up and respond to a new home-based public. The BBC didn't have to deliver its audience to commercial sponsors, but it was still a mass medium. We should drop the idea that mass culture has to be American, Hollywood, 'popular'. The BBC was central to another process: the creation of mass, British, *middle-brow* culture. To make sense of British broadcasting we have to relate it to the bourgeois best-sellers analysed in Q. D. Leavis's *Fiction and the Reading Public*, to the British commercial cinema's dependence on actors and writers and dramas drawn from the West End stage, to the values embedded in the *Daily Mail* and *Daily Express*, to the multi-media success of someone like J. B. Priestley.

The mass culture debate in the 1930s was, as Orwell implied, a debate about needs. Working class consumption, it seemed, could no longer be defined in terms of subsistence. The very idea of a 'luxury' was becoming suspect, could no longer be confined to bourgeois commodities. The prob-lem was that if new inventions, new goods, could create their own need (no-one had 'needed' a radio before it was invented) then the concept of need itself had to be re-thought. 'Real' needs were based on obvious material problems (food, shelter, warmth). 'Superficial' needs, by contrast, appeared to reflect irrational choices: why did people pick out one fashion rather than another? One sort of washing powder? One tune? Tastes and preferences became a matter of expert investigation – the National Institute of Industrial Psychology was founded in 1921 and psychologists had soon established themselves too as marketing consultants. Advertising was the symbol of mass culture as the manipulation of desire.

The BBC disdained this role and scorned, in Val Gielgud's words, 'the imbecilities of commercial sponsors', but it too had to make assumptions about audience needs, assumptions that shaped the pleasures on offer. Light entertainment, in particular, was defined in terms – balance, access, community – that cannot be separated from an account of the audience gathered round an essentially middle class hearth. Balanced entertainment thus meant not pluralism, numerous different sorts of humour and music, but relaxation, programmes guaranteed soothing ('wholesome') by their exclusion of all excesses. Balance in light music meant, similarly, avoiding both sounds that were too high-brow *and* sounds that were too low-brow.

The radio made public events accessible, brought them into the home – outside broadcasting was particularly significant for this process, but at this time *all* broadcasts were live. This was the basis for Reith's claim for radio's contribution to democracy. All listeners could take part in an event equally; no-one's living room was more or less privileged. It is a misleading claim. Domestic listening is a very peculiar form of public participation and the key role was played by the commentator, the BBC talker whose job was, in practice, to teach the audience how to join in a radio event, how to organise their experience. Access was available, then, through an authority. 'Active' listening was a matter of knowing one's place. What was on offer was access to a community, a language, a set of radio manners. To become a BBC

The wireless and domesticity. Mervyn Wilson, *Radio Times*, 18 November 1938.

listener was to join a club (children could do so literally) which clearly excluded people with bad radio manners – the tap listeners, the passive consumers. The 'I/we/you' of the BBC announcer was, therefore, subtly arranged. The message was that the BBC was honoured to enter your home; the assumption was that your home was a particular kind of place; the promise was that if it wasn't, the BBC, by entering, could make it so. Again, *Children's Hour* with its BBC Aunts and Uncles is the most direct example.

What matters about this is not that the BBC expresses 'middle-class ideology' (an obvious point), but that because of its ideology the BBC developed particular sorts of pleasure. The enjoyment of the wireless came to depend on the processes of *flattery* and *familiarity*. BBC audiences were flattered by a tone of voice, by speakers, comics, singers, addressing them directly, as if each individual listener's pleasure mattered to them personally – compare Stanley Baldwin's radio talks with traditional political rhetoric, for example. Flattery meant offering a sort of knowledge – the King speaks just to you, you can get to know him – which both confirmed the 'ordinariness' of public performers (the new definition of 'personality') but also structured the 'ordinariness' of the listener – if they're just like us, we must be just like them. Ordinariness became the measure of authenticity, confirmed listeners' sense of belonging. (This wasn't confined to the BBC, of course. The audience was constructed in similar ways by cinema newsreels and daily newspapers.) The pleasure of familiarity came partly from the radio's organisation of time – broadcasting provided a predictable rhythm to leisure – and partly from the use of repetition – the radio audience became the community of the catch phrase. Either way, expectations were always confirmed, and this, in the end, was the joy of listening. The BBC represented its listeners to themselves. What was (and is) enjoyable is the sense that you too can become significant by turning on the switch.

Notes

1. F. R. Leavis (ed.), *Towards Standards of Criticism*, London, 1976, p. xvi; B. Bergonzi, *Reading the Thirties*, London, 1978, p. 143. And see D. Hebdige, 'Towards a cartography of taste' in *Block* no. 4, 1981, pp. 42–3.
2. Quoted in Bergonzi op. cit. p. 142.
3. Quoted in P. Scannell and D. Cardiff, 'Serving the nation: public service broadcasting before the war' in B. Waites, A. Bennett and G. Thompson (eds), *Popular Culture Past and Present*, London, 1981, pp. 180–1. And see T. Burns, *The BBC: Public Institution and Private World*, London, 1977, pp. 38–9.
4. Quoted in R. Manvell, *On the Air*, London, 1953, p. 46.
5. Burns op. cit. p. 42.
6. See D. G. Bridson, *Prospero and Ariel* London, 1971, p. 205; B. Coulton, *Louis McNeice in the BBC* London, 1980, pp. 44–5; V. Gielgud, *British Radio Drama 1922–1956*, London 1957, p. 185; M. Pegg *British Radio Broadcasting and its Audience, 1918–1939*, Oxford D. Phil 1979, pp. 199, 227–231.
7. See Scannell and Cardiff op. cit.; P. Scannell, 'Music for the multitude? The dilemmas of

the BBC's music policy, 1923–1946' in *Media Culture and Society*, vol. 3 no. 3, 1981; D. Cardiff 'The serious and the popular: aspects of the evolution of style in the radio talk, 1928–1939' in *Media Culture and Society*, vol. 2 no. 1, 1980.

8. See A. Briggs, *The History of Broadcasting in the UK, volume 1*, London, 1961, pp. 235–9.

9. Young also argued that 'your wireless set, however simple or however elaborate, should never be an ugly thing.' *BBC Handbook 1928* pp. 115, 349–351. And see F. Young, *Shall I Listen. Studies in the Adventure and Technique of Broadcasting*, London, 1933, pp. 70–76.

10. Hilda Matheson, *Broadcasting*, London 1933, p. 156; C. A. Lewis, *Broadcasting from Within*, London, 1942, pp. 114–115; V. Gielgud, *Years of the Locust*, London, 1947, pp. 103–4. And see A. Briggs, *The History of Broadcasting in the UK, volume 2*, London, 1965, pp. 74.

11. Quote from Manvell op. cit. p. 57.

12. Quoted in J. C. W. Reith, *Into The Wind*, London, 1949, p. 116.

13. J. Reith, *Broadcast Over Britain*, London, 1924, pp. 147–8; Lewis op. cit. pp. 51–2, 155. And see A. Briggs vol. 1, pp. 81, 251–3.

14. Burns op. cit. pp. 19–20.

15. V. Gielgud, *British Radio Drama*, pp. 33, 5.

16. *ibid*. pp. 60–1, 68, 89. And see V. Gielgud, *Years of the Locust*, ch. IX.

17. Lewis op. cit. p. 175; J. C. W. Reith, *Into The Wind*, p. 135.

18. Marconi advertisement, quoted in S. Briggs, *Those Radio Times*, London, 1981, p. 87; Lewis op. cit. p. 176.

19. Reith, quoted in S. Briggs op. cit. p. 97.

20. *BBC Handbook 1928*, p. 34. And see M. Chanan, *The Dream That Kicks*, London, 1980, p. 148.

21. Matheson op. cit. p. 160; *BBC Handbook 1928*, p. 89.

22. Lewis op. cit. p. 176; S. Briggs op. cit. p. 148; Bridson op. cit. pp. 57–8; Jack Payne, 'This is Jack Payne', London, 1932, pp. 56–8, 83; Jack Payne, *Signature Tune*, London, 1947, pp. 109–111.

23. W. Weber, *Music and the Middle Class*, London, 1975, pp. 26, 30–33.

24. See Pegg op. cit. passim and Scannell and Cardiff op. cit. pp. 185–188.

25. Quoted in A. Briggs vol. 1, p. 256. See Cardiff op. cit. for a much fuller discussion of radio talk.

26. Bridson op. cit. pp. 51–2.

27. See Coulson op. cit. p. 42; J. C. Canell, *In Town Tonight*, London, 1935.

28. L. Henry, *My Laugh Story*, London, 1937, p. 36.

29. Payne quoted in A. McCarthy, *The Dance Band Era*, London 1971, p. 76.

30. *ibid*. 129–130. And see R. L. Taylor, *Art, an Enemy of the People*, Hassocks, 1978, pp. 145–9.

31. See S. Colin, *And The Bands Played On*, London, 1977, pp. 45, 86.

32. *The Gramophone Critic and Society Review*, Oct. 1928 and July 1929.

33. McCarthy op. cit. p. 54.

34. I discuss this is more detail in 'The making of the British record industry, 1920–1964', in J. Curran, A. Smith and P. Wingate (eds), *The Impact of the Mass Media in the 20th Century*, forthcoming.

35. See Christopher Stone, *Christopher Stone Speaking*, London, 1933, passim; R. Pearsall, *Popular Music of the 1920s*, Newton Abbot, 1976, ch. 1.

36. For the BBC's relationship with show business see A. Briggs vol. 1, pp. 251–3 and vol. 2, pp. 89–94.

37. G. Orwell, *The Road to Wigan Pier*, Penguin edition, 1962, pp. 80–1, 141.

Grahame Thompson

CARNIVAL AND THE CALCULABLE:
Consumption and Play at Blackpool

Blackpool, proclaims its 1981 Holiday Brochure, is the 'Fun City' of Europe –
'It's Got the Lot!' But what does it have the lot of? And how is this plenitude
socially organised? My focus here is on how the particular mix of leisure-
based pleasures on offer at Blackpool is presented and consumed. This will
mean opening up some of the enigmatic terms in which leisure is usually
discussed – fun, amusement, play and, especially, *pleasure* and *consumption*.
These two I see as a series of differentiated activities involving different sets
of determinations and consequences – they are more accurately pleasures
and consumptions. I am less concerned with *what* they are than with *how*
they are constructed and *how* they operate. In this, my approach differs from
those that attempt to establish a general relationship between the individual
and the social – in the manner of, say, Marcuse's argument that the reality
principle of the 'social' constrains the pleasure principle of the 'individual'.[1]
Nor does it first construct a social field of pleasures and an individual or
psychic field of pleasures and then juxtapose (or even articulate) these
together. Instead, my analysis operates *between* the social and the individual
– it picks up a series of strands from the 'social' and the 'individual' *in passing*
as it were and knits these together as they create specific effects of pleasure
within the social and the individual through particular activities. In other
words, I don't start off by assuming that pleasure is a known quantity and
then find examples of it. Instead, in examining how play is organised at
Blackpool, I try to identify the character of the effects produced within those
aspects of the social and the individual which are 'pleasurable'. The question
is not how either the reality principle or the pleasure principle dominates the
other, but rather how their existence as a series of registers within each other
is mapped with respect to particular instances of their operation in the
amusements of Blackpool.

What is it about Blackpool that attracts nearly fifteen million visits from
holidaymakers and day trippers each year? Above all, of course, Blackpool is
a sea-side resort. The beach offers a particular fascination, bringing into play
pleasurable differences between sea and land, wet and dry, nature and
culture. These offer a certain excitation for the body – its exposure to sun and
water, for example, with their supposedly health giving properties and the

uncertainties and tensions associated with them produce a relaxation of social protocols and taboos, allowing for relatively unconstrained social fraternization. The beach also provides a focus for family relaxation and play.

The spatial organization of the town has been determined by the beach in two ways. The 'front' imposes a physical boundary, broken only by the North, Central and South Piers. And people's habit of making for the sea first defines the main axis of movement within Blackpool – the east/west journey between hotel or guest house and the beach. Increasingly important, however, is the north/south axis of the promenade. Originally a leisurely, aristocratic space for taking the air, since the first real prom was opened around 1870 this has become the central focus of commercial activity – especially in the amusement arcades, eating places and shops packed into the half mile or so between the North and Central Piers, the famous Golden Mile. At night or on rainy days this fun area becomes the primary focus of attraction. And although the older generation and those with small children may still concentrate on the beach, for the young and mobile the pubs, discos and fun palaces may have more to offer.

Apart from its beach and Golden Mile, Blackpool is best known for its Tower. A glance at the brochures produced by Blackpool Corporation since the turn of the century shows the Tower, opened in 1894, to be an enduring symbol of the town and its pleasures. It also adds a third dimension to the east/west and north/south axes of movement. Rather like the beach/sea interface, it offers some specific pleasures by transcending the normal and day-to-day. It enables the holidaymaker to enjoy Blackpool from a different perspective, rather as Roland Barthes describes the experience of the Eiffel Tower.[2] The Tower looks at Paris, Barthes suggests. Its 'gaze' involves the doubly structured consumption of differentiated space – structured once through the pleasure of a panoramic vision and then through a reaction against this euphoria, articulated through a struggle to decipher the space, to recognise particular points and patterns within it. This work of the imagination (and of memory/knowledge) renders the vision of Paris comprehensible and consumable – but consumed in this instance as nothing more than a pleasurable experience.

Types of Consumption at Blackpool

The pleasures of Blackpool as a holiday resort are socially organised in part through these patterns of spatial and physical differentiation. To understand how they are offered for consumption, we should first distinguish between what is *free* and what is *for sale* – especially as these do not coincide exactly with ownership categories of *public* and *private*. Thus nearly all the sites of pleasure are owned and controlled by private interests rather than

the municipality. The Corporation is responsible for the beach and the promenade, runs the transport, provides the Illuminations and manages the town's few open spaces, including the large Stanley Park and Zoo at the rear of the town. The three piers, the Winter Gardens complex, the Tower complex and two of the larger leisure complexes are all owned by one company, Trust House Forte – which thus has a near monopoly of the major entertainment sites. The Pleasure Beach, as Tony Bennett notes, is owned by a private company including members of the founding family, but companies like Coral (and until recently EMI Entertainments) have interests in other amusement sites. Entertainment at Blackpool is clearly very big business. The Ken Dodd Spectacular, for instance, was running at the 3,000 seat Opera House in the Winter Gardens complex twice-nightly, six nights a week between June and October in 1981!

Entrance to the privately owned piers and amusement arcades is 'free', although once entered they offer the consumer all manner of pleasures which have to be paid for. The free entry, then, is a kind of loss-leader which draws the consumer into a field of paid-for activities. Equally, to sit on a deck-chair or take a donkey ride on the 'free', publically owned beach costs money. There are very few public spaces in Blackpool which do not provide a context for private commercial relations. (I am using 'payment' and 'free' in their literal sense – economists would rightly point out that much of what I designate 'free' has to be paid for indirectly, whether through cross-subsidization from paid-for activities, through the rates or whatever. Nevertheless, this free/paid-for boundary does have social consequences *as such*.)

For the purposes of this discussion, consumption is defined as a sphere of economic or commercial activity combining the act of purchase and consumption to satisfy a specific desire. It involves not the production of a tangible object but the inducement of a series of *effects* for the consuming agent. Of course, a purchase often involves buying the anticipation of a pleasurable effect, which may or may not materialize. All consumption is in that sense overdetermined by the anticipation of pleasure – the field of pleasure is never entirely exhausted by the individual acts of consumption that take place within it. The psychic economy – and to some extent the real economy as well! – is driven by the motor of the possibility of unpleasure (pain) in the pursuit of pleasure, which continually renews the conditions for discharge. This conception of pleasure and consumption has at least two advantages over orthodox economic accounts. It provides a way of theorizing the re-production of that which is to be released through or as pleasure, and it avoids the notion that commodities contain a given amount of pleasure which they gradually release during the process of consumption.

This tension between the anticipation of a pleasurable experience and the possibility of the experience being painful lends a peculiar intensity to the consumption of pleasure in the strong sense. By 'the strong sense' I mean a socially coded event in which the primary *intention* of a purchase is the anticipation of physical pleasure as such – to 'have some fun', to 'enjoy yourself' and so on – as distinct from purchase and consumption designed, say, to quench one's thirst or help in a tedious household task. These have other determinations and consequences, even though pleasure as an unconsciously articulated pleasure still cannot be ignored. But it is not a pleasurable experience as such that is being purchased. The general point, however, is that pleasure cannot really be discussed without its other – the possibility of pain – also being involved. A repetition is set up through the dissemination of tension by the (attempted) avoidance of *un*pleasure.

Goods

To exemplify these arguments I shall concentrate on my observations of the amusements that could be purchased along the Golden Mile, on the piers and, in general terms, the Pleasure Beach in the summer of 1981. In terms of buying tangible goods, this consumption of pleasure (and pleasure of consumption) contrasts markedly with day-to-day shopping at home. It could be termed *impulse leisure consumption*. This involves the – literally consumable – holiday treats of ice creams, rock, nuts and fruit, but many other goods as well. These may be as ephemeral as printed jokes and horoscopes. Masks and hats, often with saucy slogans, are very popular – JR stetsons were selling well in 1981. So were personalised T-shirts. A number of shops and stalls sell brightly coloured glass figurines. Others specialise in fluffy dolls and animals and rather garish items in 'Nottingham Lace'.

Blackpool thus offers the scope for what might be called 'working-class conspicuous consumption' – economically modest but indiscreetly vulgar in comparison with the upper-middle class variety. It is this very outlandish-ness that signifies the relaxation of the normal disciplines of consumption when on holiday. Moral and economic restraints on eating, drinking and spending money give way to indulgence and excess. The pleasure comes from breaking taboos without provoking serious consequences. But these particular types of consumption do not simply emanate from an individual-ized impulse to break rules. They are actively encouraged. Potential custom-ers are aggressively 'hailed' or 'addressed', principally through the forms of displaying goods. These use lighting and mirrors in flamboyant ways and provide unusual juxtapositions of very bright and garish colours or pastel shades. They render the ordinary bizarre by exaggerating it or putting it into an unexpected context. They bring the exotic and the taboo into play within the consumable field. People are encouraged to spend by this *disorganization* of the normal, 'acceptable' routines of consumption.

However marked the contrast with 'normal life', however, the organ-ization of consumption at Blackpool does have a clear commercial logic – this applies as much to paid-for games and amusements as to the purchase of goods. Its time régime, for instance, consists of complicated overlapping rhythms. Even though some of these may not differ that much from normal daily routines, leisure activities are certainly displaced and reorganized to increase opportunities for spending money. Amusements begin to open up around ten in the morning and continue for the most part until eleven or twelve at night. The first bingo call tends to be around 10.30 a.m., the last at 10.30 p.m. It is not uncommon to find several hundred dancers in the Tower Ballroom at eleven in the morning. Sing-alongs are encouraged in several large pubs at lunchtimes as well as in the evenings.

Playing Games

Transactions at Blackpool often involve the purchase not of goods but of the chance to take part in games or amusements – the chance to win a prize, a gambling stake, having your fortune read, a turn on a Space Invaders machine or in a shooting gallery, a ride on the dodgem cars or a roller coaster. What are the characteristic features of these different activities? According to René Caillois,[3] two important elements in games are *competition* and *chance*. In competition, the skills and ingenuity of players are pitted against each other and/or obstacles within defined limits. These rules usually attempt to equalize these differences and give each competitor a 'fair' chance to win. The fascination of games of pure chance has nothing to do with the qualities of the players but lies in their very capriciousness. Who wins is arbitrary: these games are always pregnant with the possibility of losing.

Chance and competition are therefore oppositional but complementary. They involve mechanisms for rendering down differences – or rather, for re-creating another field of differences within an alternative set of rules. Whereas in 'ordinary life' differences and antagonisms seem arbitrary and perplexing and the conditions of equality are subject to intense struggle, debate and uncertainty, in games the rules define a known, artificial 'space' in which differences are created in relations of equality. Players enter the rules of a game and then step out of them, in most cases within a defined time span and a particular arena. This enables games to offer a certain release and a certain comfort: the struggle within them is highly articulated, conditional and contingent. That is why they cannot easily be characterized by a series of generalized rules and features.

Play also involves an element of *simulation* or *mimicry* – a mixture of make-believe, illusion and imagination in which the subject both 'escapes itself' and also makes others believe and escape themselves. Presenting oneself as ridiculous – putting on masks or silly hats, posing in a hall of mirrors, fooling around – encourages a legitimate laughter. Such exhibitionism requires (or engenders) spectators, and so creates the communal complicity and fraternization essential to the enjoyment of resorts like Blackpool.

The final feature of the game form is *instability*, what Caillois calls *vertigo*. The normal steadiness of personal 'position' and perception is suddenly disrupted by a momentary shudder of panic. Many Blackpool amusements provide this escape from the 'tyranny of the ordinary'. They release the normally suppressed desire for disorder of the body by offering physical and/or mental thrills and (the possibility of) spills. Rides like big dippers or ghost trains are intense and quickly over, but there is a pleasurable tension in the knowing build-up to the actual event. There is also an element of vertigo in one-armed bandits, although the dislocation of stability is here transferred to the machine. The reels or balls are disordered momentarily by the pull of a handle or the release of a trigger.

Like competition and chance, mimicry and instability tend to elide differences – we are all open to be mimicked, we are all panicky on the roller coaster. To some extent, then, these aspects of play render us equal before them and so render into a specific relationship an otherwise disparate, non-specific and unknown series of personalized qualities and differences. Thus, along with pleasure, equity and fairness are *constructed* within the matrix of play. They are no more a natural part of play than the artificially created fairness and equality of the chance/competition combination.

All these elements of the game form can be usurped or corrupted – this is another of their pleasures. Competition can be corrupted by professional-ization, whch narrows the odds on who will win, or by cheating. In a way, cheating can actually be part of the game – it violates the rules without *disrupting* them. The real problem is the spoil-sport who won't accept the rules or won't play. There is little chance of cheating the professionals or the machines in Blackpool: the only option is not to take part. Chance can also be undermined in two ways. The first is a belief in superstition. This ascribes to chance a heart and a memory, so that it is no longer an impersonal power. This belief is manifest in the long established fortune tellers that co-exist with games of chance at Blackpool.[4] In 1981 five Gipsy clairvoyants re-mained on the Golden Mile and the Central Pier, along with innumerable mechanical devices for issuing horoscopes. The other corruption of chance is calculation – the rational assessment of risks and probabilities. Mimicry can be negated through the discomforting experience of role playing, the loss of self or fracturing subjectivity that can be brought to the surface by looking in at oneself from outside. Finally, instability itself can be usurped in a kind of double disruption. This is characterized by the search for an *acceptable* risk that simulates vertigo without provoking its full destructive implications. Rides on roller coasters, dodgem cars or The Revolution at Blackpool leave the punters fleetingly and intermittently stunned, but always return them to a state of regained equilibrium and co-ordination.

As I have already mentioned, social relations at Blackpool are more communal than elsewhere. People usually move around in groups on holiday. Such fraternization is also often a feature of play – even an apparently individualized game like bingo tends to be a *social* event for those taking part.[5] But games cannot simply be lumped under the single heading 'sociable events'. The sociability of different types of play is differently constructed and has variable consequences. Take the example of slot machines, one-armed bandits, Space Invaders and so forth. The way these are organized in amusement arcades and leisure complexes is less chaotic than it appears at first sight. Although most are based on a limited number of simple principles – shooting at targets provides the basis for ingenious variation – there is a judicious juxtaposition of machines involving a pure gamble, those offering the chance to win something and those providing the opportunity to indulge in an unfamiliar situation. Slot machines, pin-ball machines and the like are usually banked together in threes or fours.

Although the games themselves involve the attempts of one player to dominate one machine, this arrangement encourages group participation – the pleasure of *collective individuality* rather than the collective mutuality discussed by Tony Bennett.

Another attractive feature of these machines is the way they embody 'pre-decision'.[6] All the player's assessments are made *before* the game starts – the outcome is decided entirely by the playing of the machine. Afterwards there are no more decisions or arguments and no appeal against the outcome. The game is over. Its ending is usually abrupt and unexpected. This gives the games their peculiar intensity. Everything is staked before the game commences – something which does not often happen in normal life, where consequences and arguments follow after events. In playing the machines there is only a short time before the total but limited field of consequences is known absolutely. Machines like Space Invaders involve not only a short time span – one minute on average – but also a remarkably intense condensation of activities, involving sight, sound and touch. They can be quite testing, requiring both mental agility and physical dexterity and co-ordination. They require a reactive rather than a reasoned strategic approach, however. The player not only has to hit the Invaders, but also has to miss being hit by them. The constraints are clearly demarcated and this gives the player a limited but full range for the display of power. Some unexpected but not random events are built into the machine. The experienced player can eventually learn these, and so may tire of the game when the unexpected becomes the anticipated.

The machines are not innovative of themselves, which may account for the number of variations on a theme to be found in amusement arcades. People can thus move from a known machine to a similar yet different one – there is a fascination with difference and repetition. One-armed bandits can be varied by introducing STOP and NUDGE buttons. This implies a greater degree of skill from the player and pretends to add greater competition into the essentially chance based character of the machines. Variety can also be introduced through the range of cultural references and connotations incorporated into the machines and their decoration. Royal themes are common, making reference both to the royal family and to card games. Pin-ball machines especially portray popular cultural heroes like Mohammed Ali or The Rolling Stones.

Calculation and Carnival

Games and play, I have argued, are neither unstructured nor characterized by a voluptuous freedom. Rules are an inseparable part of them and govern their disorder and disturbance. This clearly applies to games based on competition and/or chance. In tennis or poker, for example, comparatively simple scoring systems build uncertainty and insecurity into the play – they foster dramatic reversals of fortune on the basis of even slight changes in the performance or luck of the competitors. These scoring systems have the effect of under-exaggerating differences in skill. In one sense, they compensate for the *lack* of chance in games based on training, ability and experience – like professional tennis, for example. Thus the degree of chance in games of competition and chance is not natural. It is a constructed characteristic, operating through the effects harnessed by the principles of calculation embodied in scoring systems.

If the order in these games is based on the principle of calculation, what about play characterized by elements of mimicry and instability? As Tony Bennett shows, these are the typical features of *carnival*, which Bakhtin saw primarily in terms of transgression.[7] That does not mean that the carnivalesque is un-ordered. Rather, it is subject to a different order – the law of transgression, a kind of refusal to define and to specify. A certain ambivalence or ambiguity thus creeps into activity in which symbolic relationships and analogy take precedence over substantive and causal relationships. New meanings can be given to (and result from) an established bricolage of activities. The carnival challenges the authority of 'social laws'. It is a rebellious event in which prohibitions and their transgression co-exist and so specify an ambiguous representation. Carnival is a play without a stage. The participant, both actor and audience, loses a sense of individuality by passing through a zero point of carnivalesque activity and splitting into a subject of the spectacle and an object of the game. The player is rendered into a *double*.[8] This is not simply a parody, which would tend to reinforce the law of the acceptable. This laughter is more provocative and serious – it undermines that law by laughing *at* it.

On the dodgem cars, for example, the normal and the acceptable are inverted. Instead of trying to avoid other cars, the object is to hit them. There are no explicit rules, but some ill-defined ones are apparent. Although the maximum effect can be achieved by hitting other cars head on, this is only ambiguously condoned. One of the ill-defined rules is not to do this – and so a driver can enjoy transgressing it by attempting the manoeuvre. At the other extreme, the 'cool' driver can transgress by deliberately avoiding *any* collisions. It is these ambivalences and ambiguities in the ill-defined rules that make the dodgems carnivalesque. A similar argument could be made about certain types of material consumption at Blackpool. There is a grotesque realism in dentures and plates of breakfast food made from edible rock or in the purchase of funny hats or masks. It could be argued that the potentially disruptive effects of these objects are rendered harmless because they are made available through commercial interests – their transgressiveness is never realized because it is overdetermined by ultra-rule governed commercial criteria. While this may be partly true, it does reveal the ambiguity of meaning in the act of purchase. From the seller's point of view it is rule-governed, rational and calculable, whereas from the buyer's point of view it is rebellious and liberational – in a word, pleasurable. The reality principle does not thereby undermine the operation of the pleasure principle. It can actually intensify its effects.

There is also a rather complex interplay between the reality principle and the pleasure principle in the competition/chance matrix. I have already argued that calculation represents an attempt to tame the element of chance in these games. Although the systematic assessment of probabilities opens up the possibility of gambling, the *pleasure* of gambling cannot be reduced to such mathematical rationalism. Its attractions also involve ingenuity and improvisation. In any case, when making a bet it is impossible to construct all the relevant data *a priori*. Error, caprice, luck and arbitrary decisions or events always play a part. So too, in a somewhat different way, does a deliberate desire to lose.[9] As we have seen, the pleasure of the game is inseparable from the risk of losing. The calculation of probabilities has its own pleasures, and this 'mathematisation' can become a game in its own right. But it takes place as it were *alongside* games and play. If it were ever to exclude the element of random chance, it would destroy them.

At Blackpool and elsewhere, then, gambling and calculation are closely connected but not identical. They exist in a relationship of tension. This may perhaps explain why gambling sometimes changes from a transient and diffused 'flutter' and becomes a *compulsion* and an *obsession*. In his essay on 'Dostoevsky and Parricide', Freud suggests that the fascination with the possibility of loss may be connected with that radical separation (loss) involving mother and child.[10] This would mean that at the unconscious level, the gambler always begins from an *already lost/won position*. He or she is trying to regain this position, and it is the possibility of winning/losing that allows this unpleasure to be lived as pleasure. The primal loss can here be replayed without its traumatic consequences – unless a combination with other personality traits dictates that the separation becomes psychically consequential. The desire to win/lose may allow unpleasure to be lived as pleasure – the two would thus not be in opposition.

Parody and Pleasure

Games and amusements at Blackpool are organized around a series of oppositions and contrasts which seem to be geared to the possibility of *disorganization* and *disruption*. But this potential is not realised. Cultural themes and motifs apparently ripe for transgression are either missing or significantly underplayed. For instance, in 1981, the year of *the* Royal Wedding, the few references to royalty tended to be laudatory – the vogue for wearing monstrous 'Prince Charles Ears' was an important but very limited exception. Nor was there any noticeable ridicule of the established

churches or of religious figures and rituals. The treatment of sex (and to a lesser extent, death) is more complex. Sex and death, I would suggest, are not transgressed or disrupted at Blackpool. Rather, they are *parodied*. Blackpool has no equivalent to Soho (I could find no magazine and aid shops or strip joints!) 'Bad taste' and spectacular displays of commercial sex are kept to a minimum – knitted 'willy warmers' seemed to represent the limit of permissable transgression. This is no doubt connected to the prohibitions characteristic of the town's municipal and commercial tradition, but there is also a peculiar coyness in the ways sex is parodied. The Ken Dodd Spectacular illustrates the attitude perfectly. Sex is continually alluded to without being confronted directly – Ken Dodd himself is like a living saucy post-card. His jokes produce a snigger or a giggle, but actually leave the existing boundaries of the sexual field perfectly in place. That is not to say that sex is unimportant at Blackpool – far from it. A wander along the promenade on a summer's day demonstrates that, despite Blackpool almost, it is provocatively on display. But the disruption of normal behaviour is brought *to* the town by the visitors. It is one pleasure that Blackpool does not offer for consumption.

A final word on pleasure. My argument has been that, far from the full potential of the release of pleasure being denied (and hence repressed) by the cultural (social) restraints placed on it by the reality principle, the excitation involved in pleasure is actually enhanced by the confrontation with the reality principle. The reality principle is thus registered within the pleasure principle as an unpleasure, but this unpleasure is then part of pleasure. In this confrontation, unpleasure is lived as pleasure – thus confirming the operation of the pleasure principle. Its heightening/enhancement/confirmation is secured as the 'obstacle' of the reality principle is 'overcome' within the field of pleasure itself.[11] One corollary of this argument is to call into question the formalistic division of pleasure into two opposed types – as in some popular renderings of the relationship between *jouissance* (bliss) and *plaisir* (pleasure). Even in the most sophisticated versions of this distinction, there remains a danger of reducing the 'social' to the 'psyche'. In examining the production of pleasures through the organization of consumption and play at Blackpool, I have tried to offer a space between these two possibilities.

Notes

1. Herbert Marcuse, *Eros and Civilization*, Boston, Beacon Press, 1966.
2. Roland Barthes, *The Eiffel Tower and Other Mythologies*, New York, Hill and Wang, 1979.
3. René Caillois, *Man, Play and Games*, London, Thames and Hudson, 1962.
4. See Tom Harrison, *Britain Revisited*, London, Gollancz, 1961.
5. D. M. Downes *et al.*, *Gambling, Work and Leisure*, London, Routledge & Kegan Paul, 1976.
6. Erving Goffman, 'Where the action is' in *Interaction Ritual*, Harmondsworth, Penguin, 1972.

7. M. M. Bakhtin, *Rabelais and his World*, Cambridge (USA), MIT Press, 1965.
8. See Julia Kristeva, *Desire in Language*, Oxford, Basil Blackwell, 1980.
9. E. Bergler, *The Psychology of Gambling*, London, International University Press, 1958.
10. S. Freud, 'Dostoevsky and Parricide' in *Standard Edition of the Complete Psychological Works of Sigmund Freud* Vol. XXI, London, Hogarth Press, 1961.
11. S. Freud, 'Beyond the Pleasure Principle', in *Standard Edition of the Complete Psychological Works of Sigmund Freud* Vol. XVIII, London, Hogarth Press, 1955.

Tony Bennett

A THOUSAND AND ONE TROUBLES:
Blackpool Pleasure Beach

BLACKPOOL PLEASURE BEACH
Europe's greatest amusement park
Home of the largest collection of
'White Knuckle' Rides in Europe

Everything here is bigger and better: the Space Tower *not only takes you to the top of its 160 feet, but does the viewing for you as it spirals around its slender column. The* Grand National *is the only double track coaster ride in Europe, whilst the* Steeplechase *is unique in having three tracks for racing. Where else can you hurtle through 360° and view* Blackpool Pleasure Beach *upside down – only here on the* Revolution *– a thrill filled sooperdooperlooper. Or experience the sensations of an astronaut in the upside-downess of the* Starship Enterprise . . . *Or hurtle round the figure of eight track on our* Tokaydo Express . . . *Or experience the unusual sensations of riding the* Tidal Wave *and racing on our own* Grand Prix . . . *all within a few hundred yards?*

Such claims, taken from a 1981 publicity leaflet, are typical of the way Blackpool Pleasure Beach represents itself, and has always represented itself – as offering the biggest, the best, the only one of its kind, the unique, the latest, the most up-to-the-minute range of thrills, spills and popular entertainment. It is always one step ahead, always changing – 'The *Pleasure Beach* is never static'[1] – constantly 'in search of new rides which will appeal to the Blackpool public', unrivalled even its claims to be unrivalled. Although in its name pleasure struts forth in an unusually brazen way, the Pleasure Beach is neatly decked out in the clothes of modernity. Not only in publicity handouts, but in the names, themes, design and lay-out of the principal rides and in its architecture, pleasure at the Pleasure Beach is rigorously constructed under the signs of modernity, progress, the future, America. Its face is the bold face of the new. Operating on the threshold between the present and the future, the Pleasure Beach harnesses for our pleasure the technologies developed at the outer limits of progress ('Bright colours and geometric shapes reflect the use of glass fibre and thermoplastics in construction'); it anticipates the future in making advanced technologies a part of the here and now (its operating monorail is 'the first of its kind in

Europe'). The past, with qualified exceptions, is as dead as a dodo. In this article, I want to consider the different types of pleasure that are available at the Pleasure Beach, the ways they are organized and the signs under which they are coded for consumption. Taken together, these constitute a distinct 'régime of pleasure' which occupies a special place in relation to the rest of Blackpool.

Modernity and Respectability

Although a *part of* Blackpool in the sense that it is central to the town's commercial well-being and, in turn, dependent on it – an independent source of attraction which brings business to the rest of Blackpool as well as feeding off the business which the rest of Blackpool provides – the Pleasure Beach is also *apart from* Blackpool, a recognisably distinct sub-system in the overall organization of pleasure which the town offers. In the first place, it is geographically separate. Located on the southern edge of the town, it is separated from the town centre leisure-pleasure complexes – the Tower, the Golden Mile and the Central Pier – by a 'pleasure-barren' half to three-quarters of a mile of hotels and boarding houses. Just south of the Pleasure Beach, Blackpool – not Blackpool as a municipal entity but Blackpool as 'fun city' – stops abruptly, as an arch over the road bids the visitor goodbye. This geographical isolation is reinforced by a circular wall which encloses the Pleasure Beach, segregating it from the terraced houses at its rear and from the promenade at its front. Nor does this wall just mark a physical separation. It also constitutes a symbolic boundary, operating definite inclusions and exclusions which, to a degree, mark off the forms of pleasure available within it from those available outside it in the rest of Blackpool.

Most obviously, many of the 'excesses' which characterise forms of consumption in the rest of Blackpool – giant foam-rubber stetsons, carnival-like masks, willy-warmers – are not available in the Pleasure Beach. This difference is accentuated by the display of these items in a short row of shops and stalls just outside the Pleasure Beach. More generally, pleasure wears a more uniform face in the Pleasure Beach than it does in the rest of Blackpool. In an impressionistic survey of Blackpool written in the 1930s, Tom Harrison, founder of the Mass Observation movement, commented on the incredibly diverse forms of pleasure competing with each other along the promenade – traditional fortune tellers, quack medicines, appeals to the orient and to mysticism, freaks and monstrosities, conjuring tricks and unbelievable spectacles jostling for space with the joke shops and amusement arcades.[2] Something of this diversity remains in the centre of Blackpool, although even here the face of pleasure has been considerably smoothed and streamlined – there are far fewer independent side-shows than there used to be even in the 1960s. The once messy and variegated sprawl of the Golden Mile, with its mass of rival stalls and side-shows, has been converted into a large, integrated indoor entertainments complex run by EMI.

In the Pleasure Beach, by contrast, pleasure is resolutely modern. Its distinctive 'hail' to pleasure-seekers is constructed around the large mechanical rides, unavailable elsewhere in Blackpool and packaged for consumption as a manifestation of progress harnessed for pleasure. There are amusement arcades, bingo stalls, rifle ranges and so on – but no freak shows, no quack medicine, no mysticism and only one fortune teller. Even those forms of entertainment that are widely available at other amusement parks and travelling fairs are here reconstructed under the sign of modernity. The dodgems were billed as 'The first in Europe direct from America' when they were first introduced around 1909. Now, according to *The Pleasure Beach Story*, 'the old Dodgem tubs of pre-war days have been transformed into Auto Skooters, which are built here at Blackpool Pleasure Beach, centre of the British Fun Industry'. They are in fact indistinguishable from dodgems elsewhere but, as a once up-to-the-minute ride which has become traditional, they have been retrieved as super-modern.

Pleasure has not always been so unambiguously coded at the Pleasure Beach. Nor have its relations to the rest of Blackpool always been the same. The Pleasure Beach occupies what used to be, in the mid-nineteenth century, a gipsy encampment where, in the summer, both the resident families and itinerant entertainers offered a variety of traditional entertainments – astrology, fortune-telling, palmistry, phrenology and so on.[3] Mechanical rides were first developed on this South Shore site (originally just a vast area of sand stretching back from and continuous with the beach) in the late 1880s – a period which witnessed similar developments in other parts of the town, especially in the town-centre at Raikes Hall, an open-air pleasure centre modelled on Manchester's Belle Vue Gardens. The South Shore site, at this time, was merely a jumble of independently owned and operated mechanical rides existing cheek by jowl with the gipsy amusements. The origins of the Pleasure Beach can be traced to 1895 when two local entrepreneurs, John W. Outhwaite, who operated the Switchback Railway on the South Shore, and William George Bean, a one-time amusement park engineer in America who operated the Hotchkiss Bicycle Railway on the South Shore, bought the forty acres of sand on which the mechanical rides and the gipsy encampment were located. Prompted by the closure of Raikes Hall, which reduced the competition for mechanically induced spills and thrills from the town centre, their aim was to develop the South Shore site as an integrated open-air pleasure complex on the model of American amusement parks.

There were two obstacles to be surmounted: the opposition of rival business interests, particularly those which had invested in the new pleas-

The nineteenth-century gipsy encampment.

ure complexes like the Tower and the Winter Gardens in the town-centre, and the continued presence of gipsy homes and entertainments on the site. Both were overcome by the election of Bean to the town council in 1907. This enabled the interests of the Pleasure Beach to be represented in the local political machinery alongside those of their rivals. Nor was it any coinci dence that, in the same year, a set of new Fairground Regulations was announced which forbade gambling, clairvoyance and quack medicine on all fairground sites in Blackpool and declared that no 'gipsy's shed, tent, caravan or encampment shall be permitted on any part of the land set apart as a Fair Ground'. This enabled the eviction of itinerant gipsies from the Pleasure Beach in the following year. (The site had been christened The Pleasure Beach in 1906, the company of The Blackpool Pleasure Beach Ltd being formed in 1909). By 1910, the last of the permanent gipsy families had left.

This campaign against the gipsies was consistent with the general drive, manifest throughout Blackpool's history, to give pleasure an air of bourgeois respectability – a drive that has always been, to a degree, thwarted as a result of the town's peculiar structure of land tenure. As John Walton and Harold Perkin have both noted,[4] land ownership in Blackpool was extremely fragmented by the beginning of the nineteenth century, largely because the sale of the Layton estate, owned by the Clifton family, allowed the centre of the town to be split into small parcels. This contrasted sharply with resorts like Southport, where the dominance of large landholders allowed an integrated and planned development to cater for the respectable and well-to-do day-trippers and holidaymakers. The morsellisation of land tenure in Blackpool inhibited attempts to develop Blackpool along similar lines as it enabled the more commercially orientated entrepreneurs, with an eye on the working-class trade of the industrial towns of Lancashire and Yorkshire, to cater for the tastes of the 'non-respectable' in spite of the opposition of local magnates.

This is not to suggest that the history of Blackpool can be construed as one of unbridled commercialism riding rough-shod over opposing principles. To the contrary, it was not really until the 1880s that the working-class market became significant enough – both in size and in spending power – to prevail over the requirements of the middle-class visitors who had previously provided the town's mainstay. Elegance, respectability and cultivation – these were the watchwords of Blackpool's early history, and the town quite deliberately sought to maintain a lofty air which would exclude *hoi polloi*. However, such attempts were consistently undercut by the ease with which entrepreneurs could buy town-centre sites and evade corporation regulations. The first pier, today's North Pier, opened in May 1863, aiming above all at dignity. It was an elegant walk-way over the sea, utterly lacking in commercial embellishment – but in 1868 it was forced to provide various forms of diversion as its revenues declined after the rival South Jetty opened. Today's Central Pier, this was known at the time as 'The People's Pier'; it offered dancing from dawn to dusk, seven days a week. Similarly, in the theatre, it took a succession of financial failures before the town's impresarios accommodated themselves to popular taste – a shift nicely encapsulated in the contrast between the founding ambition of the Winter Gardens' shareholders to provide 'high class entertainment which no lady or gentleman would object to see' to the maxim of Billy Holland, appointed manager of the Winter Gardens in 1881: 'Give 'em what they want'. The origins of The Golden Mile perhaps indicate most clearly the contradictory forces at play in Blackpool's development. As an unregulated zone, the beach had always been a trading area for itinerant hawkers, phrenologists, showmen and the like – much to the consternation of the local tradesmen who regarded these 'sandrats' as unfair competition driving away the town's 'respectable' business. Responding to this pressure, the Corporation prohibited trading on the beach in 1897, but this in turn provoked such a public outcry that the Corporation relented. 'Ventriloquists, Niggers, Punch and Judy, Camels, Ice Cream, Ginger Beer, Blackpool Rock, Sweets in Baskets and Oyster Sellers' could remain on the beach, but not 'phrenologists, "Quack" Doctors, Palmists, Mock Auctions and Cheap Jacks'. The result was that the prohibited traders merely set up shop in the forecourts of the houses fronting onto the promenade – the origins of The Golden Mile, an ideological scandal, an affront to the town's carefully constructed image of modernity and respectability.

At the Pleasure Beach, a single site under single ownership, it was possible to construct a more closely integrated régime of pleasure. Early photographs convey the impression of a quite different organization of pleasure from that which obtains today. The Pleasure Beach and the beach were virtually indistinguishable, with no physical boundaries separating the two. The rides and side-stalls were simply placed on the sand and some rival entertainments were installed on the beach itself. Pleasure-seekers moved uninterruptedly from the one to the other. They formed overlapping and merging (rather than separate and distinct) pleasure zones. The lay-out of rides was fairly haphazard, as gipsy stalls and side shows jostled for space with the big rides. The signs of pleasure were multiple and contradictory: the pleasure seeker could move from the futuristic vertigo of the Scenic Railway to the pseudo-past of a mock-Tudor village street in a few paces. During the pre- and immediately post-war years, the Pleasure Beach was not so much transformed as added to, mainly in the form of rides imported 'direct from America': the House of Nonsense, containing 'over 60 of the latest American Amusement Devices'; the Gee Whiz, 'The latest Invention and Most Intriguing Ride in Blackpool'.[5] Even the past was constructed under the sign of science. According to a contemporary report on a reproduction of the Battle of Monitor and Merrimac: 'With the aid of fine scientific

The Pleasure Beach, Easter 1913.

appliances, history has been made to live.' This appeal to America, to the future and to a super-modernity was not the only sign-ensemble under which pleasure was reconstructed during this period. There was also and still is a latent democracy of pleasure. The Social Mixer aimed to make 'Everybody Happy, Happy, Happy.' 'Everybody's Doing It' proclaimed the House of Nonsense, and the local paper recommended the Joy Wheel as a great social leveller: 'Nobody can be pompous on the Joy Wheel: we prescribe it as a cure for the swelled-head.' But the appeal to modernity was becoming the dominant form of 'barking'.

This was even more apparent in the 1920s and 1930s, when the Pleasure Beach began to acquire the collective form and identity that is still recognisable today. The extension of the promenade, which had hitherto stopped at the northern entrance to the Pleasure Beach, finally separated Pleasure Beach and beach into distinct zones. It was also at this time that the Pleasure Beach was walled off. More important perhaps, especially in the late 1930s, the Pleasure Beach hauled its architecture unequivocally into the age of the new. In the period around the Great War, many of the main architectural features had been imperial in their references. The Casino, the main entrance to the Beach and its architectural show-piece, was con-

The Casino, 1921.

structed in 1913 in the style of an Indian palace and many of the individual rides echoed this in their imitation of various other outposts of Empire. But now these recurring motifs of the oriental, the ornate and the exotic were swept away. Leonard Thompson, Bean's son-in-law and managing director of the Pleasure Beach at the time, commissioned Joseph Emberton, a leading modernist architect, to redesign the whole Pleasure Beach in a single style. The Casino became a clean white building with smooth lines and no frills, totally functional in appearance. The Fun House, heir to the timber House of Nonsense, was rebuilt in reinforced concrete to harmonise with the new Casino. The Grand National, in the same style, replaced the Scenic Railway. Even the architectural minutiae were modernised. The interior of the River Caves was restyled in cubist designs: so were the animals on the Noah's Ark, giving them an angular, futuristic appearance – a bizarre modernisation of the past! By the end of the 1930s, the Pleasure Beach looked resolutely modern. Its architecture of pleasure had taken on a streamlined, functional appearance. And the sand had been covered by asphalt. 'If you can see a foot of asphalt in August,' Leonard Thompson said, 'we aren't doing well'. The situationists of 1968 might have responded that, by the end of the 1930s, the Pleasure Beach had managed to bury 'la plage sous les pavés'.

Since the 1930s, the architectural modernity of the Pleasure Beach has been updated from time to time. In the 1950s Jack Radcliffe, designer of the Festival of Britain in 1951, was commissioned to give it a new look – largely by superimposing an American jazz and glitter on Emberton's clean white facades. In the 1960s most of the new rides were stylistically indebted to innovations pioneered in world fairs and exhibitions. This was merely following a time-honoured pattern of development for Blackpool as a whole – the Tower was modelled on the Eiffel Tower constructed for the Paris Exhibition of 1889; the giant Ferris Wheel which dominated the Winter Garden sky-line from 1896 to 1928 was based on the one designed for the Oriental Exhibition at Earls Court in 1895, in turn modelled on the first Ferris Wheel exhibited at the Chicago World's Fair in 1893. In like vein, the chair-lift (1961) was inspired by one used at the World Fair in 1958, the dome of the Astro-Swirl (1969) was based on the design of the American Pavilion at 'Expo 67' in Montreal, and the Space Tower (1975) was a smaller replica of an exhibit in Lausanne in the early 1970s. Since then, the Pleasure Beach has acquired a series of rides derived from American amusement parks, many of them still with futuristic references – the Revolution in 1979, and, in 1980, the Tokaydo Express and the Starship Enterprise.

The Pleasure Beach and Blackpool

I have already noted that the Pleasure Beach is to some degree separate from Blackpool. Unlike the town-centre pleasure complexes – the Tower, the Golden Mile, the piers – which hail the passer-by and rely on impulse consumption, the Pleasure Beach is a place to be visited, perhaps just once or twice in a holiday, for a special occasion. It offers something different. Yet that 'something different' is not in reality distinct from Blackpool. Rather, it is a heightening of Blackpool, a synecdoche of the town's constructed image.

From its earliest days as a sea-side resort the by-word of Blackpool, recurring again and again in its publicity brochures, has been *Progress*. This has always had a particular local, Lancashire articulation, a kind of capping of Lancashire pride in the period when Lancashire claimed to be the workshop of the world. If Manchester used to claim that what it thought today, London did the next day and the world heard about the day after, then Blackpool's claim was to be even one step ahead of Manchester. Nor was the claim an idle one. Blackpool has an impressive number of 'firsts' to its credit – the first town in Britain with electric street lighting (1879) and the first town in the world to have a permanent electric street tramway (1885), for example. Furthermore, its achievements were all the product of northern capital and of northern capitalists. Virtually all the investment which fuelled Blackpool's development came from local entrepreneurs, from the town Corporation or from the business communities in Halifax and Manchester. London capital did not get a look in – at least not until the 1960s when most of the town's leisure-pleasure complexes passed into the hands of what is now Trust House Forte (the three piers) and EMI (the Tower, the Winter Gardens, the Grand Theatre and a part of the Golden Mile). A shining testimony to the power and verve of northern capital, Blackpool offered the working people of the industrial north a place in the vanguard of human development in their leisure analogous to that which the ideology of progress constructed for them in their work-places. The Pleasure Beach's claim, quite simply, has been to have capped the lot, to have done yesterday what the rest of Blackpool is only thinking of getting round to today – all this, and the product of local capital too!

There is little doubt that this has been the explicit aim of the Pleasure Beach management. They seem always to have regarded it as the spearhead of Blackpool, with distinctive interests not necessarily in line with those of the town as a whole. In its early days, the Pleasure Beach company extracted some very shrewd concessions from the town council. In agreeing to the extension of the promenade beyond its northern entrance, for example, it was able to stipulate that no entertainment sites should be constructed beyond its southern boundary for a period of fifteen years. But if it is to a degree in competition with the rest of the town the Pleasure Beach has differentiated itself only by being Blackpool to the nth degree, more Blackpool than Blackpool itself. Just as the town has its Tower, so there is a tower at the Pleasure Beach too – not a rusty old iron thing that you go up and down in an old-fashioned lift and have to walk round when you reach the top, but an aggressively up-to-date tower which, using the very latest technology, 'does the viewing for you as it spirals round its slender column'. Provocatively placed at the very front of the Pleasure Beach, the Space Tower makes Blackpool Tower look quaint, the relic of an outmoded technology. To travel from the town-centre to the Pleasure Beach is to travel through time – but only to reach an exaggerated, up-dated version of your point of departure. Blackpool's ideological centre is located not in the town-centre but at the South Shore, in the Pleasure Beach where there are no scandals to embarrass its aspirations to progress and modernity. As an executive of the Pleasure Beach told me, 'The Pleasure Beach *is* Blackpool'.

A Site of Pleasures

'The Pleasure Beach,' according to Leonard Thompson, 'provides a conglomeration of thrills, spectacles and a myriad of activity, so arranged together for providing that operation known as separating the public from their money as painlessly and pleasantly as possible'. In this, it is spectacularly successful, attracting over eight million visitors annually. It has remained so consistently profitable that the original company remains in private hands and is still run as a family concern by the grandson of one of its co-founders. Given the size of the Pleasure Beach and the considerable capital costs incurred in its development – plus the fact that the company also owns an amusement part at neighbouring Morecambe – it would seem that the provision of pleasure at Blackpool has paid handsome dividends. Whereas most amusement parks have only one or two roller-coaster type rides, the Pleasure Beach boasts four – along with something like seventy major rides or features. In addition, there are the usual side-stalls by the dozen, several large amusement arcades, an ice-drome and a huge indoor entertainments complex incorporating several bars, a nightly floor show and restaurants.

What most impresses, however, is the sheer diversity of the thrills, spills and entertainments. Theoretically speaking, this is something of a problem as it would not be difficult, with a little imagination, to find confirmation for virtually any theory of pleasure you cared to mention. Is the never-endingly laughing clown in front of the Fun House a testimony to the bubbling-up of Kristeva's semiotic chora? And the hall of mirrors – or '1001 Troubles' as it is called at the Pleasure Beach – brazenly advertises a multiple troubling and cracking of self-identity that might tempt the unwary Lacanian into an excess of instant theorisation. For the most part, however, the Pleasure Beach addresses – indeed assaults – the body, suspending the physical laws that normally restrict its movement, breaking the social codes that normally regulate its conduct, inverting the usual relations between the body and machinery and generally inscribing the body in relations different from those in which it is caught and held in everyday life. However, it is equally important to stress the self-referring structure of the Pleasure Beach. A strong sense of 'intertextuality' prevails in the way that different rides allude to the pleasures available on other rides – either by mimicry, inversion or by a recombination of their elements. As the pleasure-seeker moves from ride to ride, he or she is always caught in a web of references to other rides and, ultimately, to the Pleasure Beach as a whole.

The major rides and features at the Pleasure Beach can be divided into five somewhat crude categories, although particular rides may overlap these. The largest category consists of the big open-air 'thrill rides' – the Roller Coaster, the Grand National, The Revolution, the Steeplechase, the Log Flumes, the Big Dipper and so on. These are not only the main attraction of the Pleasure Beach. They also serve as the centre of its system of pleasure – constantly alluded to by other rides, but not themselves referring outward to these in a reciprocal fashion. The pleasures offered by these rides are complex and diverse. In some cases, the dominant appeal is that of liberating the body from normal constraints to expose it to otherwise unattainable sensations. The Revolution, the Starship Enterprise (rather like the Ferris Wheel, except that the rider is placed on the inside of the wheel and travels upside down) and the Astro Swirl (based on the centrifugal training equipment used by American astronauts) all defy the laws of gravity. In releasing the body for pleasure rather than harnessing it for work, part of their appeal may be that they invert the normal relations between people and machinery prevailing in an industrial context. More generally, the thrill rides give rise to a pleasurable excitation by producing and playing on a tension between danger and safety. The psychic energies invested in deliberately placing the body at risk – only partly offset by assurances of safety (faith in technology put to the test) – are pleasurably released at the end of the ride. The public nature of these rides adds to this pleasure of tension and its release. Thresholds are important here. To pay the price of an entrance ticket is to commit oneself – there's no going back, except through taunts of 'chicken'. The psychic thrill of physical danger is therefore intensified by the pleasures of bravado, by the public display of conquering fear.

The pleasures afforded by the thrill-rides differ according to whether they are addressed to small groups or larger collectives. Most of the rides are for couples – two in a car. Others address groups of four to five – The Reel, for example. Rides like the Roller Coaster are for couples within larger groups. Two rides incorporate an element of competition – the Grand National ('the only double track coaster ride in Europe') and the Steeplechase. In the case of the Grand National, it is groups that are in competition

The 'white knuckle' rides.

with one another as distinct from the individual competitions available in the amusement arcades. Like these, however, the competitive rides effect an equalisation of the competitors with respect to the machinery. The outcome of the race is entirely fortuitous – it cannot be influenced by the participants – and, except momentarily, is inconsequential. Finally the Tidal Wave, a huge mechanical swing, seating dozens at a time, is for an undifferentiated mass – the 'body of the people', the romantic might say, swinging in unison. This appeal to groups is a characteristic trait of the Pleasure Beach as a whole, again distinguishing it from the piers and promenades. No place for the solitary, and least of all for the leisurely *flâneur*, its pleasures are pleasures only if shared by a group or, as its minimal 'pleasure unit', a couple. To go there alone is to do something odd, a tactless reminder of singularity in a world which, except for its amusement arcades, respects and addresses only plural identities.

Enclosed rides offer two main types of pleasure. There are the pleasures of looking afforded by imaginary transport to other worlds – the exotic, the remote, the fantastic, the quaint. The Goldmine, Alice in Wonderland (*à la* Walt Disney) and the River Caves, 'a boat journey through exotic scenes from every culture in the world' are the clearest examples, especially the last in its claim to offer the public sights otherwise unseeable. Geoffrey Thompson, currently managing director of the Pleasure Beach, capped these claims when he told the local paper, on the completion of the construction of a replica of the temples of Ankora Watt in Cambodia: 'The temples are no longer on view to the Western World since the Khmer Rouge took over Cambodia so you could say that we are offering people the only chance they will get to see them.'[6] Other rides function as abbreviated narratives, mimicking the tensions produced by popular fictional forms. The Ghost Train is the clearest example: a journey through an enclosed universe where you encounter all the imaginary terrors of the Gothic novel and horror film before coming into the light of day again. Here, as with the thrill-rides, thresholds are important – once in, there's no going back – but, as in the hall of mirrors, it is the psyche that is (flirtatiously) exposed to assault.

A number of enclosed walk-through features like Noah's Ark and the Haunted Hotel use mechanical contrivances to expose the body to unexpected perils (moving floors) and ritual insults (wind up the skirts). The Fun House is especially worthy of mention as it inverts the usual relations between the body and machinery at the Pleasure Beach. On most thrill-rides, the body is surrendered to the machinery which liberates it from normal limitations. In the Fun House, the body competes with the machinery, tries to conquer it and is forcibly reminded of its limitations. Most of its activities involve trying to get the better of various mechanical devices – walking through a revolving drum, attempting to stay at the centre of a spinning wheel, crawling to the centre of a centrifugal bowl or climbing impossibly slippery slopes. The sense of crossing a threshold in the Fun House is quite strong. Before getting into the main entertainment area, the body is subjected to a number of ritual assaults – you are buffeted by skittles, the floor shifts beneath your feet and you have to cross a series of revolving discs. These obstacles also mark a boundary between the Fun House and the rest of the Pleasure Beach – a sign of a reversal of the relations between the body and machinery, a warning that in the Fun House the body will be opposed by machinery rather than assisted or transported by it, and that the body must resist machinery and struggle against it rather than surrender itself to it.

A degree of intertextuality also characterises the new 180° indoor cinema shows like Journey into Space and Cinema USA. These allude to the thrill-rides in two rather contradictory ways. Whereas thrill rides take the normally stationary body and hurtle it through space, they hurtle the vision through space whilst fixing the body as stationary. Yet the cinema shows also compete with the thrill rides by claiming to outdate them, to reproduce all the thrills and excitement of the big rides by means of a more advanced, simpler and safer technology. Nestling beneath the Revolver, the Cinema USA – which includes a film of the largest roller coaster ride in America – seems to declare the 'sooperdooperlooper' redundant, a mass of unnecessary machinery. Rule breaking is also evident in the placing of familiar activities in new contexts. This is especially true of various self-drive rides – the Auto-Skooters, Go-Karts, Swamp Buggies and Speedboats. Clearly, the Auto-Skooters, where the aim is to hit other cars rather than to avoid them, invert the usual rules of driving. More generally, our normal expectations of transportation are suspended as travel is presented as a self-sufficient, functionless pleasure, rather than a means of getting from A to B. You can also travel by all possible means of transportation. 'You can travel by land, sea or air when you come to Blackpool Pleasure Beach: by land on the Pleasure Beach Express, on water by Tom Sawyer's Rafts, and in the air along the one-mile Monorail or the Cableway.' This, however, is to speak of the various through-site transportation systems – a markedly distinctive feature of the Pleasure Beach. You can travel through and around the Pleasure Beach by a small-gauge railway, through it and over it by the monorail, over it by cable-cars; you can survey it as a whole from the top of the Space Tower. In these ways the Pleasure Beach offers itself as a site of pleasures to the gaze of the passing spectator.

Finally, the self-referential structure of the system of pleasure in operation at the Pleasure Beach is clearly evident in miniaturised duplications of many of the major rides. The Wild Mouse is a miniature of rides like the roller-coaster and, more generally, there are miniaturisations of the Auto-Skooters, Go-Karts and Speedboats – small, electronically controlled vehicles which confer on the user total control over the machinery as distinct from surrendering yourself to it, as on the thrill-rides, or being opposed by it, as in the Fun House.

A World Turned Upside Down?

In view of the degree to which the rules and constraints which normally hem in the body are either inverted or suspended at the Pleasure Beach, it might be tempting to draw parallels between the Pleasure Beach and the world of carnival, to view it as 'a world turned upside down'. Tom Harrison commented on a general and pervasive confusion of categories in Blackpool, directly reminiscent of the world of carnival;

> 'The motif of sea and land, east and west are inextricably confused. On the sand a great teapot serves refreshments, while the name Central Beach refers only to the tangle of pleasure shows on the prom, and Pleasure Beach refers to Emberton's shining white permanent Wembley . . . The rams are ships of land. Over the inland pleasure zone of Olympia towers a pseudo-lighthouse.'[7]

At the Pleasure Beach, direct allusions to the world of carnival are not hard to find. The revolving figures at the front of the Fun House – various heads which rotate so that a different face appears according to whether they are upside up or upside down, although it's impossible to determine which of these is which – make clear reference to the 'world turned upside down' aspect of carnival. Similarly, a frequent mixing and confusing of categories effects a carnival-like dissolution of opposites – the most obvious juxtaposition is that between the laughing clown, a King of Mirth, in front of the Fun House and the laughing death's head (itself merging and dissolving opposites: Life laughs at death, death mocks life) which presides over the Ghost Train roughly at the centre of the park. There are numerous allusions to the world of the fantastic (the Alice Ride, the giant figure of Gulliver that supports the monorail), to the tradition of what the Soviet literary critic Mikhail Bakhtin called 'carnivalised literature', an incorporation of the transgressive potentialities of carnival into a subversive literary tradition.[8]

But although such connections are undeniable, it would be misleading to draw them too tightly or to take them at their face value in construing the Pleasure Beach as an anticipation of a people's utopia of pleasure, as Bakhtin conceived of carnival. Indeed, as Terry Eagleton has noted, Bakhtin's populist utopianism has its limitations even in regard to carnival:

> 'Carnival, after all, is a *licensed* affair in every sense, a permissable rupture of hegemony, a contained popular blow-off as disturbing and relatively ineffectual as a revolutionary work of art . . . Carnival

laughter is incorporative as well as liberating, the lifting of inhibitions politically enervating as well as disruptive. Indeed from one viewpoint carnival may figure as a prime example of that mutual complicity of law and liberation, power and desire, that has become a dominant theme of contemporary post-Marxist pessimism.'[9]

Even accepting these limitations, a populist construction of the Pleasure Beach would reflect a serious misunderstanding of Bakhtin's position. For Bakhtin, the carnival of the late medieval period was not just a festival of transgression. It was characterised by the inversion not just of everyday rules and behaviour, but of the dominant symbolic order. As his study of Rabelais makes clear,[10] carnival was a festival of *discrowning* in which the axial signifiers of medieval ideology were scandalously and often scatalogically debased, tumbled down from heaven to earth, trampled over and sullied by the heavily material feet of the people's practice – as well as being opposed and overwhelmed by the 'popular belly' of carnival in its anticipatory celebration of a world of material surfeit. The Pleasure Beach is simply not like that, not even remotely. The body may be whirled upside down, hurled this way and that, but, in the coding of these pleasures for consumption, the dominant symbolic order remains solidly intact and unwaveringly the right way up. It has not always been so. Tom Harrison records that imitation bosses once figured prominently at the Pleasure Beach, and there used to be a dummy policeman in a stationary car on the dodgems, but this was abandoned as the figure was smashed up in no time at all – which suggests many possibilities as to what a 'people's fair' might look like! And outside the Pleasure Beach, debasements of the dominant symbolic order are relatively easily purchased – in 1981, street-sellers were offering dartboards printed over with a full-face picture of Margaret Thatcher.

Inside the Pleasure Beach, however, the brash themes of modernity and progress dominate all. This does not mean they are the only themes in operation. Subsidiary themes are in evidence on individual rides and attractions – particularly the reference to other universes, to imaginary pasts (the Gaslight Bar, done out in Edwardian decor), to popular narrative universes (the Goldmine, Diamond Lil's Saloon, the Starship Enterprise) and to the exotic (the River Caves). In all such cases, however, it is an assimilated otherness that is on offer, an already recuperated and tamed fantastic – *Walt Disney's* Alice, a *functional* Gulliver, and so on. (Although he may not have been much fun to take to the Pleasure Beach, Adorno would definitely have been an instructive companion!) What most needs to be stressed is the ultimate subordination of such divergent themes to the theme of modernity articulated at the level of the Pleasure Beach's collective hail to its visitors.

This is due not solely to the quantitative preponderance of this theme over others but also to the structure of 'barking' in operation on the site. In its economic relations, the Pleasure Beach has two levels. The whole of the site is owned by Blackpool Pleasure Beach Ltd, which also runs all of the major rides and features as well as the indoor entertainment complexes. Most of the smaller rides, side-shows and small stalls, by contrast, are run by independent operators, or 'concessionaires', who make over a portion of their take to the company in return for the right to operate. This dual economy has definite consequences for the structure of 'barking'. Traditional forms of aggressive salesmanship survive only in the independently operated side-shows and stalls where relations of competition persist. The large rides and features are run as an integrated business rather than as separate enterprises. They are staffed by uniformed employees and, following the practice at Disneyland, the visitor is increasingly encouraged to buy books of tickets giving access to all rides rather than to pay for rides individually. Given these economic relations, it is the collective 'hail', getting people into the Pleasure Beach, that is important. Once there, it is immaterial how they spend their money so long as they spend it. As a consequence, few of the individual rides aggressively solicit custom – there's no address made to the public and, mostly, they contain merely the name of the ride, its price and a notice saying which class of ticket applies. It is by the collective hail of the Pleasure Beach as a whole – by its architecture, its public address systems, and its claims to be the biggest, the best, the latest – that the individual is placed as a pleasure seeker under the sign of modernity.

Yet such interpellations can be refused or, at least, negotiated. It is easy to get a one-sided impression of the Pleasure Beach by concentrating solely on the system of pleasure constituted by the nature of its rides, their disposition in relation to one another and the signs under which they are coded for consumption. The Pleasure Beach is not just a site of pleasures, not just a set of buildings and rides conceived as uninhabited structures; there are usually people there too, mostly in groups of different sizes, shapes and complexions and with different histories, traditions and purposes. Usually to go to the Pleasure Beach is a cultural event, a distinct moment in the history of a group, be it a couple, a family, a youth-club or neighbourhood outing or a works trip. Far from imposing its 'régime of pleasure' on a series of individuals, construed as puppets of its organization, the Pleasure Beach is used and negotiated in different ways by different groups in accordance with the cultural relations and processes characterising the group concerned. The group context in which you go to the Pleasure Beach, as well as the timing of the visit, make a difference to the way it is experienced. To go in the daytime, as a parent, is one thing: you are a custodian in a complex initiation ceremony as terror quickly gives way to the no-hands sang-froid of a six year old pestering to go on the Revolution. But go there in the night with a group of friends and it's quite different. Pleasures are less surreptitiously taken than in the daylight. Space is compressed – by other people and by the darkness pressing in – and there's the added edge of an assertive pleasure that refuses and conquers the life-denying darkness, friends to egg or be egged on by, to dare and double-dare. It's one thing to go in 'Glasgow week' – not my scene, personally – and, as an Oldhammer, quite another to go in 'Oldham week'.

For Bakhtin, carnival was, above all, a practice of the people. It possessed not a sedimented form in fixed and permanent structures, but a vibrant and changing form, living only in the street-theatre of the people. If carnival enters the Pleasure Beach – and sometimes it does – it is through the people who tumble in from the promenade with their stetson hats, group swagger and bravado, appropriating the Pleasure Beach for a different practice as they break the rules of its laid-out and provided pleasures – by marching arm-in-arm down the walk ways, dipping one another in the pools by the River Caves and splashing passers-by, whooping it up in the Ghost Train, trying to sink the logs on the Log Flume, taking the piss out of the laughing clown, rocking the Roller Coaster. The Pleasure Beach is not a site of transgressions. It is a site to be transgressed but one which, to a degree, invites – incites even – its own transgression. In its constructed separateness from the outside world, materially bracketed by the enclosing walls, the Pleasure Beach engenders expectations of untramelled pleasures which the ideological coding operative within it can only partly contain.

Notes

1. All quotations, unless otherwise indicated, are from Steve Palmer, *The Pleasure Beach Story*, published by Blackpool Pleasure Beach Ltd.
2. Tom Harrison, 'The fifty-second week: Impressions of Blackpool', *The Geographical Magazine*, April 1938.
3. I am indebted to Brian Turner and Steve Palmer, *The Blackpool Story*, Cleveleys, Palmer and Turner, 1981 for most of the historical perspectives developed in this article. We are also grateful to Steve Palmer for his help in finding the illustrations.
4. See J. K. Walton, 'Residential Amenity, Respectable Morality and the Rise of the Entertainment Industry: The case of Blackpool, 1860–1914', *Literature and History*. vol. 1, 1975 and H. J. Perkin 'The "Social Tone" of Victorian Seaside Resorts in the North West', *Northern History* no. 11., 1975/6.
5. These legends are taken from contemporary photographs. I am most grateful to Blackpool Pleasure Beach Ltd for letting me see them.
6. *Blackpool Evening Gazette*, 21 March 1977.
7. Harrison op. cit. p. 393.
8. See M. Bakhtin, *Problems of Dostoevsky's Poetics*, Michigan, Ardis/Ann Arbor, 1973.
9. Terry Eagleton, *Walter Benjamin, Or Towards a Revolutionary Criticism*. London, NLB, 1981.
10. M. Bakhtin, *Rabelais and his World*, Cambridge, Massachusetts, MIT Press, 1968.

FEMINIST FILM PRACTICE
AND PLEASURE: A Discussion

In planning *Formations of Pleasure*, three general considerations were identified. These were the role of pleasure in the formation of subjectivity, the social management of pleasure, and the socialist-feminist reformation of existing patterns of pleasure. In the discussion that follows, three feminist film-makers consider how these intersect with their concerns. Taking part are Dee Dee Glass, a television documentary producer-director, Laura Mulvey, a teacher at Bulmershe College of Higher Education and film-maker (*Penthesilea*, *Riddles of the Sphinx*, *Amy!*), and Judith Williamson, who writes about film for *City Limits*, the London arts and politics magazine, and has recently completed her first film. The discussion revolves around three main areas of interest.

A) The Pleasure of Activity

Women as producers, makers of meaning, film-makers – these are fundamental new pleasures for women who have been largely excluded from the production processes of mainstream capitalist cinema. In the past decade, the impetus of the Women's Movement and the new opportunities afforded by technical changes – the availability of 16mm and 8mm film, for example – have encouraged women's intervention within film making. Their experiences are contradictory. On the one hand, there may be the pleasure of agency and directorship, but the institutional conditions of production, in both film and television – tight budgets and limited time schedules, all-male film crews and so forth – create conflict and constraint.

B) Feminism, Pleasure and the Audience

Several years ago I went to see Chantal Akerman's *Les Rendez-vous d'Anna* at a Regional Film Theatre. The usual audience was swelled by a large number of women who had been alerted to this showing of a 'feminist' film by a laudatory article on Akerman in *Spare Rib*. Much of this audience was angry and disappointed at the end – 'So much for that as a feminist film!' I suspect that the laconic, highly formalised yet superbly timed progress of Aker-

156

man's film about film-maker Anna's travels and encounters in Europe as she takes her film from regional showing to regional showing failed to provide the expected pleasure of feminist identification with a narrative about women or with a heroic female character. Most of the feminist audience was probably unfamiliar with the particular traditions of film making from which and on which Akerman works. Rather than the theoretically informed stylisation of *Les Rendez-vous d'Anna*, the audience had anticipated a feminist experience couched in the familiar and pleasurably reassuring conventions of realism. The question raised here is this: what do feminists expect from films? What sort of films offer them what sort of pleasure?

A different approach to these questions has been developed within feminist film theory, both in teaching and in journals like *Camera Obscura* and *Screen*. Here the emphasis has been on what feminist *readings* can discover in explicitly non-feminist films – the pleasures of knowledge, analysis and deconstruction. Are the pleasures of traditional film forms and feminism incompatible – or are they there to be reworked?

C) Feminism, Theory and Pleasure

How do we transform the disappointment of a feminist audience anticipating the traditional narcissistic pleasures of cinema – ego-ideal identification, the search for maternal plenitude, the bisexual fantasy of the 'active' phase – yet confronted with feminist interventions precisely in and against those ideologically potent structures of visual pleasure? Feminist theoretical work in photography as much as film confronts this problem. A 'theory vs. practice' hostility expresses not only a fear of excessive intellectualism but also a suspicion about the alienating effect of theoretical work for a feminist audience. Yet as Laura Mulvey herself argued in 1975, the deconstruction of the pleasures of narrative cinema (identification, narcissism and imaginary release) is a vital political project.

> 'The magic of the Hollywood style at its best (and of all the cinema which fell within its sphere of influence) arose, not exclusively, but in one important aspect, from its skilled and satisfying manipulation of visual pleasure. Unchallenged, mainstream film coded the erotic into the language of the dominant patriarchal order. In the highly developed Hollywood cinema it was only through these codes that the alienated subject, torn in its imaginary memory by a sense of loss, by the terror of potential lack in phantasy, came near to finding a glimpse of satisfaction: through its formal beauty and its play on his own formative obsessions. This article will discuss the interweaving of that erotic pleasure in film, its meaning, and in particular the central place of the image of woman. It is said that analysing pleasure, or beauty,

destroys it. That is the intention of this article. The satisfaction and reinforcement of the ego that represent the high point of film history hitherto must be attacked. Not in favour of a reconstructed new pleasure, which cannot exist in the abstract, nor of intellectualised unpleasure, but to make for a total negation of the ease and plenitude of the narrative fiction film. The alternative is the thrill that comes from leaving the past behind without rejecting it, transcending outworn or oppressive forms, or daring to break with normal pleasurable expectations in order to conceive a new language of desire.'[1]

Much subsequent writing about the question of pleasure has been influenced by Laura Mulvey's argument in 'Visual pleasure and narrative cinema'. But the article, partly because of its author's simultaneous engagements in film making, also belongs in a network of practices beyond the purely theoretical and critical. Film strategies were developing which already called into question the normative processes of visual pleasure in film – Jean-Luc Godard's severance of the semiotic codes by separating image and sound is but one example[2] – and these found an echo in the separation of the visual and the textual in art discourses. Since 1975, photographic and film practices generated within feminism and associated political perspectives have produced a variety of work which can be recognised as components of a new language of desire, productive of new order, new visual pleasures.[3] What are these? How do they function? How are viewers to *read* them?

'The Time and the Energy', the photographic essay that follows the discussion, has been produced as part of this debate. Marie Yates's work is both a contribution to and a reflection on this intersection of theories, practices and pleasures. She reassembles a range of strategies – the cinematic movement of images *versus* stillness, the repetition of words, interwoven texts, images, voices and so forth – to suggest how new formations of pleasure can be discerned within the practice of analysis, on the other side of theory.

Griselda Pollock

Women's Culture and Colonization

Dee Dee Glass: I do think there is some kind of common women's culture. So addressing women is fairly easy because if I adopt an attitude and show certain images around it, I feel other women are going to be able to identify with that attitude. But then, it's easier for me to say that because, in terms of film language, the documentaries I work in are much more conventional than, say, the language Laura works in.

Judith Williamson: So one important pleasure for you would be that identification in the sense of getting across to your audience?

Griselda Pollock: But identification is not something which happens spontaneously in the viewer – it's a result of processes actively putting you in the position that you think you're identifying with spontaneously. Often when talking about feminist film culture there is a kind of idealism – the idea that you the film maker are just evoking something that's already there. It's almost like the romantic theory of art as a bridge between the person who makes the film and her audience. And while I'm interested in the question of evoking a hidden sense of a public, I think that feminist film might have to consider the question of how identifications are actually constituted.

Laura Mulvey: I was struck, Dee Dee, by what you were saying about women's culture and women's experience being something separate – that you appeal to it in turning the private and the personalised into a visual experience. There you were talking about a popular experience the dominant culture hadn't bothered to take into account. You seem to be trying to find areas of life which dominant mass culture hasn't explored and exploited. One can see that search for the uncolonised in quite a lot of alternative work, and in feminist work as well. It was also one of the impulses behind *Riddles of the Sphinx* – taking the question of motherhood and the mother-child relationship as an area that patriarchy has relegated to the nursery. So one can see various gestures towards discovering and exploring things in these 'other' areas: the fact that they're small and 'not important' makes them of greater importance.

JW: That's actually what my film was about, from a different angle. The brief was very general – it was supposed to be about advertising, based on my book.[4] I didn't want to do it that way, because it's now six years since I wrote *Decoding Advertisements* and I have become much more interested in the debate raised by your film. At that point I was trying to work out whether there really are uncolonised areas – which I think is fairly dubious. What I've brought to the topic of advertising on this occasion is work I've been doing about the way that not feminism but capitalism constantly attempts to find uncolonised areas.

LM: What do you mean?

JW: That there is a desperate search which feeds off the desire which Dee Dee is describing. It's a real desire to find new areas, but it's also an economic one. We are using 'colonisation' as a metaphor. Our way of life is based on the rise of industrialism, and that was made possible in this country by going outside the domestic cultural sphere to colonise 'wild', untouched areas. Today, the equivalent search seems to be for uncolonized areas *within* society – geographically, we cannot go outside anymore. There's a really good chapter in *Woman's Consciousness, Man's World:*[5] where Sheila Rowbotham talks about the boom in products for women's personal use and in health products – the move into fringe areas, into the body, into private areas, in fact.

LM: I'm sure you can consider that movement as having two directions – the turn to nature and then a move inwards to the private, the body.

JW: Images of the wild and the natural have now been overtaken by images of the woman. And because they seem to be uncolonized, they're like a diversion. They are the other side of what is acceptable in modern life. It reminds me of insurance adverts – slave away and pour your money into things so that over here, you can have your wife and family, your home. The areas that justify everything else are the personal ones.

DG: I think the significant issue here is capitalism's relentless search for areas within a culture that can be colonised. Take the absorption of the Black Power movement and the women's movement in America. You have Afro sprays and all that, and you have the Virginia Slims cigarette 'You've come a long way, Baby' campaign which uses the image of the successful woman. You take whatever the women's movement has accomplished and you colonize it, you sanitize it and you make it safe. In purely capitalist terms, it's extremely successful. But what I really wanted to ask you goes back to the question of audience. Do you think that by making what I think are feminist films and putting them onto television, I am allowing them to be colonized? Television is like an enormous sandwich, so you may see *Mind Your Language* before my film goes on and then some appalling Sussex vicar talking about God and family life after it. Is that somehow colonizing my films?

JW: Not necessarily. I also think that women who aren't consciously feminist see things on television which affect them. I remember seeing a programme in my teens about pre-menstrual tension. It was an ordinary documentary, but the fact that it was on television, that it was public, was very powerful. I remember feeling identification and a kind of triumph that this should be regarded as a subject for a documentary in fairly prime time. Although one can go into all the things behind that, the way that television seems to validate certain things, you can't just push it aside and say that if you work in the mainstream everything you do is colonized.

DG: Well, it's very difficult to work that one out. For example, I made a film about anorexia for Southern Television in which I used half a dozen clips from the Disney *Sleeping Beauty* and *Snow White* cartoons – images of the witch giving Snow White the apple, the Sleeping Beauty being awoken by the prince, the slaying of the dragon and all that. Even though they only made up a total of perhaps ten minutes, it was actually very difficult to prevent them taking over the film – because they are such powerful images from our collective childhoods.

JW: I had the same problem using advertisements in my film. My strategy – which I don't think was very successful – was to mix archive and contemporary adverts with very plain, slow tracks. No quick cutting or zippy camera movements, everything square, a very ex-RCA[6] puritanical style – very recognizable to me now. So there was a contrast between what I had shot and then, suddenly, these fast, exciting adverts. Although there are some shots that I still like, especially pans and camera movements where there was something else happening in the frame, this plain section now seems a bit pedantic. That problem of the pleasure of the advertising material leads into a more general argument about pleasure in film – the debates that Laura's work started off. Although I accept that a lot of the pleasure in mainstream films is gender based – the pleasure of looking at women and so on – I know that I still get another kind of pleasure from watching films which comes from particular combinations of camera movements, from other movements, from music, and things like that. So the question of whether to produce pleasure or combat it becomes broader – a question of style and how you make films. When I was at film school you were regarded as reactionary, you were virtually fascist if you did anything in your film that produced a kind of cinematic pleasure. There was a closed-in feeling, based on a critique of mainstream films, that you musn't do any of these little exciting things.

LM: But do you think that's a kind of functionalism, like the rejection of Victorian style by the Bauhaus – a rejection on an aesthetic level?

JW: I think it was a rejection of a style *and* a rejection of pleasure. It ties in with something deeper – with a puritanical attitude which feminism has only recently become really aware of and started to tackle. At first, I think, a lot of the feminist movement had a very ambiguous relationship to puritanism as opposed to pleasure – in the debates about pornography, for example, which I'm certainly not very clear about. In combating traditional forms of pleasure, how far are you combating all pleasure? And in that case, what kind can you retain in your own film making?

Theory and Practice

DG: As you both started making films after you had worked on them theoretically, do you feel that your attitudes about the pleasure they give you and also your theoretical attitudes have shifted at all?

LM: Do I see films differently?

DG: Yes – and how do you see films differently? I mean, I can read an essay about John Ford and know from the inaccuracies and the technical mistakes that the author has never been near a film set. Decisions about how to shoot and how to put shots into a film, which I assume you picked up from working, are often non-theoretical. In other words, you see this wonderful wide shot in which Ford has the sun setting behind John Wayne, and you can write fifty pages about the meaning of life, the lone man in the desert and all the rest of it. Then it actually turns out that the shot was like that because the studio said this was the last day of filming, the light was going and so there was only time to shoot that one shot. So the reason wasn't to do with the meaning of life – it was actually to do with practical considerations.

LM: That's difficult to answer because I don't think my way of looking at films has been much affected by my own way of making films – which is so different from a Hollywood set in the studio system, it's almost like chalk and cheese. I don't think I have learnt much that I could apply backwards, though I do feel I constantly learn from the body of cinema and try to think that through even though the conditions of production are so different.

Where I have learnt most is probably through teaching and looking at films in great detail. Obviously one teaches films that seem aesthetically successful, but actually I think rather the opposite to you. What astonishes me is how much more was thought out than one might have imagined. That sense of intense detail of construction is one of the fantastic pleasures of Hollywood cinema. I think it's something that comes from that very, very controlled way of working in the studio and on the set, where very little happened by accident. It's very different from the location-based Hollywood of the '60s and '70s, which is much speedier.

JW: In making my film, I was working in a very straight set-up, mostly on a set, with an ordinary crew, all of them were men – I was the director. That's what I really couldn't cope with. When you've only got ten minutes left before everyone is on triple overtime and the fuse has gone on the video thing, so you can't do the shot you planned and so you've got to rewrite something very quickly – in those situations you're still forced into making definite choices, even if you're not consciously thinking theoretically. So I disagree with Dee Dee's point that practical, working decisions aren't theoretical – the idea of 'theory' may be a red herring, because it sounds deliberate, but your decisions are still based on how you want the film to look, what you want it to mean and how you want it to give an impression to people. And those things *are* precisely what 'theoretical' criticism looks at. In fact I think that often it's when you're under greatest pressure, like making snap decisions, that your underlying *assumptions* about film get put into practice, whether deliberately or not. If the light's going and you can only do one shot, what that one shot is will say an awful lot about the meaning you want it to achieve. Anyway, in answer to your question, when I see films by other people, I feel tremendous admiration and jealousy that they have managed to make things happen the way they wanted, that they've got a grip on these details.

Feminism, Pleasure and Film Making

GP: Even if all production is more or less materially determined, I don't think that can be reduced to the question of practical constraints. Although the technical area hasn't been adequately incorporated into theoretical explanations of film, I don't think a theory/practice opposition will get us anywhere. In terms of feminist film practice, the theory/practice contrast just doesn't work – on two levels. First of all, if you use the argument about material determination, there wouldn't be any feminist film. We actually have to go out in the first instance and create the conditions for financing, to get together the collectors or companies to provide backing, to exploit the independent circuits. To make feminist films requires quite an active policy.

DG: That only applies if you don't believe in subversion.

GP: But you do have to construct spaces as part of a much broader movement actually to create the possibility of an alternative independent film culture. And secondly, you have to think about what kinds of films feminists should be making and what kinds of jobs they are going to be doing. Whether you call it theory or you don't call it theory, it means trying to understand the nature of the film culture into which you may be intruding.

DG: I think it's less a debate between theory and practice than a debate about where you start from. I'd be very unhappy if I had to sit down and decide how feminist films ought to be constructed.

GP: No, I'm not saying we should decide how feminist films *ought* to be constructed, but that any feminist making a film makes decisions which are informed by a sense of what a film is. You make decisions, that's essential. Now those decisions can either be programmatically conjured out of your back issues of *Screen* or Noël Burch's *Theory of Film Practice*[7] – identify every law of film and break it. That's an easy way to an alternative film culture. Or, in the sense we're talking about, those decisions depend on the ways that feminist film can mobilize features we've come to understand, appreciate or be amazed at in cinema – recognising the ideological significance of certain moves and realising how feminist film can avoid being merely oppositional, a negation, but go into those spaces. That requires an informed knowledge about the film tradition we've gone back to.

JW: But to an extent we're already in those spaces, in two distinct ways. In studying and teaching Hollywood films – films that weren't consciously made as feminist – it's possible to draw out a feminist dimension that can be discussed. Secondly, there are feminists already in structures like television. So it's not just a question of feminists wondering, how shall I make a film? What's really important is where these things tie up – having found elements in mainstream films and other kinds of film making that not just feminists or women can use or enjoy. So the question isn't just, does being a feminist mean you make a feminist film? There are all these different possibilities – you get women and feminists, you get feminist films made by women who aren't setting out to be feminists. In a way my film isn't deliberately feminist. I'm a feminist, I'm making a film about advertising, but it wasn't specifically to do with advertising and women. It reminds me of an argument at the Co-Op[8] once about a simplistic version of Laura's idea that the male view is the basis of 'the look' in traditional cinema. Some people were arguing that there had to be a camerawoman shooting, otherwise the look would be a male look – having a camera*man* was absolutely out. I think it's difficult having a cameraman on your crew if you're a woman making a film for other reasons.

DG: I don't think anyone would argue with you on that point!

JW: There are all these questions about what makes a feminist film. What you were saying implied that a feminist would sit down and think, well, how do I make a feminist film?

GP: I don't see why not. We don't have to get into the problems of categorizing. We agreed that there are ways that feminists discover and make use of critical, subversive elements in films that don't ostensibly claim to promote the cause of women. But if you ask yourself what constitutes a feminist practice, then what sort of things are you concerned to do?

LM: I think that takes us back to the question of pleasure. You can only make a film in a way that actually pleases you. I think it's really significant that I feel I can learn a lot from Hollywood movies and you don't feel you can, Dee Dee, because the kind of movies we make and our approaches to film are very different. It's essential to realize that I couldn't make films like you do because I just couldn't! I could enjoy your films and learn a lot from them, but I couldn't make them. A problem one sometimes faces in talking about a film after you present it is that people ask you, why did you do that? Wouldn't something else have been better? People often seem to want to re-make your film for you. It's difficult to answer, because often you've done it that way because that's the way it pleases you.

JW: Having that confidence in your ideas, in what you want to see and how you want to make it look and the things you want to do seems quite feminist in itself, given the difficulties facing a woman making a film. It's like women in the movement reclaiming the way they feel or their right to do things. Rather than asking what is a feminist film practice, I'd ask what is *my* feminist practice. I probably wouldn't even put 'feminist' in because I know I'm a feminist and I wouldn't need to say it to myself when I was at my desk.

GP: This seems to me the classic fetishism of the artist. Granted, there are special difficulties in mobilizing the resources, finances and machinery needed to get a film made. But why is your practice as a film-maker different, for instance, from my practice as a writer about cultural artefacts and history? I wouldn't just say, I'm a feminist and that inevitably comes through. I ask myself, what is it to do feminist history or feminist art history? What have other feminists done? Where does that end them up? How did they produce cultural myths about artists and notions about the aesthetic which are ideologically regressive? It seems to me that the project of feminism has to include not just a pluralistic individualism, but a question-ing of ourselves and what we do. That's not a moral imperative or a unitarily imposed programme – 'This is what a feminist film is.' But you ask yourself that question because you know that everything you carry with you – from what turns you on in the cinema to what happy memories you have – are both potentially progressive *and* positively regressive. They have to be negotiated with some care.

JW: One reason I feel so vehemently about this is because I now think that parts of my film suffered because I felt pressurized to stick to certain ideas about radical film making. They were bound up with my particular situa-tion, the women around me, the group I was in, being at the RCA – ideas that this was a radical thing to do, this was a feminist thing to do, you must have a woman doing this or that. There were various things I felt I ought to do as a feminist and as a marxist, and that was very restrictive. I still think the most successful parts of the film – which are no less marxist or feminist – are those where I did follow through an idea I had or something I wanted to do. It sounds like your classic artist!

GP: The point I was making is that the myth is there for us to fall into. Putting it crudely, there are so many traps which have to be negotiated by nourishing a constantly evolving political consciousness.

IM: Yes, but talking in terms of pleasure, Griselda, the point was that there should be a pleasure in what you're producing even if the work is a minimal one and may not appear pleasurable to the people consuming it. It may seem like an ultimate demand on the spectator to work, but for the person who is making the film, there must be some kind of pleasure involved in producing it. Even from the point of view of seeing yourself as a woman film maker, as Judith described herself, or as a feminist film maker, which is more as Dee Dee describes herself, you can see how utterly diverse these instances of pleasure are. That can take you back to the actual psychoanalytic individual – which I think is possibly the right theoretical approach. Rather than dismissing this as a romanticism of the individual artist, you can see that – even while we've all been part of a struggle to create a feminist culture and an alternative, feminist way of looking – at the same time our own psychoanalytic stances are valid. And that produces very varied practices.

GP: There's a point underlying that which really intrigues me – it only dawned on me recently when writing about women artists. Women artists are up against the notion that the artist in the most general sense of our culture is the most self-fulfilling and privileged forms of creative actor.

LM: Oh, now I know what you are talking about. It's like that discussion at the ICA[6] – there was total misunderstanding between two sides of the room . . .

GP: Yes, and it led me onto this. The problem is that on the one hand, women have been denied cultural creativity both in terms of recognition and in terms of practice. And on the other hand, think of the place women occupy in the work scene – the antithesis of self-fulfilling creative work, not just alienated labour but repetitive drudgery. They are the replaceable secretary, nurse, clerical worker, housewife.

What interested me is the way that women involved in making either art or film are demanding a creative individuality (or at least recognition of their own creative individuality within a profession where it is denied them) on behalf of *all* women – who have generally been seen as non-creative. Yet at the same time there is a reasonable criticism of the mythology, the romanticism of the creative individual.

LM: The film community, if one can roughly call it that, appears to have rather different problems from the visual arts. I was really surprised that afternoon to see how strong the desire to be an artist was among the women there. They felt that was a position denied them, but they wanted to get at it by delving into a particular sensitivity that was in itself feminine. Out of that they would produce feminine art or feminist art.

The film community is quite different in various ways. I don't know if the others would agree, but I think one thing that has marked many of us is the historical moment. Alternative practices in cinema, the availability of 16 millimetre equipment and stock, and so on came on the scene at a crucial moment. It coincided, on the one hand, with the development of alternative politics in the US – the anti-war movements and women's movements – and quickly became a political instrument. You can see a first wave of alternative films that were specifically politicized, made by people who didn't see themselves as artists and used the film as a weapon of agitation. Then on the other hand, on the aesthetic front, you can also see film being adopted by people in the art community who were questioning the place of the artist – photography became important to some artists around the same time. So that kind of experimental film is also marked by a questioning of traditional views of art. What's interesting about independent avant-garde films is the way these two tendencies have cross-fertilized at various points whilst staying apart.

At the same time, here we are sitting around talking in a way I don't think would be possible about any other medium at the moment. It's our background in film *and* in the women's movement which has made this kind of thing possible, whereas in the visual arts there hasn't been that kind of traumatic history.

DG: On your initial question about what gives us pleasure, I keep coming back to the word collectivity – the collectivity of film making or of making television programmes. Judith was saying she felt ill-equipped for directing a film with a bunch of men around because it was a role we as women are not trained to do. When I was first directing television, there were no other women film directors in that company and no other women in my office except for secretaries, who refused to treat me as anything but a director. So it took a long time before I had anything like an equal relationship to them, on top of which I had to use staff crews on the first two films I made. What happened was that without noticing it, I became a 'man'. I went home after making my first film and my husband was chopping the veg or something for dinner. I just walked into the kitchen and said, 'Look, why don't you put the potatoes on before you do the carrots.' And he turned round to me and said, 'Just sit down and stop directing this dinner. I'm doing the dinner, you're going to eat the dinner, pull yourself together.' It was extremely important that people were saying things like that to me because that happens to most women who produce and direct television programmes, and actually to women who enter any kind of power structure.

Eventually two other women started work as researchers in my office and we formed a sort of united front against the world. But one can also prevent the process by becoming involved in collective organizations either around one's work or completely outside it. There are groups of women in which one is supported not because one makes £500 a week and can control a budget of £60,000, but through a process of collective questioning which is both challenging and supportive.

GP: That theme around the actual conditions of production has come up a couple of times. What do you think are the priorities for change in the organizational base for feminist film? Ages ago, Judith, we were talking about how difficult it had been to make your film and you mentioned the contrast with the way Sally Potter made *Thriller*[10] – how it might be more possible to achieve the 'feminist look' within a collective because other members of the crew share your concerns and premises. I'm interested in the question of how the formal problems we can discuss in relation to different types of feminist film are related to the way the films are actually made.

JW: I remember that conversation. I wasn't really contrasting my own position with the way Sally Potter was working in a collective. What I was saying was that there wasn't a great division of labour. I remember going to the Co-Op and finding her working on *Thriller*. The film was in black and white, and she had done just about every single thing herself. She was alone in the little cutting room. It was very peaceful and she had plenty of time. There wasn't someone saying, I've got to have this in three weeks time, will you have completed it by then? The Co-Op has the facilities for developing your own film, so you don't have to rush up and down hassling the people at the labs. So that's what I was talking about – this feeling of her working in her own time, in her own way, controlling every part of the process.

DG: But Sally Potter is allowed to do that and Laura is allowed to do what she does on her films because they're outside the power structure. Once you're filming on 35 millimetre or if the film's going to be transmitted on television, then you're going to come closer to various problems, like how you are going to deal with the ACTT.[11]

LM: Basically we work with union people.

DG: But the real problem we haven't addressed is that I think many people who make independent films have decided, consciously or unconsciously, that what's important is the *process* rather than the product or what happens to the product. That's to say, a few hundred people are going to see the film and they're all going to know what you're doing anyhow – so to a great extent it's going to act as a reinforcement. Now I've made the crude political decision that because films are so expensive and because I want most people to see my films, I am willing to fight within television to get them made. How do you reconcile these two approaches? If all feminist film makers are independent film makers, then they would have to answer the question, 'Are you doing the same thing as an artist painting squares and circles or wrapping polythene around the west coast of Scotland? Are you doing it just for your own pleasure?'

JW: It would be awful if there were no feminist interventions in television – both things have to be going on side by side. You can't abandon television but, because of the women's movement and the work of women teaching, there are other contexts than film societies in which to show films like Laura's. If my film was finished, it would mainly be shown in colleges, perhaps to sixth formers in schools and also to women's groups. People often want to use a film in a meeting or discussion – so the audience for independent films isn't really so select.

DG: One of the basic tenets of feminism is reaching out to other women. If, like me, you believe that there are things which all women have in common and it's vitally important to analyse these things, then feminism has urgent reasons for getting feminist films seen by as many people as possible.

LM: Whereas when Peter Wollen and I made *Riddles of The Sphinx*, we wouldn't have thought it could really benefit either the film or anyone to have it shown on television. Partly that's because of the way it was shot – it's very much a film film rather than a television film – but it's also because at that stage we were really trying to experiment with film. We see those films not as final products but as part of what's generally called 'ongoing discussion' – they come out of that and so have to appear within it. If they were just plonked on television they wouldn't have the same meaning. They weren't made with a wide audience in mind but with the intention of changing particular people's attitudes to film – on the one hand, women interested in questions of representation and, on the other hand, people involved in film and interested in film and politics. I think there is a place for that kind of work and for research and experimentation in film. This isn't to say that there wasn't an aesthetic drive and pleasure at the same time for me in making the films, but I don't see them having a place outside an area of discussion. As the area of discussion changes, it expands and the context changes.

JW: It's also interesting the other way around. When I was working on *Time Out*, I remember typing out the programmes for a season of Women's Films at the Institute of Contemporary Arts. They mixed together independent films made at the Co-Op with straight half-hour television programmes about an aspect of women's lives. There was much more interaction between the two fields than had been possible before – it would have been unthinkable a while ago for the ICA to show this mixture of early films made by women in 1916, contemporary independent feminist films and also the television films. By putting them alongside each other as women's films, it showed how feminism has broadened interest in women's issues and in women's film making. I think all of that is really important and it has been broadened by the women's movement.

Notes

1. Laura Mulvey, 'Visual pleasure and narrative cinema', in *Screen*, vol. 16, no. 3, 1975, p. 87.
2. See Colin MacCabe, *Godard: Images, Sounds, Politics*, London, BFI/Macmillan, 1980.
3. See, for example, Victor Burgin, 'Seeing Sense' in *Art Forum*, February 1980; Angela Martin, 'Chantal Akerman's Films: a dossier' in *Feminist Review* no. 3, 1979; Yvonne Rainer, 'Looking Myself in the Mouth' in *October* no. 17, 1981; Ann Sargent-Wooster, 'Yvonne Rainer's Journeys from Berlin, 1971–1980' in *Drama Review* no. 2, 1980; Gillian Swanson and Lucy Moy-Thomas, 'An interview with Sally Potter' in *Undercut* no. 1, 1981.
4. Judith Williamson, *Decoding Advertisements*, London, Marion Boyars, 1978.
5. Sheila Rowbotham, *Woman's Consciousness, Man's World*, Harmondsworth, Penguin, 1973.
6. Royal College of Art, London.
7. Noël Burch, *Theory of Film Practice*, London, Secker and Warburg, 1973.
8. The London Film-makers' Co-op.
9. The reference here is to a discussion at a conference held at the Institute of Contemporary Arts, London, in association with the exhibition *Issue: Social Strategies by Women Artists* selected by Lucy R. Lippard, 14 November – 21 December 1980.
10. *Thriller* directed by Sally Potter, 1979. See Sally Potter 'On *Thriller*' and Jane Weinstock 'She Who Laughs First Laughs Last', in *Camera Obscura* no. 5, Spring 1980.
11. The Association of Cinematograph, Television and Allied Technicians.

Marie Yates

THE TIME AND THE ENERGY

On the left, pleasure and desire are largely unaddressed, despite a growing recognition of their importance for the development of a number of diverse practices. The separation of the visual and the textual in art discourses finds echo in the separation of pleasure and desire from politics and theory in other perhaps more vocal discourses. Laura Mulvey suggested that 'desire born with language allows the possibility of transcending the instinctual and the imaginary'* and maybe it is time to consider this.

When watching moving images the visual codes manipulate the mechanisms of our pleasure to the perfect pitch of satisfaction by rapid shifts of emphasis of the look, from voyeuristic gaze to identification and back. The sound echoes the image to create a coherence which encloses us within these identifications and positionings.

Current image production has developed counterpoint techniques to intervene in these mechanisms, and these practices are referred to in this work. It is therefore necessary to view the textual images as if they are moving across a screen with all the processes of pause, delay, repeat, relay and change implied.

* Laura Mulvey – *Visual Pleasure and Narrative Cinema* 1977.

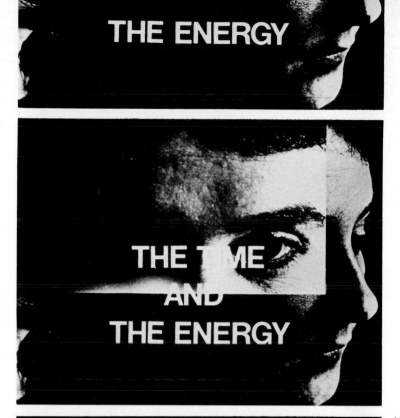

Voice. Reclaiming pleasure for the artistic text.

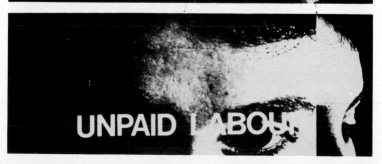

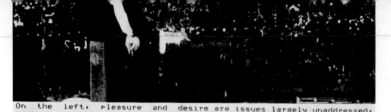

On the left, pleasure and desire are issues largely unaddressed, despite a growing recognition of their importance for the development

Voice 1.   I don't know . . . . but if you are a woman and an artist, compared to a man in a similar position, you seem to be generally condemned to an existence which is well . . . definitely not on a par.

Voice 2.   Yes, your sphere of activity will be radically smaller, possibilities for wage-earning distinctly limited, particularly if you compare men and women in the so-called 'mid-stage' of their careers, say at around forty-five—there will be less in the bank, if any, housing conditions will be poorer, less prospects for retirement—few pensionable posts available in art for women, and art funding and support . . . .

Voice 1.   Oh, why is art funding so discriminatory, particularly at that point in a woman's career?

Voice 2.   This sounds like a moan and complaint without particular political direction but when you are so close inside a situation like this—you can't articulate it . . . it' so emotional . . . . what can you do?

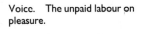

Voice. The unpaid labour on pleasure.

Voice. . . . . pleasure has an intellectual and a political level. Intellect has a pleasure level. Politics . . . .

pleasure and desire from politics and theory in other perhaps more vocal discourses. Laura Mulvey suggested that 'desire born with

language allows the possibility of transcending the instinctual and
the imaginary, and maybe it is time to consider this.

Voice 1.   When I'm working, I
go into a kind of trance-like state
. . . .

Voice 2.   I think I shall always
live alone . . . . . I prefer it that
way . . . .

When watching moving images the visual codes manipulate the
mechanisms of our pleasure to the perfect pitch of satisfaction by

LANGUAGE
PLEASURE
DESIRE / IMAGINARY
INSTINCTUAL

rapid shifts of emphasis of the look, from voyeuristic gaze to

identification and back. The sound echoes the image to create a

coherence which encloses us within these identifications and
positionings.

Voice 1.   As a couple . . . . , it
should be possible to take it in
turns with your art practice: one
earns the money for living . . . . . .

Voice 2.   And expenses for the
art work.

Voice 1.   Yes, and subsidizes the
other one's practice. But wait, it
is then SO hard on the one who Is
wage-earning because they will
have to work full time and
overtime plus to earn enough . . . .

Voice 2.   And there may be
children too . . . .

Voice 1.   Yes, but the hardest bit
is that the one who is wage-
earning, if they are lucky enough
to find anything at all now, will be
DEAD professionally for the
period of the turn, inactive   like
only having one pair of shoes
between you, and how many jobs
can you leave and take up again
later . . . .

Voice 2.   And what about the
awful guilt about that, If your'e
the one being 'active' . . . .

Voice 1.   It's so hard to think
rationally about it . . . . .

Voice 2.   Yes, ... but for two
women the problem is
compounded.

Current image production has developed counterpoint techniques to
intervene in these mechanisms, and these practices are referred to in
this work. It is therefore necessary to view the textual images as if
they are moving across a screen with all the processes of pause,
delay, repeat, relay and change implied.